# *Hazards and Responses*

## Second Edition

## Victoria Bishop

Lutterworth Upper School and Community College

ollins

*IDMARK GEOGRAPHY*

Published by Collins Educational
77–85 Fulham Palace Road
London W6 8JB

An imprint of HarperCollins*Publishers*

©Victoria Bishop 1998, 2001

First published 1998
Second edition 2001

10 9 8 7 6 5 4 3 2

ISBN 0 00 711431 1

Edited by Melanie McRae

Designed by Sally Boothroyd

Indexed by Marie Lorimer

Picture research by Caroline Thompson

Computer artwork by Jerry Fowler
Cartoon Fig. 5.1 by Richy K Chandler

Printed and bound by Printing Express Ltd.
*Cover picture*
Tornado on the horizon
(GettyOne Stone)

*Maps*
Fig. 3.20, US Geological Survey
Fig. 7.31, Environment Agency

## Acknowledgements

Every effort has been made to contact the holders of copyright material, but if any have been inadvertently overlooked, the publishers will be pleased to make the necessary arrangements at the first opportunity.

*Photographs*
The publishers would like to thank the following for permission to reproduce photographs:
Associated Press, AP, Figs 3.16, 3.25, 6.12, AP Photo/John McConnico, Fig. 4.9, AP Photo/Rick Rycroft, Fig. 5.11, AP Photo/Gregory Bull, Fig. 6.19, AP Photo/Austin American-Statesman, Ted S Warren, Fig. 6.20, AP Photo/L M Olero, Fig. 6.28, AP Photo/Mark Fallander, Fig. 5.38, Associated Press, US Forest Service, Fig. 6.42, AP Photo/Franco Castano, Fig. 7.5, AP Photo/Fabrice Cottrini, Figs 7.7, 7.9, AP Photo/Andy Mettler, Fig. 7.11, AP Photo/Charlie Riedel or Tannen Maury, AP Photo/Karel Prinsloo, Fig. 7.18
Jim Holmes/Axiom Photo Agency, Fig. 4.7
Victoria Bishop, Figs. 4.5, 4.8, 4.20, 4.23, 4.24, 4.27
Leigh Green/Bournemouth News, Fig. 2.13
Yann Arthus-Bertrand/Corbis, Fig. 2.1, Gary Braasch/Corbis, Fig. 4.1, Macduff Everton/Corbis, Fig. 4.11, Library of Congress/Corbis, Fig. 4.13, Earl Cowell/Corbis, Fig. 4.14, Raymond Gehman/Corbis, Fig. 4.34, Corbis-Bettmann, Figs. 4.35, 6.17, Corbis-Bettmann/Reuter, Fig. 5.5
Environment Agency, Bangor, Figs 7.33, 7.34
Jerry Laizure/Getty Images, Fig. 6.26R
Kyodo News Service, Fig. 3.27
Reproduced by kind permission of Leicester Mercury, Fig. 7.24
NERC Satellite Station, University of Dundee, Fig. 7.22
NOAA/National Climatic Data Center, Fig. 2.9
Jeremy Hartley/Panos Pictures, Fig. 2.15
Popperfoto, Fig. 6.15
Popperfoto/Reuters, Figs 3.24, 3.26, 7.4
Rex Features, Figs 4.16, 7.14;
Science Photo Library, Figs 2.12, 3.1, 6.26L
P Robert/Sygma, Fig. 1.4, EPIX/Sygma, Fig. 3.13, L Frances Jnr/Sygma, Fig. 3.14.

*Internet addresses*
The following Internet addresses were correct at the time of writing. They are intended to be a starting-point for using the Internet to research natural hazards. However, addresses do change so be prepared to use your search engine to find other Web sites. University and government departments are the most informative for hazard studies. Happy surfing!

United States Emergency Management Agency (FEMA) – tropical storms, reducing risk, preparedness, kinds of disaster and lots more at http://www.fema.gov/

Natural Hazards Mitigation Group, University of Geneva at http://www.unige.ch/hazards/

TORRO (tornadoes) at http://www.torro.org.uk/

National Skywarn Hurricane and Tropical Cyclones at http://www.skywarn.org/tropical.html

El Niño information at NOAA at http://www.pmel.noaa.gov/toga-tao/el-nino/forecasts.html

Atlantic and Pacific hurricanes data at http://wxp.eas.purdue.edu/hurricane

United States Geological Survey earthquake information at http://quake.wr.usgs.gov/

Northern California Earthquake Data Centre at http://quake.geo.berkeley.edu

Seismosurfing–earthquake Internet connections at http://www.geophys.washington.edu/seismosurfing.html

Hawaiian Volcano Observatory at http://www.soest.hawaii.edu/hvo/

USGS National Landslide Information Centre at http://geohazards.cr.usgs.gov

Atlantic Oceanographic and Meteorological Laboratory, Miami, Florida, at http://landsea@aoml.noaa.gov

PHIVOLCS (Philippines): at the time of writing this book the PHIVOLCS homepage was under construction. Type 'PHIVOLCS' into your search engine to find.

# Contents

# 1 Defining and classifying hazards

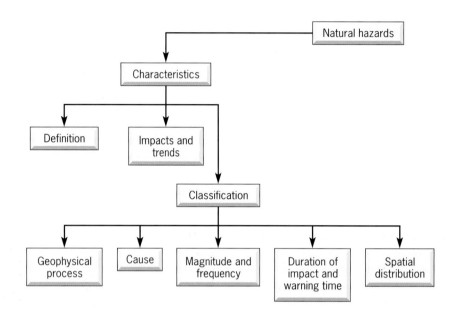

## 1.1 What is a hazard?

We are all familiar with newspaper and television headlines which show that natural processes can cause loss of life, injury and damage to property. Our awareness of these events is increased by improved global communication systems and the sometimes distressing images that are flashed across our television screens. The **geophysical processes** operating in the lithosphere, hydrosphere, atmosphere and biosphere provide people with opportunities and constraints. The opportunities are the resources we use: for example, forests, fertile crop land on flood plains or near volcanoes, water and energy resources. People have adapted their social and economic systems to what they perceive as the 'normal events' within these geophysical systems.

However, more extreme events can endanger human life and possessions, as shown in Figure 1.1. We can define a natural hazard as a naturally occurring process or event which has the *potential* to cause loss of life or property. The key understanding is that hazards are not just natural events, since without people they are just that – natural processes. It is the interaction of people and the environment that defines a hazard (Fig. 1.2). When studying natural hazards we need to understand both the geophysical processes involved and the human systems.

**Figure 1.1 Sensitivity to environmental hazards: geophysical processes and human systems (*After:* Smith, 1996)**

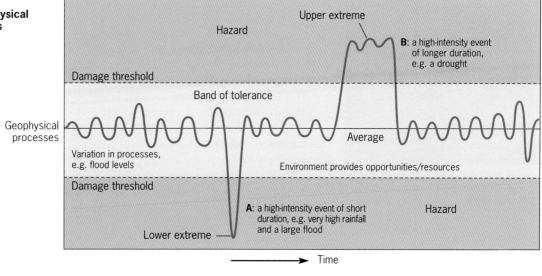

Human systems are adapted to 'normal' conditions within the environment (the band of tolerance) but will be disrupted by more extreme natural events. People's use of rivers is a good example, for benefits are gained from living on a fertile flood plain. Flooding is a normal process in the functioning and evolution of river systems, most floods being relatively small and frequent. People have adapted to and benefit from this flood cycle: the soil water store will be refilled, crops irrigated, and houses built above flood levels. However, a large flood may disrupt this human activity, causing loss of crops. A larger area of land will be flooded resulting in loss of life, property and disruption of communications. The flood is now a hazardous event and outside the range of tolerance. Floods are short-term hazardous events (A). A longer-term hazardous event (B) would be a drought, which would cause the river to dry up and disrupt people's activities over a longer period of time.

In 1969 Sheenan and Hewitt defined disaster losses as:
**a** at least US$1 000 000 damage
**b** at least 100 people injured
**c** at least 100 people dead.
One or more of the criteria had to be satisfied for the event to be defined as a disaster. More recently (1990), the Swiss Reinsurance Company defined disaster losses as either or both of:
**a** at least 20 people killed
**b** insured damage of at least US$16.2 million.

**?**

**1** Why is it difficult to define a disaster?

**2** What are the problems of assigning monetary values to disaster losses?

**3** Suggest how different definitions of a disaster will create problems of making comparisons (**a**) of different places at the global scale and (**b**) comparing disasters at different times (temporal comparisons).

Figure 1.2 introduces another term used in hazard studies – that of disaster. A disaster is difficult to define but may be seen as 'the realisation of hazard, although there is no universally agreed definition of the scale on which loss has to occur in order to qualify as a disaster' (Smith, 1996). There are various attempts to put loss boundaries into the definition of a disaster, but these depend upon many variables and the assignment of monetary values becomes quickly dated.

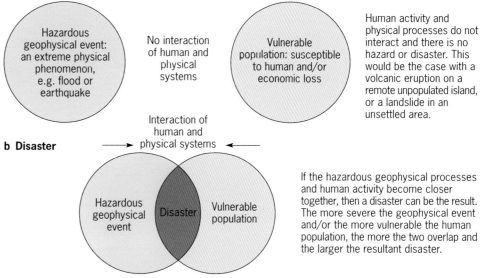

**a No hazard or disaster**

Human activity and physical processes do not interact and there is no hazard or disaster. This would be the case with a volcanic eruption on a remote unpopulated island, or a landslide in an unsettled area.

**b Disaster**

If the hazardous geophysical processes and human activity become closer together, then a disaster can be the result. The more severe the geophysical event and/or the more vulnerable the human population, the more the two overlap and the larger the resultant disaster.

**Figure 1.2   The disaster equation: the relationship between hazard, disaster and human vulnerability (*After:* Dregg, 1992)**

**Figure 1.4  A family in Kobe, Japan, made homeless by an earthquake in January 1995**

# 1.2 Hazard impacts and trends

The impact of a hazard produces direct and indirect losses and disruption (Fig. 1.3) to human systems, including death and injury, property damage, and disruption of social services and communication systems. There is likely to be a need for help from outside the affected area, i.e. other parts of the country or the international community (Fig. 1.4).

The impacts of disaster are not equal at the global scale. Some 90 per cent of hazard-related deaths occur in the less economically developed countries (LEDCs), while 75 per cent of the economic losses occur in the more economically developed countries (MEDCs). In MEDCs the number of deaths has decreased from an average of 38 deaths per hazard during the period 1947–67 to 19 deaths per hazard in 1969–89. In LEDCs, however, the death toll continues to rise from 1000 per hazard during 1947–67 to 2000 during 1969–89. The type of impact is dependent upon the type of hazard (Fig. 1.5).

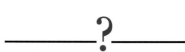

**4** Study Figure 1.3.
**a** Classify the impacts into short-term impacts (few days) and long-term impacts (weeks or years).
**b** Which impacts can be easily assigned monetary values (i.e. are tangible impacts)?
**c** What factors will affect (i) how severe the hazard impacts will be on people and (ii) how long the impacts will last?
**d** When disaster reports in the media say that the costs were put at US$X million, what costs do you think these include?
**e** Why is it difficult to give monetary values to some impacts?

**5** Study Figure 1.5.
**a** Which hazard types cause the most (i) deaths, (ii) injuries, (iii) homelessness and (iv) affect the most people?
**b** Which single hazard type would you say caused the most human suffering? Justify your answer.
**c** What do you think is meant by 'affected' in Figure 1.5(c)? Figure 1.3 may help your answer.

**Figure 1.5  People's suffering caused by different types of natural hazard as a percentage of the people affected throughout the world, 1968–92**

**Losses**

**Direct**
• Deaths
• Physical damage to property/infrastructure
• Injury

**Indirect**
• Long- and short-term damage to mental health
• Loss of employment
• Loss of ability to earn money as a result of injury
• Disease (e.g. cholera epidemics)
• Disruption of social and economic activity
• Negative multiplier effect (e.g. falling property values, rise in unemployment, less money spent by consumers)

**Gains**

**Direct**
• Aid (national and international)
• Reconstruction grants
• Fertile land (e.g. from flood silt or volcanic ash)

**Indirect**
There is little research into this aspect of hazards

**Figure 1.3  Impacts of natural hazards**

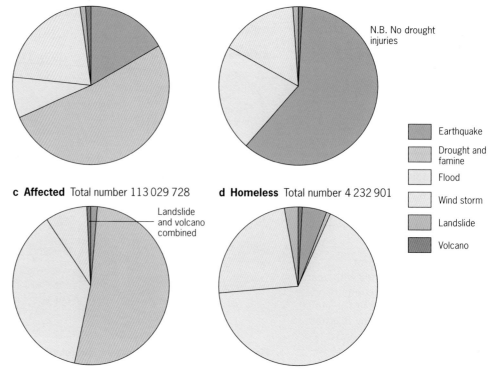

**a Killed** Total number 140 315

**b Injured** Total number 54 111

N.B. No drought injuries

**c Affected** Total number 113 029 728

Landslide and volcano combined

**d Homeless** Total number 4 232 901

- Earthquake
- Drought and famine
- Flood
- Wind storm
- Landslide
- Volcano

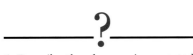

**6** Describe the changes in reported disasters shown in Figure 1.6.

**7a** Describe the overall trend shown by the graph in Figure 1.7.
**b** What are the implications for insurance companies?

The number of hazardous events (Fig. 1.6) and the scale of impacts (Fig. 1.7) from natural hazards has shown an upward trend in recent decades. In the 1960s, fewer than 50 million people were affected each year, but by the mid-1990s the number had risen to 250 million each year. The 1990s was the United Nations International Decade for Natural Disasters Reduction (1990–99). Despite the efforts to reduce the impacts of natural hazards, the death toll and damage to property continued to rise. Higher death tolls were recorded from storms and floods during the period 1997–2000 than during 1990–97 (O' Hare, 2001). Although global warming is expected to result in increased atmospheric and flood hazards, current data does not show this as yet. The growth in disaster impact is because more people are placed at risk from potentially hazardous events (remember the definition of a hazard). This is due to many factors, including population growth, land pressure, urbanisation, increased vulnerability, economic growth producing more property to be damaged, and political change which may reduce a government's commitment to internal and international welfare. There is also an increase in the number of reported disasters due to the development of mass media and communications.

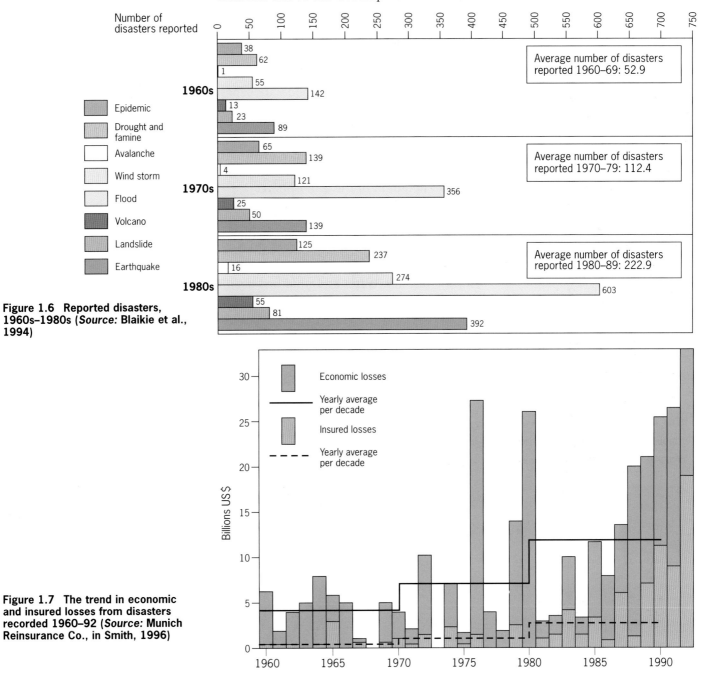

**Figure 1.6  Reported disasters, 1960s–1980s (Source: Blaikie et al., 1994)**

**Figure 1.7  The trend in economic and insured losses from disasters recorded 1960–92 (Source: Munich Reinsurance Co., in Smith, 1996)**

# 1.3 Classifying hazards

Hazards are extremely variable in type, magnitude (size), frequency (how often they occur), geographical location and scale of impact. Classification helps us to focus on the key characteristics of different hazards so that they can be more clearly understood. Then the human response to hazards can be managed by governments, planners, hazard managers and insurance companies, as well as by the people directly at risk.

## Geophysical processes

Geographers have traditionally classified hazards based upon the geophysical processes which cause the hazard (Table 1.1). This approach is used in the structure of this book, but it is not without its problems. The classification is simple and easily understood but there are problems with accuracy. Many of the geophysical divisions become blurred since some hazardous events produce responses in other geophysical systems. For example, a volcanic eruption can produce landsliding, floods and fires. In some cases more than one geophysical system combine to produce the hazard, as with river flooding and coastal flooding which can result from a combination of atmospheric and geomorphological processes and conditions.

## Cause

The hazards studied in this book are generally considered to be *natural hazards*, but there is increasing concern about this term. Some hazards are entirely natural in origin, such as an earthquake or volcanic eruption resulting from large-scale tectonic processes. Other hazards may not be entirely natural. For example, there is some evidence of an increase in atmospheric extremes, such as storms and cyclones, which result from the global warming impacts of human pollution of the atmosphere.

Increasingly, floods are exacerbated by human activity as urban development or deforestation increases runoff processes. The flash-flood disaster which killed over 83 people on a campsite in Spain on 8 August 1996 resulted from localised very heavy rainfall which was impossible to forecast. However, local people blamed recent deforestation of the Pyrenean foothills for the disaster. Water and mud had been impounded behind a small bridge which, when it burst, resulted in a huge torrent rushing down the valley. Such hazards, which to some degree are a consequence of human activity, are termed *quasi-natural hazards*, although in reality it may be difficult to separate them from a more 'natural' hazard.

**Table 1.1  Classification of natural hazards by geophysical processes**

| *Geophysical processes* | Tectonic (geological) | Geomorphological | Atmospheric | Biological |
|---|---|---|---|---|
| **Hazard** | Earthquake<br>Volcano<br>Tsunami | Flooding – river<br>Flooding – coast and tidal surge<br>Mass movement, e.g. landslide and avalanche<br>Subsidence<br>Blowing sand | Hurricane/cyclone<br>Storm<br>Tornado<br>Drought<br>Snowstorm/blizzard<br>Hail<br>Lightning<br>Fog | Forest and grassland fire<br>Insect plague<br>Disease, e.g. malaria |

# Time and water run out for China
## Years of neglect and modern life have led to a devastating drought

**John Gittings** in Hong Kong

China is struggling to cope with a catastrophic drought that has turned the Yellow river into a trickle, dried up deep wells and turned vast areas of farmland into arid waste. After decades in which politics took precedence over the environment, China's prime minister, Zhu Rongji, is trying desperately to reverse the balance.

'Let trees sprout on mountains again, stop growing grain on hilly land and keep your livestock in its pens,' he said recently in a written edict to farmers.

Much of the drought is caused by reckless overuse as China's new consumer society demands more water. Two-thirds of China's cities, including Beijing, face severe water shortages.

'Beijingers do not appreciate their precious resource,' said the Beijing Youth Daily in a survey of the city's water crisis. The three most wasteful outlets, it concluded, are the 'bottled water industry, on-street car-washes and luxury bathing and beauty salons'.

The drought area covers most of north and central China in the interior provinces stretching from the Yellow river to the Yangtze.

The northern province of Hebei, which surrounds Beijing,

has been worst hit. About 12 000 square miles of farmland will bear no summer crops and planting has been delayed on another 2000 square miles. In the next province of Henan, rainfall last year was only 14% of the average.

Rainfall in Henan and Anhui provinces last week came too late to save threatened crops and it is no comfort that flood warnings are being issued for the summer in central China. Much of the water is expected to run off uselessly.

Experts have warned that China's plans to develop the less-advanced western provinces could wreak further damage. The western area provides the source waters for the Yellow, Yangtze and other main river systems.

But Mr Zhu, who leads the government task force for western development, is insisting that the ecological balance be maintained.

China is finally having to reckon the hidden cost of massive hydro-electric schemes which have interfered with the natural flow of its great rivers, allowing more water to be diverted and lost by evaporation.

The Yellow river has been worst hit, with no more than a trickle of water flowing in its bed from Henan to Shangdong province on the coast. Authorities

at the Xiaolangdi hydro-electric plant are now opening their sluices to let the water run freely and save the farmers' fields downstream.

No solution has yet been found to the well-known paradox that southern China has a surplus of water and has been hit by increasingly severe floods. But long-discussed plans for a south-north water transfer are being revived.

'By the year 2010,' said Wang Xucheng, the water conservancy minister, 'city-dwellers in Beijing are likely to be drinking Yangtze river water.'

And some cities are at least beginning to charge water users according to consumption. Weihai in Shandong has taken the lead, raising the price in the past year from 7p a cubic metre to £3.

Residents have been forced to reuse the same water to wash themselves and flush out their lavatories. There are complaints that some restaurants are cleaning dirty dishes with just rags.

The most tragic stories come, as always, from the countryside. A reporter from the popular newspaper Southern Weekend – which devoted an entire issue to the drought – found villagers in Henan queueing for a trickle that

took half an hour to fill a bucket.

Other peasants told of vain attempts to save the lives of thirsty water buffalo by putting damp blankets on their backs.

As fields dry up, desperate farmers are planting their crops in river waterbeds although they know that these may suddenly flood when the weather breaks.

The drought in north China comes after weeks of sandstorms in the early spring, blamed on the loss of tree cover and excessive reclamation of natural waterlands.

Much of the damage was done in the1950s and 1960s when peasants were mobilised in campaigns to increase immediate crop yields without considering the long term.

The new economic reforms of the 1980s, which allowed peasants to shift to profitable cash crops, have also led to overuse as boreholes are drilled even deeper.

Most of the water is wasted – only about 40% is used effectively in dry areas. Some farmers continued to irrigate crops which had no chance of ripening before the water ran dry.

The Yellow river flow is rationed to the provinces through which it passes, according to a fixed formula, but this is ignored.

**Figure 1.8  News article: Time and water run out for China (*Source: The Guardian*, 8 June 2000)**

**8** List the physical causes of the drought.

**9** How has the economic development added to the severity of this drought?

**10** Would you describe this as a natural hazard or a quasi-natural hazard? Explain your answer.

## Magnitude and frequency

*Magnitude* is the size of a natural hazard event or process and represents the amount of geophysical work done by the event, e.g. in the release of built-up energy by an earthquake, or mass movement of material in a landslide. Low-magnitude events tend to have less impact on people than high-magnitude events, and it is difficult to identify precisely at what point the process becomes hazardous. Many geophysical processes have magnitude scales which help us to understand the event and likely impacts, such as the Richter scale for earthquakes, and the Saffir–Simpson scale for hurricanes. *Frequency* is the number of events of a given magnitude that occur over a period of time (Figs 1.9 and 1.10).

Data from monitoring geophysical events tend to be relatively recent and cover a few decades. It is therefore difficult to predict events with long-term return periods, since there may be no record of these.

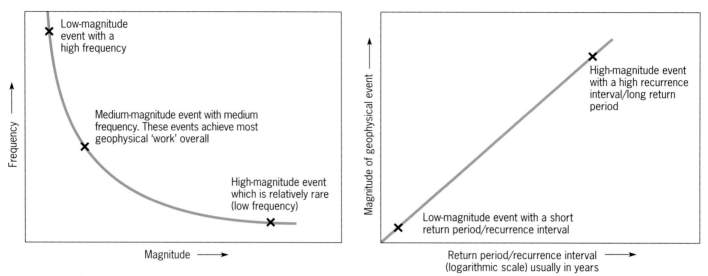

**Figure 1.9  The relationship between magnitude and frequency**

**Figure 1.10  The relationship between magnitude and return period**

---

**?**

**11** If you were a resident of California, how would you react to a 30 per cent prediction of a high-magnitude earthquake in the next 30 years? Would you take immediate action or not? What type of action could you take? Explain your answer.

**12** Study the list of hazards in Table 1.1. Suggest which hazards will show a seasonal occurrence.

---

Figure 1.11 indicates the approach used to predict hazards by giving statistical probabilities of an event occurring and which thus enables responses to be made. In California, the statistical record of earthquakes extends over the last 150 years. This is a shorter time than the likely recurrence interval for a major earthquake, and so there is an incomplete record of events which makes prediction uncertain. However, in 1988, using past records, seismologists forecast a 30 per cent probability of a magnitude 6.5 earthquake in the Loma Prieta area of the northern San Andreas fault by 2018. In 1989, a magnitude 7.1 event occurred. Using this type of data, decisions can be made about the nature of the threat, the degree of risk and whether protection measures will be taken.

Hazards may follow the pattern of Figure 1.9, or they may be seasonal, or even both. For example, a hurricane may be seasonal in occurrence but the magnitude will vary according to magnitude–frequency relationships. Other events such as lightning and fires are random in occurrence.

---

Observed results are used to extrapolate the frequency and return period for unobserved events. For example, if a river flood record covers the last 50 years, the largest flood recorded would be represented by **B**. This has a recurrence interval or return period of 50 years, or put it another way, there is 1:50 chance of that magnitude event happening each year. At point **C** there are no records of such a high-magnitude flood, but by extrapolation this would have a recurrence interval of, for example, 100 years, or a 1:100 chance of occurring each year. As more data is collected , the recurrence intervals will be revised.

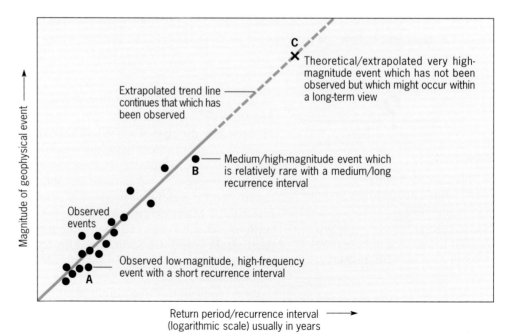

**Figure 1.11 Probability of hazardous events**

## Duration of impact and warning time

Hazards can be classified by the length of time involved in the impact on people and the warning time that is available before the event happens. *Sudden impact hazards*, such as an earthquake (measured in seconds) to tornadoes (minutes) or flash floods (hours), are judged by their casualty and damage figures since warning times are usually short. *Slow onset* or *creeping hazards* may take weeks or months, e.g. drought, some volcanic eruptions, or even years with some types of ground subsidence. These hazards usually affect larger areas and have longer warning times. In reality, however, it is difficult to divide all hazards into these two distinct groups, and there is a continuum of impact duration and forewarning times (Table 1.2).

The duration of the impact needs to be extended when we consider human systems and the post-disaster period (Fig. 1.12).

## Spatial distribution

Hazards vary in the spatial characteristics of both their occurrence and their impact (Table 1.3). Some hazards are associated with distinct geographical areas: for example, tropical cyclones occur only in parts of the tropics and earthquakes/volcanoes tend to be associated with tectonic plate boundaries. A further group of hazards are more widespread in occurrence, as with river flooding and mass movements. The scale of impact varies from local to international, with occasional global impacts such as dust and short-term climatic change resulting from large volcanic eruptions.

The impacts of hazards also vary spatially. This is the result of the spatial distribution of the hazardous events and variations in the vulnerability of the population. Data from the OFDA (US Office of Foreign Disaster Assistance) shows that the six most disaster-prone countries in the world are India, the Philippines, Bangladesh, China, Indonesia and Japan. Asia suffers the greatest in terms of deaths due to its large population in vulnerable locations and the relatively large number of people living in poverty (Table 1.4). Africa also suffered great impacts in terms of damage to economies and the number of people affected.

**13** Study Figure 1.12.
**a** Describe the stages of disruption at different phases of the hazard event.
**b** Suggest how these will differ for an event in an LEDC and an MEDC.
**c** The pattern shown in Figure 1.12 is for a sudden-impact hazard, e.g. an earthquake. How will the pattern of change vary for a slow-onset hazard such as a drought? Redraw the diagram to explain your answer.
**d** How will the pattern on the diagram be affected by (i) a very high-magnitude event, (ii) frequent medium- and low-magnitude events?

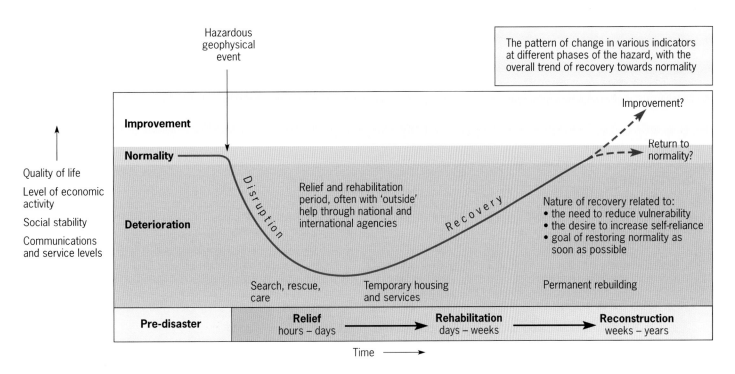

**Figure 1.12  Hazard impacts on human systems (*After:* Park, 1991)**

**Table 1.2 Classification of hazards by duration of impact and length of forewarning (*After*: Alexander, 1993)**

| Type of hazard | Duration of impact | Length of forewarning |
|---|---|---|
| Lightning | Instant | Seconds–hours |
| Avalanche | Seconds–minutes | Seconds–hours |
| Earthquake | Seconds–minutes | Minutes–years |
| Tornado | Seconds–hours | Minutes |
| Landslide | Seconds–decades | Seconds–years |
| Intense rainstorm | Minutes | Seconds–hours |
| Hail | Minutes | Minutes–hours |
| Tsunami | Minutes–hours | Minutes–hours |
| Flood | Minutes–days | Minutes–days |
| Subsidence | Minutes–decades | Seconds–years |
| Windstorm | Hours | Hours |
| Frost | Hours | Hours |
| Hurricane | Hours | Hours |
| Snowstorm | Hours | Hours |
| Forest fire | Hours–days | Seconds–days |
| Insect infestation | Hours–days | Seconds–days |
| Fog | Hours–days | Minutes–hours |
| Volcanic eruption | Hours–years | Hours–decades |
| Coastal erosion | Hours–years | Hours–decades |
| Drought | Days–months | Days–weeks |

**Table 1.3 Classification of hazards by spatial occurrence and scale of impact**

| Hazard | Spatial occurrence | Scale of impact |
|---|---|---|
| Earthquake | Global, but distinct zones | Local/regional |
| Volcano | Global, but distinct zones | Local/regional, but sometimes global |
| Tsunami | Global, but distinct zones | Local |
| River flood | Widespread | Local/regional/international |
| Coastal flooding | Widespread | Local/regional |
| Mass movement | Widespread | Local |
| Subsidence | Widespread | Local |
| Blowing sand | Restricted to arid/semi-arid/coastal | Local/regional |
| Fires | Seasonal drought | Local/regional |
| Insect plague | Widespread | Local/regional/international |
| Disease | Widespread | All scales |
| Hurricane | Tropics | Local/regional/international |
| Storm | Widespread | Local/regional/international |
| Drought | Widespread | Regional/international |
| Snowstorm/blizzard | Temperate/high latitudes | Local/regional |
| Hail | Temperate/high latitudes | Local |
| Lightning | Widespread | Local |
| Fog | Temperate/high latitudes | Local/regional |

?

**14** Present the data in Table 1.4 graphically using a spreadsheet package, or as located proportional symbols on a world map. What are the key features shown by this data?

**Table 1.4 Number of significant disasters by continental areas, 1963–1992**

| | Number of deaths (at least 100) | Significant damage (at least 1% of GNP) | Affected people (at least 1% of population) | Total | Per cent |
|---|---|---|---|---|---|
| Asia | 378 | 51 | 138 | 567 | 37.1 |
| Europe | 44 | 8 | 8 | 60 | 3.9 |
| Africa | 113 | 60 | 181 | 354 | 23.1 |
| Caribbean and C. America | 32 | 59 | 65 | 156 | 10.2 |
| North America | 41 | 2 | 0 | 43 | 2.8 |
| South America | 77 | 31 | 51 | 159 | 10.4 |
| Australia and Oceania | 101 | 30 | 60 | 191 | 12.5 |
| | | | | 1530 | 100.0 |

*Source:* Adapted from Department of Humanitarian Affairs (1994)

## Summary

- A natural hazard is a geophysical event which has the potential to cause loss of life or property. Hazard studies represent a key interaction between people and the physical environment.

- Hazard impacts include direct and indirect losses and gains in human systems. The nature of the losses varies at the global scale with highest loss of life in LEDCs and highest economic losses in MEDCs.

- Hazards may be classified by geophysical process, cause, magnitude and frequency, duration of impact and warning time, and spatial distribution.

- Hazard impacts continue to increase due to a range of factors including population growth, land pressure, urbanisation, increased vulnerability and political change.

# 2 Hazards and responses

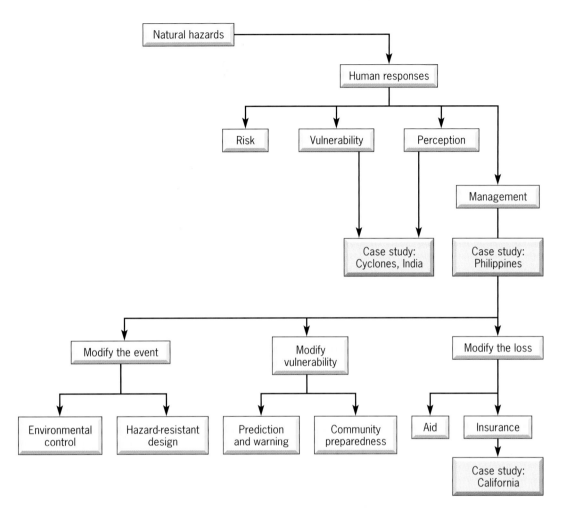

## 2.1 Risk

We are all familiar with the concept of risk, and we face risks every day, to some degree, as we travel to school or work, or take part in sporting activities which may produce injury. Risk is therefore the exposure of people to a hazardous event. These present a potential threat to people or their possessions, including buildings and structures. Generally, people perceive greater risk from events which threaten themselves than those which threaten their possessions. People may consciously place themselves at risk from natural hazards, but why do they do this? There are several related factors involved, identified by Park (1992).

### Unpredictability
Hazards are not always predictable, and it may be difficult to know when or where an event may occur or what the magnitude of the event will be.

### Lack of alternatives
People may stay in a hazardous location: for example, near an active fault line at risk from earthquakes, along a coastline subject to tropical cyclones, storm surges or tsunami, or in regions subject to drought or insect infestation. It is not easy to uproot and move to another location. This may be because of economic reasons linked to their livelihoods or a lack of alternatives, e.g. shortage of land and a lack of knowledge.

**Figure 2.1 The location of Paris on a floodplain makes it particularly vulnerable**

## Changing dangers

Natural hazards vary in space as well as through time, so that places that were once safe are now at risk. For example, low-lying coastal areas may experience more flooding in the future as a result of global warming, and river floodplains may experience more and greater-magnitude floods as a result of deforestation changing hydrological processes. These examples show clearly how humans can change the location or increase the number and magnitude of hazardous events. Remember, we need to be careful when we call some hazards 'natural', since they may be exacerbated by human activity.

## Russian roulette

People tend to have an optimistic outlook, and turn a 'blind eye' to known risks and accept them as part of the cost of living in a place or as 'God's will'. This clearly shows the importance of hazard perception and how an understanding of this is important in hazard management (see section 2.3).

## Costs versus benefits

The resources or benefits of a hazardous location may well outweigh the risks involved in staying there. For example, in California, the earthquake risk is high, but there are many benefits to living in the state (Fig. 2.2).

# 2.2 Vulnerability

People live in hazardous environments for many complex, interrelated reasons, and place themselves at risk from hazardous events. However, is this risk equal for all people? The hazardous event may be natural, but the impact and the scale of the resulting disaster is largely determined by human factors (Fig. 1.3). Just as there are differences in how people benefit from the resources in the environment, so there are differences in how they are vulnerable to the risks. For example, in California, recent earthquakes (Fig. 2.2) caused large economic losses but relatively little loss of life compared with similar-magnitude earthquakes in the developing world. Even within one society some people are more vulnerable than others, as shown by the 1995 Kobe earthquake in Japan, which killed mainly older and poorer members of the city who lived in older housing not designed to withstand earthquakes. The richer people suffered less physical damage and were able to move away from the area rather than remain in the camps for the homeless. Vulnerability refers not only to the hazardous event itself, but also to the ability to recover afterwards.

People's wealth and level of technical ability can affect the degree to which they can protect themselves from a natural hazard – for example, by building homes more able to withstand an earthquake or tropical cyclone. Education is also important, particularly the level of awareness of the hazard and what protection measures can be taken. The organisation of a society can be crucial in determining the impact of a hazard. Groups of people working together either informally or at the local/national government level can prepare themselves better before a hazardous event and organise relief efforts afterwards. Health and vulnerability are related to income, but age is also

**1** Read the article, Figure 2.2.
**a** How do Californians react to the risk from the earthquake hazard?
**b** What environmental advantages seem to outweigh the risks involved?
**c** How does the unpredictability of events affect people's views of natural hazards?

# Is California worth the risk?

*Absolutely, 30 million residents will say – and they're no different from Americans who smoke, drive, hang-glide, eat apples or fly DC-10s*

There should be plenty to talk about this week at the annual conference of the Society for Risk Analysis. (Yes, there really is one.) The 800 or so actuaries, social scientists, lawyers and psychologists who are expected to attend will gather in – what better place? – San Francisco. They will need only step outside their hotels to see a city that has become a vast society for risk analysis. All around the Bay Area these days, amid the tumbled roadways and jolted buildings left by the earthquake, people are asking themselves: Is it crazy to live on a fault line?

Though that question is never entirely out of mind in California, it usually just withers in the sun, overwhelmed by the seductive arguments of the natural beauty and friendly climate. But now the palpable and sometimes painful memories of the Pretty Big One, as the locals are calling the recent quake, have lent a certain sharpness to the prospects of further shake-ups. Last week scientists were telling Californians that the state faces a 50% chance that another quake as strong as the recent one could happen 'at any time' during the next 30 years. 'And that means tomorrow,' says Don Anderson, director of the seismological laboratory at the Californian Institute of Technology.

Even so, few are rushing to catch the next plane east. In Santa Cruz, near the epicenter of the quake, county officials are awaiting the judgement of geologists as to whether homeowners should be allowed to rebuild on the fractured hillsides, where landslides may now become a perennial headache, Many residents are nonetheless eager to rebuild. True to their reputation for mellowness and impregnable cool, Californians are generally unfased by the fault-line threat.

'The earth shakes and rolls under my feet,' shrugs novelist Wallace Stegner, a 40-year-old resident of Los Altos Hills. 'It's never particularly alarmed me.' Brokers insist that San Francisco's booming real estate market has not subsided. 'Obviously the quake was a drawback,' concedes Katherine August of First Republic Bancorp, which specializes in loans for luxury homes. 'But I don't think it will have a lasting effect on the market. We closed one deal the day after the quake.' Says pollster Mervin Field: 'Sure it shook people up. But look at the World Series game that was interrupted at Candlestick Park. A few minutes after the quake, you had 58,000 people chanting 'Play ball! Play ball!'

Is this the same California that has been sensitive to risks from every kind of environmental threat? Three years ago, the state's voters approved Proposition 65, a law that mandates warning labels on any substance found to carry a 1-in-100,000 lifetime risk of causing cancer. As a result, cautionary notices now appear on gasoline pumps, in hardware and grocery stores and on the walls of Napa Valley wineries.

In fact, Californians are no different from other Americans when it comes to risk. The national temperament seems to have a fault line all its own. On one side of that psychic divide, Americans shrug off demonstrable threats: they build houses on eroding beaches, speed without wearing seat belts, go hang-gliding and expose themselves to cancer-causing rays of the sun. On the other side, they suffer a bad case of the jitters about the smallest threat to personal well-being. They flee from apples that might bear a trace of Alar and fret about radon, nuclear power and DC-10s.

F. Scott Fitzgerald once suggested that 'the test of a first-rate intelligence is the ability to hold two opposed ideas in the mind at the same time'. If so, America has developed a perverse sort of genius. Yet both national moods – the urge to deny risk and the urge to insist that we can protect ourselves from it entirely – may be traceable to the same unfailing optimism. In a culture that has long fancied itself a New World paradise, disasters seem impossible either to imagine or to tolerate. People expect to conduct the pursuit of happiness along a road that is straight, well lighted and free of bumps.

Experts on risk perception generally agree that people tend to be less concerned about dangers they incur voluntarily, like cigarette smoking and fast driving. They are more resentful of risks they feel have been imposed upon them, like the threat of mishaps at a nearby nuclear plant. They are more sensitive to risks they can control – for instance, through laws that ban pesticides or require safety warnings – than they are to those they feel they can do nothing about – like acts of nature. 'People choose what to fear,' says Aaron Wildavsky, co-author of *Risk and Culture.* 'What can you do about an earthquake?'

There is evidence that it takes repeated batterings to shake people's tenacity. Natural disasters do not often occur in so predictable a manner. Mary Skipper is getting ready to replace her mobile home near Charleston, S.C., in a spot hit hard by Hurricane Hugo in September. 'I know this is a flood plain,' she explains. 'But something like Hugo may never happen again for another 100 years.'

Californians cannot count on the same lengthy intervals between disasters. After a moderately powerful quake shook the area around Whittier in 1987, a University of Southern California survey of 235 people in Los Angeles County found that most of those questioned were not interested in leaving. But 30% said they might make plans to go if another quake of the same magnitude shook them.

'Applied to San Francisco, it means that a second quake there in a year or two would have a much greater impact. We could expect to see a significant out-migration from California,' says geologist Curtis C. Roseman. 'One quake doesn't do the job.'

To say that Californians have been willing to tolerate the risks arising from life on a fault line is not to say they have been indifferent to them. The recent quake was comparable in magnitude to the one in Armenia last December, which killed 25,000. 'A substantial contributor to the much lower death rate in California was that California was conscious of the risk and made significant investments as a precaution,' says M. Granger Morgan, head of the Department of Engineering and Public Policy at Carnegie-Mellon University. But after last week, earthquakes are going to be viewed as a much more persistent risk than they were before. That will force many communities to choose which risks to take seriously. Says Bruce Bolt, a seismologist at the University of California, Berkeley: 'If you have only a certain amount of dollars to spend on risk mitigation in a particular area, do you spend it on seismic upgrading or on asbestos removal?'

**Figure 2.2  Magazine article: Is California Worth the Risk? (*Source: Time*, 5 November 1989)**

important. Many disasters affect the old or very young to a disproportionate degree. People's resilience may depend upon their income and social class, as these affect their ability to absorb the losses incurred to their possessions. From this overview, a key understanding is that vulnerability is not necessarily the same as poverty. If we return to our earthquake example, it is possible for the middle classes to be more affected by the collapse of their unsafe homes because of the ground movement than the poor in shanty towns whose flimsy homes collapse and cause little damage.

It is the increasing vulnerability of people which accounts for the increasing impact of natural hazards identified over recent years (see section 1.2). As the world's population has increased, so too has the number of people living in more hazardous areas. The higher population and rates of population increase in the LEDCs, the greater their vulnerability relative to the richer nations. In poorer countries people have been moved on to more marginal and vulnerable land for a variety of reasons. For example, in Bangladesh the landless are increasingly forced to live on the very flood-prone areas due to a lack of alternatives, and in growing cities, shanty towns have developed on unstable hillslopes or floodplains. However, in the MEDCs people place themselves knowingly at risk – consider the development of Tokyo and Los Angeles in hazardous, earthquake-prone regions.

There is a spectrum of vulnerability from the poorest countries such as Bangladesh and Ethiopia, with high fatalities and low economic losses, to the richer nations such as Japan and the USA, where fatalities are low but economic losses are high. These economic losses may be offset by insurance schemes (see case study). In between are those countries showing rapid development which may experience both high economic losses and high fatalities, such as Mexico and the Philippines (see Chapter 6).

**Figure 2.3 Location of the world's 100 largest urban areas (1985) in relation to earthquake zones, volcanoes, tsunami-affected coasts and windstorm hazards (*After:* Dregg, 1992)**

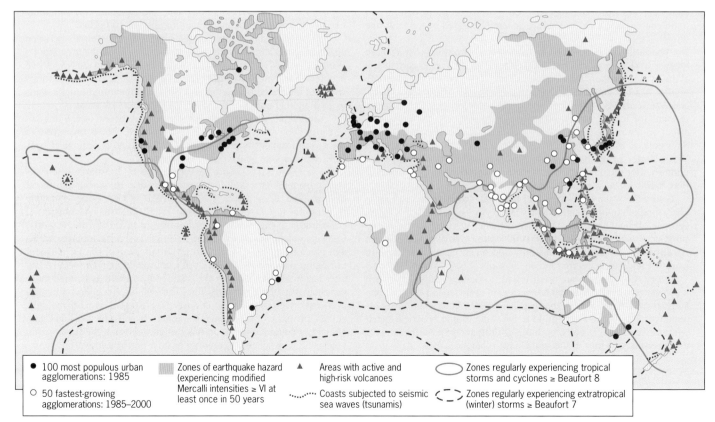

- ● 100 most populous urban agglomerations: 1985
- ○ 50 fastest-growing agglomerations: 1985–2000

Zones of earthquake hazard (experiencing modified Mercalli intensities ≥ VI at least once in 50 years)

- ▲ Areas with active and high-risk volcanoes
- ⋯⋯⋯ Coasts subjected to seismic sea waves (tsunamis)

Zones regularly experiencing tropical storms and cyclones ≥ Beaufort 8

Zones regularly experiencing extratropical (winter) storms ≥ Beaufort 7

**Figure 2.4 Urban hazard exposure: ranked exposure values of the largest cities in the developed and developing world (*After:* Dregg, 1992)**

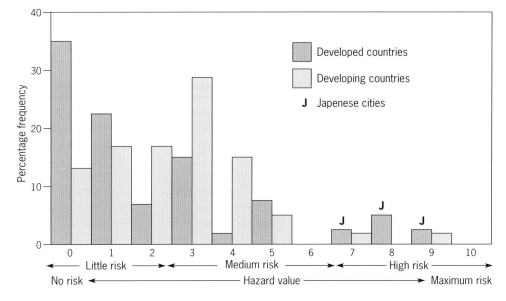

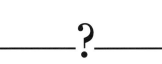

2 Study Figure 2.3.
**a** Describe the geographical location of natural hazards shown and draw a map to show the most hazardous regions.
**b** What natural hazards are faced by the following cities: Mexico City, Los Angeles, London, Rio de Janeiro, Cairo, Tokyo, Beijing, Manila, Jakarta and Melbourne?

3 Study Figure 2.4.
**a** Construct a table to compare the hazard exposure of developed and developing world cities in terms of exposure to (i) little risk (classes 2 or less); (ii) medium risk (classes 3–6); (iii) high risk (classes 7–10).
**b** Are developing world cities most at risk from natural hazards? Explain your answer.

## Vulnerability of the world's largest cities

Dregg (1992) studied the location of the world's largest and fastest-growing cities in relation to natural hazards which may threaten them, i.e. earthquake, volcanic eruption, tsunami, storm and tropical cyclone (hurricane). Figure 2.3 shows the location of the cities in relation to these hazards, and Figure 2.4 the results of the analysis.

Modifying people's vulnerability is therefore an important aspect of hazard management, along with approaches which centre on the hazardous event. Tackling the economic aspects of vulnerability is complex and long term, while hazard management, which focuses on people's self-protection and social protection by local groups or government, is therefore more realistic.

# Vulnerability to the cyclone hazard in eastern India

## Background

The Bay of Bengal is at risk from cyclone (hurricane) development just before and after the monsoon phases, i.e. in May, October and November. The coast of Andhra Pradesh (Fig. 2.5) has experienced 65 severe storms and cyclones in the last 100 years making it the most cyclone-prone region of India. There is a well documented record of cyclone impact (Table 2.1). The region is relatively poor economically with high rural population densities. This case study considers the vulnerability to impacts of the cyclone hazard using one example. However, important generalisations can be made from this.

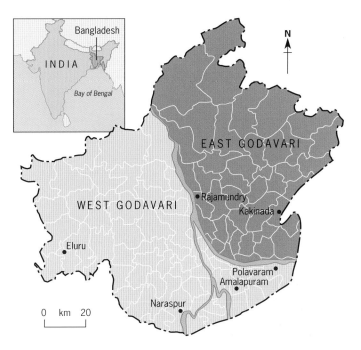

**Figure 2.5 The Godavari delta region, Andhra Pradesh, India. Each district is divided into administrative units called *mandals*.**

## Vulnerability in Indian Society

Vulnerability has been defined by Blaikie, et al (1994) as the characteristics of a person or group in terms of their capacity to anticipate, cope with, and recover from the impact of a natural hazard. The cyclone hazard results from three main physical events: the storm surge (coastal flooding); high winds; and heavy rainfall, producing floods.

Some groups are more vulnerable to the impacts of such a natural disaster and have more difficulty recovering from the financial and resource losses. These groups will generally show greater vulnerability to all natral hazards, although in this example, the focus is on the cyclone (hurricane) hazard. Particularly vulnerable groups are:
- low caste communities, e.g. tribal castes in India
- ethnic minorities
- women, especially widows
- aged men and women
- children, especially girls
- disabled
- low-income or daily-income groups
- those in debt
- those isolated from infrastructures including transport, communications and health services.

Research (Agarwal, 1990)has shown that the rural poor in India have five main survival strategies:
- diverifying sources of income, including seasonal migration
- drawing upon communal resources
- drawing upon social relationships including patronage, kinship, friendship and informal credit networks
- drawing upon household stores (food, fuel, etc.) and adjusting currrent consumption patterns
- drawing upon assets.

**Table 2.1  The impact of cyclonic depressions, tropical storms and hurricanes along the coast of Andhra Pradesh, 1978–96**

| Year of cyclone heavy rains and floods | Districts affected | Population affected ('000s) | Human deaths | Livestock loss | Houses damaged | Crop area damaged ('000s ha) | Estimated loss (Rs million) |
|---|---|---|---|---|---|---|---|
| Aug 1978 | 16 | 49 | 52 | 1 465 | 22 000 | 951 | 1 500.0 |
| May 1979 | 10 | n.d. | 706 | n.d. | 748 000 | n.d. | 2 426.5 |
| Aug 1983 | 8 | 158 | 58 | 1 726 | 94 218 | 714 | 895.6 |
| Feb 1984 | 3 | 1 900 | 7 | 3 976 | 8 244 | 192 | 555.3 |
| Dec 1985 | 11 | 1 175 | 16 | 4 | 3 196 | 214 | 405.0 |
| Aug 1986 | 13 | n.d. | 309 | 22 000 | 423 000 | 853.2 | 16 867.4 |
| Nov 1987 | 10 | 3 204 | 119 | n.d. | 110 550 | 961 | 1 264.8 |
| July 1988 | 11 | 2 343 | 88 | 4 233 | 10 621 | 906 | 2 454.0 |
| July 1989 | 22 | 8 944 | 232 | 10 905 | 227 000 | 593 | 9 135.0 |
| May 1990 | 14 | 7 781 | 817 | 27 625 | 1 439 659 | 563 | 21 372.7 |
| Aug 1990 | 10 | 1 245 | 50 | n.d. | 76 420 | 173 | 1 798.6 |
| Oct – Nov 1991 | 9 | 18 | 192 | n.d. | 97 470 | 499 | 3 673.2 |
| Nov – Dec 1993 | 5 | n.d. | n.d. | n.d. | n.d. | 52 | 1 304.5 |
| July – Aug 1994 | 6 | 281 | n.d. | n.d. | n.d. | 52 | 1 304.5 |
| Oct – Nov 1994 | 7 | 286 | 3 | n.d. | 2 587 | 452 | 6 259.3 |
| May 1995 | 10 | 256 | 26 | 3 260 | 42 665 | 320 | 4 718.6 |
| Oct – Nov 1995 | 19 | 230 | 229 | 3 663 | 146 525 | 665 | 9 170.0 |
| Oct 1996 | 5 | 137 | 338 | n.d. | 450 000 | 1 029 | 8 432.7 |
| Nov 1996 | 2 | 7 100 | 1 059 | 6 845 | 646 000 | 236 | 61 264.7 |

## Hurricane 07B

The storm reached the Godavari Delta of central Andhra Pradesh during 6–7 November 1996. The delta is a fertile agricultural area with paddy fields, coconut, bananas, sugar cane and horticultural crops. The population is 9 million with a growth rate of 1.8 per cent per year. About 67 per cent of the population work in agriculture with high population densities, especially near to the coast (Fig. 2.8a).

Figure 2.7 shows the development of the cyclone. At 5 p.m. on 6 November the cyclone was at its most intense with winds of 220 km per hr and a vortex diameter of 400 km as it crossed the delta area. The rainfall reached between 100–200 mm in the delta region, although beyond this there was little impact. For example, Vishakhapatnam received no rain. 7.12 million people, representing over 80 per cent of the delta's population, were affected by the storm.

The impacts of the storm were relatively severe for its size (Table 2.1). There were three main reasons for this.

- The Indian Meteorological Department pinpoint the atypical nature of the storm as factor. It developed very rapidly and did not give the usual precursors such as increased cloudiness, high winds and heavy rainfall in the day or two before landfall. Thus people had little 'natural' warning of the event.
- Wind speeds of 200 km/hr were twice that forecast and this allowed a high storm surge of up to 2.5 m to sweep 6 km inland.
- The storm arrived earlier than expected, i.e. 5 – 6 p.m. rather than midnight.

## People at risk

The most at risk are the rural poor, especially the landless and those without regular employment. The rural poor tend to live in houses with mud walls and thatched roofs which are easily damaged or destroyed by hurricane winds. Higher income farmers and landowners have brick and concrete houses which are less susceptible to damage. Most of the delta farmers are small-scale (less than 5ha) but most were able to rely on savings and assets to tide them over to the next harvest.

### Migrant workers

One of the most vulnerable groups is the rural landless labourer especially lower caste women and girls who are migrant workers from Orissa State. They tend to have no financial or food reserves to use in times of crisis. Their coping strategies were individual rather than part of a community response. These included begging, selling possessions (mainly jewellery), domestic service in nearby towns and migration elsewhere. In the past landowners may have provided handouts but this traditional response has largely broken down.

### Fishing communities

Another highly vulnerable group were the coastal fishing communities. Their poverty, physical and social isolation, and their location in relation to the hurricane hazard i.e. in the coastal area of first landfall and storm surge, put them at risk. Many children died due to the storm surge but more than 1000 deaths were fishermen and their sons drowning at sea (Fig 2.8b). They had been unaware of the rapidly advancing storm. As well as loss of life, this group lost their fishing boats, i.e. they lost their livelihoods. In contrast to the migrant workers, however, their response was collective and drew upon communal resources. The fishing communities are close-knit and independent. Most stayed in their villages to recover. Some worked for other fishermen and the communities helped each other by rebuilding houses and sharing food (Fig. 2.8c).

**Figure 2.6 Typical height of storm surges from severe storms and hurricanes along the eastern coast of India**

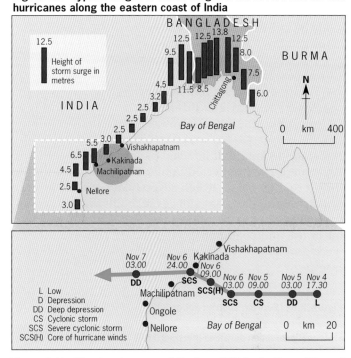

Figure 2.7   The development of Cyclone 07B in the Bay of Bengal

## Cyclone mitigation strategies

There are three approaches to cyclone hazard management in India. These are all essentially top-down apporaches; they are developed and imposed from outside the local communities.

### Physical approaches

This is the capital-intensive, technological fix approach of building defences, embankments and surge-proof buildings. These were not used by the people as they have no food or other service and they are afraid the dilapidated and disused shelters might collapse. The shelters are externally imposed and generally viewed with some suspicion.

### Early warning and evacuation procedures

Satellite-based cyclone forecasting and evacuation procedures are in place for India. The Cyclone Warning and Dissemination Systems (CWDS) implemented along Andhra coast in 1978 has reduced the death toll from major cyclones. For example, contrasting two category-5 cyclones, in November 1977 there were 10 000 deaths compared to 1000 deaths in May 1990.

Warning systems are not without their problems. They are issued up to 24 hours ahead by telephone, teleprinter, telex and television. Many of the poor fishing communities in the Godavari Delta do not have access to these. Although radio stations also give hourly warnings, a recent survey by the Indian Meteorological Service showed that only 30 per cent of fishermen carry radios and these may not be tuned into the right station. The signal was often too weak.

Evacuation is a problem due to poor communications. Only half of the roads are all-weather surfaces and up to 20 per cent of the villages are not connected by road. Had evacuation occurred, it would clearly have saved lives. There is also some concern when warnings are issued which turn out to be inaccurate. People are less likely to respond quickly the next time a cyclone threatens.

### Aid

The state organised basic relief by providing rice and kerosene for each affected family. Poor communications meant that it took between several days and two weeks to reach remote coastal villages, if at all. Compensation payments were made for injuries and death as well as for house and boat damage (Fig. 2.8d). However, there were problems with or proving the losses in some cases.

## Conclusion

The different social groups and communities in the Godavari Delta area of India affects the variation in the hazard vulnerability within one geographical area. The spatial impact of the hazard, position of people within society and other social characteristics such as age, and gender all affect the variation. Many researchers argue that disasters will continue to happen unless the management strategies are changed. Figure 2.9 shows such a disaster in November 1999. This disaster occurred towards the end of the UN Decade for hazard reduction. The poverty and social ordering of Indian rural society needs to be considered. External imposed technological systems do not appear to be fully appropriate. Strategies need to:
- raise risk awareness through education schemes
- improve risk avoiding abilities
- be bottom-up and community-based. For example, the village leader is often the only person with real local authority.

**Figure 2.8** (*Source:* District records)

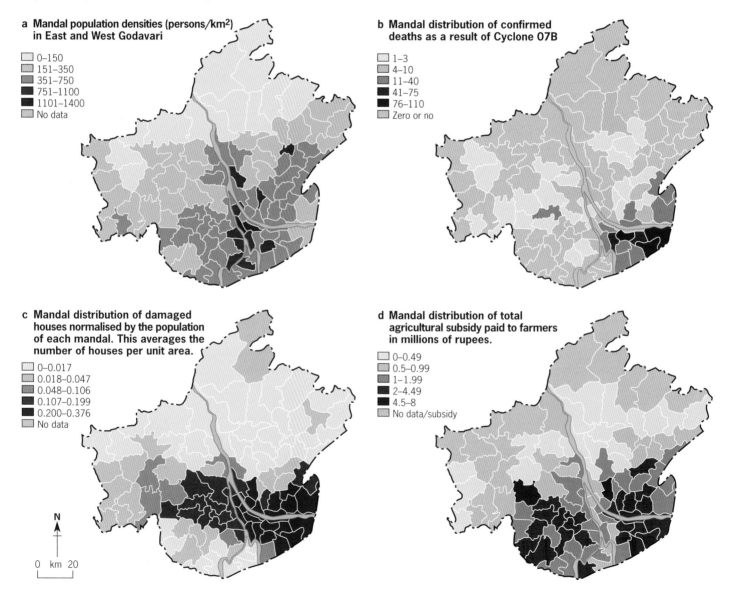

**a Mandal population densities (persons/km²) in East and West Godavari**
- 0–150
- 151–350
- 351–750
- 751–1100
- 1101–1400
- No data

**b Mandal distribution of confirmed deaths as a result of Cyclone 07B**
- 1–3
- 4–10
- 11–40
- 41–75
- 76–110
- Zero or no

**c Mandal distribution of damaged houses normalised by the population of each mandal. This averages the number of houses per unit area.**
- 0–0.017
- 0.018–0.047
- 0.048–0.106
- 0.107–0.199
- 0.200–0.376
- No data

**d Mandal distribution of total agricultural subsidy paid to farmers in millions of rupees.**
- 0–0.49
- 0.5–0.99
- 1–1.99
- 2–4.49
- 4.5–8
- No data/subsidy

N

0   km  20

?

4 Interrogate the data in Table 2.1.
a Consider whether the impacts of cyclones in Andhra Pradesh is increasing or decreasing. Explain your conclusion.
b What factors will affect the differing impacts of the cyclones in Table 2.1?
c Was Cyclone 07B a relatively damaging storm (Table 2.1)?

5a What survival strategies would your family use if your home was destroyed by a storm?
b How do these compare to those used by the rural poor of India?

6a Describe the distribution of storm surge heights in the Bay of Bengal.
b Compare the storm surge hazard of Bangladesh and eastern India.

7a Use Figure 2.7 to describe the development of storm 07B.
b Calculate the average speed of the storm between 17.30 on 4 November and 03.00 on 7 November.

c For how long was the storm classified as a severe cyclonic storm SCSC(H)?

8 Describe and explain the distribution of deaths from the cyclone (Figure 2.8b).

9 Describe and explain the distribution of damaged houses (Figures 2.7 and 2.8c).

10 Suggest why the agricultural subsidies paid (Figure 2.8d) is not the same as the distribution of deaths and house damage.

11 Evaluate the effectiveness of cyclone hazard management strategies in India.

12 Why is it suggested that these strategies are not fully appropriate?

13 Suggest the types of strategies that might be more community-based. How can these develop the successful aspects of the current strategies?

# India in the eye of 'Biblical' cyclone

A 'supercyclone' of 'Biblical' proportions has hit India's east coast, destroying the homes of more than 1.5 million people. The death toll is not yet known, but the Indian prime minister, Atal Behari Vajpayee, says it may run to thousands.

Villages up to nine miles inland of the Bengal Sea yesterday remained under water, and power and roads to much of Orissa remained cut. At least 200 fishermen have been reported missing and more than 4000 are feared dead after being caught in winds reported to have reached 160 mph.

Continuing storms meant Indian air force helicopters were yesterday unable to deliver food and fuel to the affected areas. Troops and medical teams trying to clear the roads to the region have been unable to reach those needing help. As well as cutting off power, the storm has cut off water supplies and almost all communications. Even the police wireless system has been destroyed. 'You can't imagine the damage,' Orissa State Chief Minister Giridhar Gamag told reporters.

The cyclone struck around noon on Friday and is now heading further inland and slowly weakening. The state government of Orissa has sent an emergency request to Delhi asking for massive mobilisation of resources to help supply relief. Federal minister Naveen Patnaik called for faster assistance from the capital. 'There has been tardiness in providing relief to the worst affected areas,' he said.

The storm has also damaged parts of the neighbouring states of Andhara Pradesh and West Bengal.

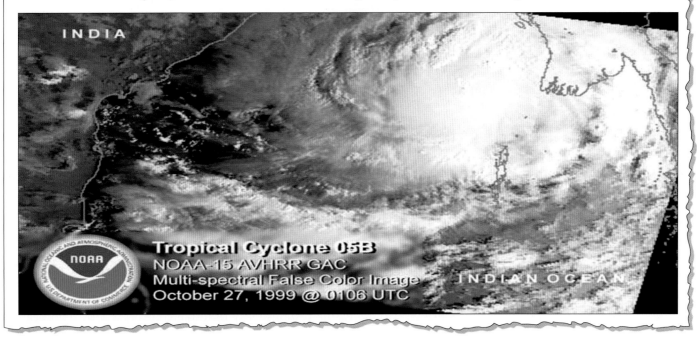

**Figure 2.9 The Bay of Bengal remains vulnerable to the cyclone hazard (*Source: The Observer*, 31 October 1999)**

## 2.3 Hazard perception

We react to the threat from natural hazards in different ways because we receive, filter and distort information as part of human perception. This perception, along with the variability of hazardous events, means that we have a selective and partial view of natural hazards. These result in differing responses which aim to modify the event or the human systems (Fig. 2.10).

**Figure 2.10 Model of human perception and response to natural hazards (*After:* Kates, 1992)**

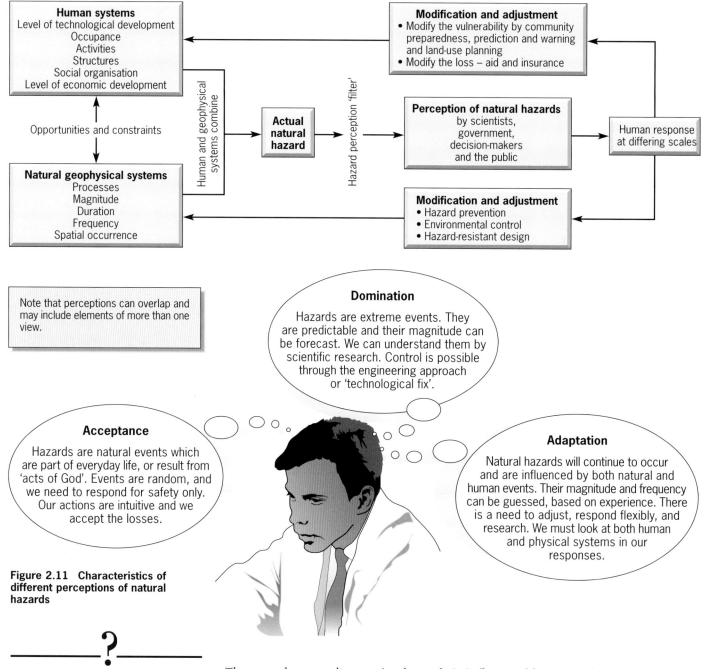

**Human systems**
Level of technological development
Occupance
Activities
Structures
Social organisation
Level of economic development

Opportunities and constraints

**Natural geophysical systems**
Processes
Magnitude
Duration
Frequency
Spatial occurrence

Human and geophysical systems combine

**Actual natural hazard**

Hazard perception 'filter'

**Modification and adjustment**
• Modify the vulnerability by community preparedness, prediction and warning and land-use planning
• Modify the loss – aid and insurance

**Perception of natural hazards**
by scientists, government, decision-makers and the public

**Modification and adjustment**
• Hazard prevention
• Environmental control
• Hazard-resistant design

**Human response at differing scales**

Note that perceptions can overlap and may include elements of more than one view.

**Domination**
Hazards are extreme events. They are predictable and their magnitude can be forecast. We can understand them by scientific research. Control is possible through the engineering approach or 'technological fix'.

**Acceptance**
Hazards are natural events which are part of everyday life, or result from 'acts of God'. Events are random, and we need to respond for safety only. Our actions are intuitive and we accept the losses.

**Adaptation**
Natural hazards will continue to occur and are influenced by both natural and human events. Their magnitude and frequency can be guessed, based on experience. There is a need to adjust, respond flexibly, and research. We must look at both human and physical systems in our responses.

**Figure 2.11 Characteristics of different perceptions of natural hazards**

**?**

**14a** How might the perceptions of scientists differ from those of the 'general public'?
**b** What factors will influence these perceptions?

**15** Why is the perception of the decision-makers in government and organisations so important?

The way that people perceive hazards is influenced by many factors, including past experiences, attitudes, personality and values, and expectations for the future. Past experience has been shown to be very important in hazard perception. People's perceptions are complex, and range from those that believe that hazards are due to fate (external control) or are outside their responsibility, to increasing responsibility (internal control) where action can be taken. The results can be divided into three broad groups of perception and response (Fig. 2.11). The assessment of the hazard threat and hazard perception combine to influence the type of human response.

# 2.4 The human response to hazards

People respond to natural hazards and the threats they pose to human life and possessions in a way that is designed to reduce the risk. This response can occur at a range of levels, from the individual and local communities to national or international level. The response(s) chosen, if any, will depend upon the nature of the hazard, past experience of hazardous events, economic ability to take action, technological resources, hazard perceptions of the decision-makers, knowledge of the available options, and the social and political framework. People and organisations may not adopt all the available strategies, since resources of time and money are needed for this. The relative importance of the threat from natural hazards compared with other concerns such as jobs, money, education, for individuals or governments, will be major factors. People and governments must be willing and able to put resources into reducing hazard impacts (**hazard salience**).

The range of responses available can be divided into three broad groups: modify the event, modify human vulnerability, or modify the loss. These will be discussed for each group of hazards in each relevant chapter.

## *Prevent or modify the event*
These management strategies aim to control the physical processes involved by the 'technological fix', and therefore modify or prevent the hazardous event. This can be achieved in two ways.

### Hazard prevention and environmental control
The ideal would be to prevent the hazardous event occurring. However, for most hazards prevention is unrealistic at present levels of understanding and technology. Environmental control aims to suppress the actual hazardous event by diffusing releases of energy over a greater area or period of time, and ultimately aims to prevent the hazardous event occurring. Flooding is the main hazard which has been managed by this method. Flood waters are diverted by a wide range of engineering structures, such as dams, levées and channel changes, or afforestation measures. Control of atmospheric processes, e.g. cloud seeding to end droughts, have had little success to date.

### Hazard-resistant design (protection)
This method aims to protect people and structures from the impacts of hazards. The focus is upon building design and construction of engineered defences such as sea walls. Buildings can be designed to withstand earthquakes, cyclones/hurricanes and floods. Most public buildings such as roads, dams and bridges will incorporate appropriate hazard-resistant features in areas of perceived risk.

## *Modify vulnerability*
This response aims to change human attitudes and behaviour towards hazards, either before the event or during it.

**?**

**16** To what extent do you consider hazard management strategies to be (a) individual responsibility, and (b) government responsibility.

**17** How will economic resources affect the choice of strategies available in MEDCs compared with LEDCs?

**Figure 2.12  Weather forecasting at the Meteorological Office at Bracknell, UK**

**?**

**18** Suggest how people could respond to a warning of (a) a flood, (b) a tropical cyclone and (c) a volcanic eruption.

**19** What will be the impacts of a false warning?

**20** Explain why technology is so important in prediction and warning.

**21** What differences will MEDCs and LEDCs have in (a) technological availability for monitoring, (b) scientific knowledge to interpret the data, and (c) dissemination methods?

**Forecast** – a relatively imprecise statement of the time, place, and nature of the expected event

**Prediction** – a relatively precise statement of the time, place and, ideally, the nature and size of an event, i.e. a precise forecast

Forecasts and predictions can be either long term or short term. For example, to a vulcanologist, 'short term' can mean hours to months, whereas 'long term' means decades or longer.

### Prediction and warning

If a hazard can be predicted before the event then action can be taken to reduce its impact. In order to achieve the greatest benefit, predictions need to identify when the event will occur, how often, the area affected, and the magnitude. This is not always possible for all hazards with the current understanding of geophysical processes and the technology available. However, improved monitoring, information and communications technology (Fig. 2.12) means that predicting hazards and issuing warnings have become more important in recent years, especially for volcanic eruptions, floods, tropical cyclones and tornadoes. Prediction of such hazards will not stop the event, but it does allow warnings to be issued so that people can prepare or evacuate the area. The purpose of prediction, therefore, is to reduce the impact on people and property. Insurance companies (see page 26) spend large amounts of money trying to predict natural disasters (Fig. 2.13). This is important in setting the cost of insurance against these events, since a major disaster can cause huge financial losses. Between 1970 and 1995, 28 of the 30 most expensive losses at Lloyd's of London were due to natural disasters. Hurricane Andrew in 1992 resulted in a huge US$16 billion in claims. Improved modelling and prediction can enable companies to set higher premiums in areas of higher risk.

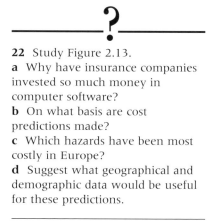

**?**

22  Study Figure 2.13.

**a**  Why have insurance companies invested so much money in computer software?

**b**  On what basis are cost predictions made?

**c**  Which hazards have been most costly in Europe?

**d**  Suggest what geographical and demographic data would be useful for these predictions.

---

Insurance companies can go hi-tech to predict the cost of damage from floods and storms

# Disaster warning ahead

On Monday 28 October, the tail end of Atlantic Hurricane Lily swept over the south and west coasts of Britain, causing severe damage to buildings and property.

With the wind blowing to force 12 and the tide rising two metres higher than predicted, insurance companies all over the country assessed the extent of their financial liability – but because of some very special software, some already knew just how much was at risk.

The two pieces of software, UKWIND and UKFLOOD, developed by an international company, EQECAT, allow insurance companies to make accurate assessments of damage and potential cost of major natural disasters.

They forecast the potential cost of flood and storm damage, and even make predictions concerning the integrity of sea defences.

EQECAT software, which cost more than £10 million to develop, relies upon an extremely detailed analysis of the area at risk, and uses both geographical and demographic data to make its cost predictions.

Every aspect of the area is considered, from the nature and value of the buildings to the occupants and social status of the inhabitants.

David Whitling of EQECAT said: 'It is important to consider every conceivable detail when assessing the cost of damage. We know the risk areas very well indeed – even down to the number of television sets that people own.

'Wind storms have been the most damaging and costly natural disasters to date in Europe, and our products are designed to calculate just how expensive they can be.'

Advance warning of potential losses allows insurers time to make sufficient funds available to deal with their liabilities, and allow them to offer a faster service at a

**Waves from Hurricane Lily batter Bournemouth seafront**

time when it is most needed.

Insurance company portfolios show properties at risk all over the country, but the companies can now use UKWIND and UKFLOOD software to show how much they are covering in any part of the UK.

This allows insurance companies to spread the financial load if one area shows a concentration of properties which could all be the subject of a disaster claim.

**Figure 2.13  Newspaper report concerning the forecasting of the damage and potential cost of major natural disasters** (*Source: The Times*, 13 November 1996)

A warning is a message which informs people at risk of an approaching or impending hazard. Prediction and warning depend upon adequate monitoring and evaluation of the data received, then the dissemination of the warning via television, radio or community personnel, such as police officers. If this approach is to be successful, the community must understand and then respond to the warning.

### Community preparedness

This involves prearranged measures which aim to reduce the loss of life and property damage. The measures involved include public education and awareness programmes, evacuation procedures, and provision of emergency medical, food and shelter supplies (Fig. 2.15). The importance of preparedness and education in successful hazard management has been shown by various programmes which have reduced losses. An example is the volcanic emergency plan devised in the 1980s for Rabaul, Papua New Guinea, which was largely responsible for the effective evacuation and low loss of life when major volcanic eruptions occurred in 1994.

### Land-use planning

This aims to prevent new development from occupying hazardous areas. The main problem is that it is not applicable to existing developments. Success depends upon knowledge of the nature, location and recurrence intervals of hazards.

## Modify the loss

The most passive response is to simply accept the losses incurred. This is rarely an acceptable strategy, especially with higher-magnitude events. More commonly, the strategy is to share the losses. This can be achieved in two ways: aid and insurance.

### Aid

Aid is normally provided at community, national or international level for relief, rehabilitation and reconstruction purposes (Fig. 2.15). High-magnitude events often result in the hazard area being designated a 'disaster area' by national governments, and the losses shared throughout the tax-paying population. This approach raises issues concerned with individual responsibility, and to what extent help should be given to those who have taken no measures to protect themselves or to those who are on high incomes and are able to recover without aid.

At the international level there may be political problems with providing aid, and issues of national pride which can make some countries reluctant to ask for international help. Organisations such as the United Nations Department of Humanitarian Affairs (DHA), set up in 1992, aims to deal more effectively with political difficulties in providing humanitarian aid (Fig. 2.16). There are also several charitable non-governmental organisations involved in aid, such as the Red Cross, the Red Crescent and the Save the Children Fund. One of the main problems with this approach is that sudden high-magnitude events tend to generate more donations than slow-onset hazards such as droughts.

**Figure 2.14 The risk management cycle, showing the sequence of assessment, response and education which is essential for successful disaster reduction (*Source:* Smith, 1996)**

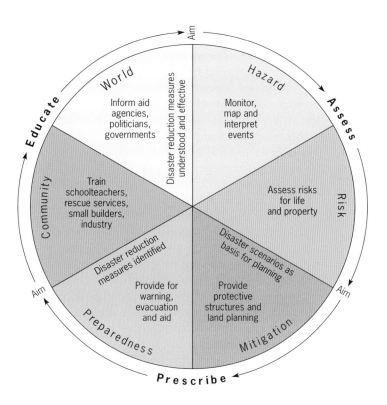

**Figure 2.15 Aid being delivered to flood victims at Khartoum, Sudan**

# Tehran appeals for quake aid from the West

IRAN'S Islamic Government last night appealed to the United Nations for help after a powerful earthquake devastated villages in the mountainous northeast of the country. Latest estimates put the death toll at some 2400.

The earthquake, measuring 7.1 on the Richter scale, on Saturday levelled houses in scores of villages across the saffron-producing province of Khorasan, which borders Afghanistan and Tajikistan. Some 10000 families are believed to have been made homeless.

Tehran officially called for emergency shipments of food, tents, blankets, clothing, four-wheeled drive vehicles, ambulances and water tankers, life detectors and white sheets, presumably for use as shrouds.

Kofi Annan, the UN Secretary-General, urged the international community to 'respond promptly and with generosity', and several Western governments immediately stepped forward with contributions of help.

The UN Department of Humanitarian Affairs announced an emergency grant of $50000 (£30000) for the local purchase of relief supplies. It also put a small disaster assessment and co-ordination team on standby for immediate dispatch to the area.

**Figure 2.16 Newspaper report concerning an earthquake in Iran (*Source: The Times*, 12 May 1997)**

## ?

**23** Should national governments provide insurance protection rather than profit-making companies? What would be the advantages and problems of this method?

**Insurance**
This is a key strategy in the MEDCs. The principle is that people join with a financial organisation to spread the costs. An individual needs to perceive that a hazard exists and be prepared to take action by purchasing a policy, the payment of a premium spreading the cost over several years. The insurers need to ensure that the property they cover is spread over a wide geographical area so that, following a disaster, the claims for losses will be less than the premiums paid. Some hazards, such as earthquakes or tropical cyclones, can cause widespread damage and cause huge insurance claims which can be financially disastrous for the insurance companies. For example, during 1994, insurance companies in California collected $500 million, but paid out $11.4 billion for damage resulting from the Northridge earthquake. As a result, in high-risk areas such as those which are regularly flooded, insurance will be very expensive or may even not be available. Research suggests that most of the property insured is commercial and industrial rather than residential.

One advantage of insurance as a management measure is that it can encourage individuals to take preventive measures for themselves – for example, the insurance company may only provide cover if the policyholder reduces the risk by using certain building materials and methods.

There are doubts about insurance as a future response. As claims increase (Fig. 1.7), the costs of premiums will rise, or companies will increasingly refuse to provide cover. Concern centres on the upward trends in atmospheric hazards which may result from global warming.

# Is insurance an effective hazard management strategy? The example of earthquake insurance in California, USA

## *Earthquake preparedness*

California has a high risk of earthquakes, but it seems that California's residents are reluctant to protect themselves from the hazard by voluntary measures to reduce or mitigate the impacts of an earthquake. These include buying earthquake insurance, and taking other measures to secure their homes and their contents: for example, conducting practice drills, securing appliances and heavy furniture, and more expensive measures such as chimney brackets and joining vertical and horizontal house beams to make the structure more stable. This is in spite of the loss of life and property which has occurred in California, expensive campaigns to increase public awareness of the hazards, and the availability of measures which people can take to protect life and property. Less than 50 per cent of California's residents have insurance against earthquake damage other than the small policy which is a state legal requirement. A 1977 survey of 1450 residents of Los Angeles showed that most households were unprepared for an earthquake (Table 1.5), and 41 per cent believed that they cannot prepare for an earthquake. However, people did make suggestions concerning what the government should do. More recent studies confirm this general low level of earthquake preparedness.

Many factors interact to determine whether awareness and knowledge of a hazard is turned into action. These include age, income, gender and level of education. However, five other factors have been shown by research to be most important.

## Resources

The individual or household must have the resources available to adopt effective mitigation measures. These resources include money, intellectual skills, and time to consider, select and adopt them.

## Perception

People vary in the degree to which they believe they can do anything about the hazard. Those who come to 'own' the earthquake risk are more likely to take action. In California there are two conflicting cultural factors which may be important. There is a tendency to think that technology can solve problems, and so they do not need to take action themselves (such as by building earthquake-proof buildings and structures). Against this is the characteristic American view that individuals are responsible for their own well-being, which results in the long-term consequences of the earthquake hazard falling on the individual household.

## Risk

Individuals personally calculate the probabilities that a given hazard will affect them. This may result in a perception of the likelihood of the hazard occurring which is very different from that predicted by scientists.

## Time

The time-frame used in decision-making affects a person's response. People who feel committed to an area for a long time period are more likely to take low-probability hazards into account than those who are only short-term residents.

## Hazard salience

This is the relative importance of the earthquake risk compared with other concerns in their lives, such as personal or family problems, unemployment, or fear of crime.

## *Earthquake Insurance*

In California, earthquake insurance has been available since 1916, and since 1984 all insurance companies offer earthquake insurance as an option to all householders when buying general household insurance. The cost of earthquake insurance is relatively high, especially in terms of the deductibles (called 'excess' in the UK) which operate. Deductibles are the amount that the householder would pay themselves, and this is usually 10 per cent of the value of the house. The deductible varies with how earthquake-proof the house structure is, so older buildings which are most at risk would cost more to insure.

**Table 2.2  Earthquake preparedness of Los Angeles residents**

|  | Per cent |
|---|---|
| Had a working flashlight | 70 |
| Had a working battery radio | 50 |
| Had a first-aid kit | 50 |
| Stored food | 30 |
| Stored water | 20 |
| Enquired about earthquake insurance | 23 |
| Actually bought earthquake insurance | 13 |
| Structurally reinforced home | 11 |
| Told children what to do in an earthquake | 50 |
| Set up emergency procedures for the household | 35 |
| Planned for the family to reunite after an earthquake | 25 |

## Results of the pre-Loma Prieta earthquake study

Research by the University of Chicago into earthquake insurance was undertaken just before the 1989 Loma Prieta earthquake (Chapter 3), and provided an excellent opportunity to requestion the people after the earthquake to see how the event had affected attitudes and behaviour (Fig. 2.19).

The survey showed that there was no relationship between those living nearest to active geological faults and those buying insurance, except for the San Fernando Valley (Los Angeles County) where insurance purchase reached 60–80 per cent, probably as a result of the 1971 San Fernando earthquake.

Insurance purchase was not related to age, length of tenure, children in the household, income, or the value of the property. The most important factor was perceived risk. The key factor was that if people believed that they were vulnerable they bought insurance.

## After the earthquake – results of the post-Loma Prieta earthquake study

The four study areas experienced different levels of impact from the earthquake. Santa Clara County had the most direct impacts. In Contra Costa County the impacts were less severe. However, residents were constantly reminded of the earthquake as commuting was disrupted by road and bridge damage for several weeks after the earthquake. The two southern counties of Los Angeles and San Bernardino had little direct impacts, but since these two counties are also situated on the San Andreas Fault, news stories highlighted their vulnerability for several months afterwards.

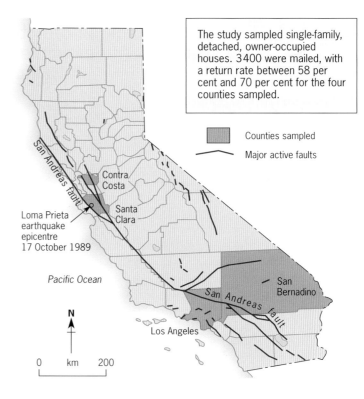

Figure 2.17 **Major active faults in California and the study counties in the pre- and post-Loma Prieta surveys** (*Source:* **Palm and Hodgson, 1992**)

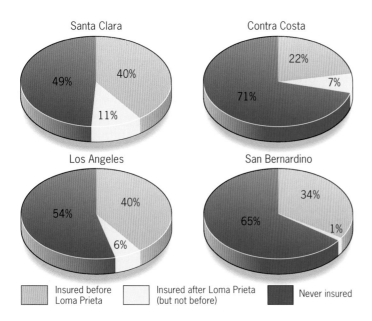

Figure 2.18 **Insurance status before and after Loma Prieta for all respondents in the four study areas** (*Source:* **Palm and Hodgson, 1992**)

As a result of the earthquake, 31 per cent and 10.5 per cent of householders in Santa Clara and Contra Costa counties, respectively, spent something on earthquake mitigation measures, compared with only 6 per cent in Los Angeles and San Bernardino. However, in many cases this investment was small (less than $30) and involved bolting furniture to the walls and floors. Changes in insurance purchases are shown in Figure 2.18.

Before the earthquake, the reasons for not purchasing earthquake insurance were given as: too expensive (52–61 per cent); not necessary (19–34 per cent) and the high deductible (3–11 per cent). After the earthquake the reasons given showed some dramatic changes (Fig. 2.19).

The study showed little change in behaviour and attitude between 1989 and 1990. Overall, only 6 per cent bought earthquake insurance following the earthquake, indicating very little shift in either perception or behaviour. People's perception of their risk is often inaccurate, with 77 per cent of people perceiving themselves to be further away from active faults than they really are (Fig. 2.20). Those whose perception was closest to the reality were most likely to buy insurance or adopt other mitigation measures.

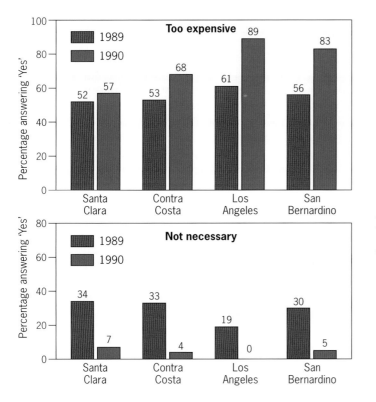

Figure 2.19  **Percentage of all uninsured respondents in each county indicating that they did not purchase insurance because it was either too expensive or not necessary** (*Source:* **Palm and Hodgson, 1992**)

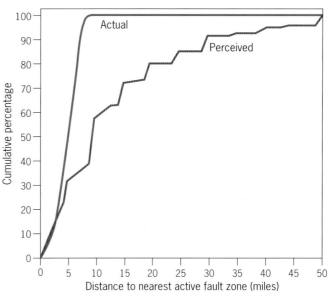

Figure 2.20  **Cumulative frequency curves of the actual and perceived distances between home locations and the nearest active surface fault** (*Source:* **Palm and Hodgson, 1992**)

## New legislation

Following the Loma Prieta earthquake of 1989, householders wanted the insurance companies to provide cover for the first $15 000 of damage. The companies were not prepared to do this. The Californian state government has since stepped in to provide mandatory insurance of up to $15 000, mainly to cover the losses caused by the insurance companies' deductibles. The government levies a surcharge on all residential insurance policies, which goes into an emergency fund. Interestingly, the earthquake hazard does not seem to affect house prices in California. Those in the seismically most active areas are not cheaper.

**?**

**24**  Describe and suggest reasons for the changes shown in Figure 2.18.

**25**  Use Figure 2.19 to analyse the reasons for not purchasing insurance before and after the earthquake, and by geographical area.

**26**  From Figure 2.20
**a**  What is the cumulative percentage of households who perceived themselves 5 miles, 10 miles, 20 miles and 40 miles from the nearest active fault ?
**b**  Compare these figures with the actual percentages.
**c**  What implications do these results have for risk perception and insurance purchase?

**27**  The survey was of relatively wealthy residents of the four areas. How do you think the purchase of insurance will vary with lower-income groups?

**28**  The researchers conclude the study by stating that 'if portions of the population are found to be highly resistant to adopting voluntary mitigation measures, then mandatory measures that will decrease the vulnerability of these populations may be called for'.
**a**  Do you agree with this statement? Explain your answer.
**b**  Write a report to the government of California making recommendations for future management of the earthquake mitigation measures. Justify your recommendations, using evidence from this case study.

# Hazard management and vulnerability in the Philippines

The Philippines in SE Asia (Fig. 2.21) are subject to a range of hazards, notably earthquakes, tsunami, volcanic eruptions, typhoons (hurricanes) and flooding. The Philippines is a lower-middle income country with relatively high population densities. The rapidly expanding population puts increasing pressuure on the country's resources with deforestation resulting from pressure to develop further agricultural development.

## Vulnerability analysis

### Housing

Most Filipinos live in single-family houses, with about 2 per cent living in impoverished structures called *barong-barong*, built of salvaged material. For the sixteen major cities, 23 per cent of the population live in low-income, self-built slums, representing 10 per cent of the whole Filipino population. Within Manila, 1.7 million people live in 415 slum areas. In rural areas, homes are built using local materials with light roofs of bamboo. In urban areas, most roofs are made of galvanised iron, aluminium, tiles, stone or wood. The older concrete buildings and slum settlements are at high risk from typhoon and earthquake damage. Concrete-framed houses at low density in modern parts of the cities are relatively low risk. The east coast is expected to receive wind speeds of over 200 kph, with a return period of 15 years. These speeds would cause total destruction of high-risk structures and moderate damage to low-risk structures.

### Infrastructure

Infrastructure can be badly damaged by severe typhoons: electricity supply can be lost for weeks or even months, for example. Landsliding and earthquake damage can be severe, particularly to mountain roads.

### Social vulnerability

Throughout the country, poverty and the high proportion of children increase vulnerability to hazards. About 49 per cent of families live below the poverty line, and there are seven million people under 9 years old or over 70 years old. There is little information at the local village (*barangay*) level for a detailed social and economic vulnerability analysis to be undertaken, so most data is only available at the regional scale.

There is no information available on the level of education, awareness and preparedness of people regarding hazards. People's perception of risk is not known but is likely to vary. There is some evidence of a lack of awareness of the risks from hazards. For example, during Typhoon Sisang in 1987, the coastal residents in Sorsogan (Region I) refused to evacuate because storm surges had not caused loss of life or property before. In 1984, at the time of Typhoon Undang, residents in Taguig, Manila, preferred their own flood warning prediction of worms leaving their holes and climbing walls to the official warning systems.

### Economic vulnerability

Hazard impacts on the economy of the Philippines are devastating to the country's efforts for economic growth. As with most LEDCs, the country has a high foreign debt, of approximately £17 billion, or £270

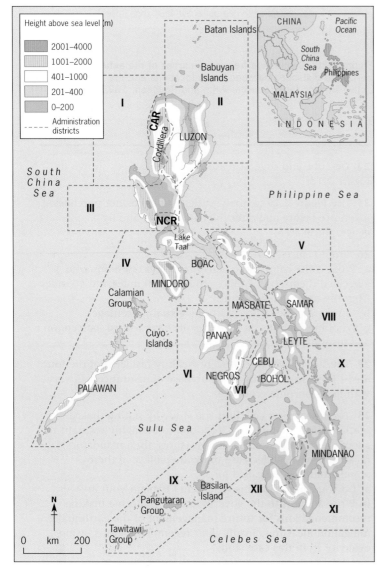

**Figure 2.21 The Philippines**

for each Filipino. Overall, agriculture suffers most, especially from typhoons. Plantation crops such as coconuts are very vulnerable to strong winds. Rice is the most important annual crop, and its planting season coincides with the rainy season when there is the highest risk of typhoons and flood damage. The fishing sector is vulnerable to damage by typhoons. All hazards impact on buildings and infrastructure.

Quantifying the economic impacts is not easy. One example which attempted to achieve this is a study of the impacts of typhoons in 1988–9 (Table 2.4). The net result of these two years on the economy was a reduction in the growth of the economy overall and the agricultural sector of £98 million. An estimated 62 000 jobs were lost. The impacts of this can be appreciated if it is assumed that each worker would have four dependants, and that the lost jobs could have fed 310 000 people. The loss in employment for these two years alone was costed at £12.8 million. Put another way, the loss of GNP from the typhoons could have bought 800 000 typhoon shelters, irrigated 51 243 ha or built 412 district hospitals. Currently, the

Philippines does not practise cost–benefit analysis of disaster mitigation projects.

The combined effects of the 1990 earthquake and 1991 eruption on the economy are shown in Table 2.5. In addition, the Filipino people, government and economy had to bear the impacts of the usual battering by typhoons and the international Gulf crisis (Table 2.3).

**Table 2.3 Damage to the economy of the Philippines, 1987–91**

| | (£ billion) |
|---|---|
| Typhoons | 0.78 |
| Earthquake (July 1990) | 0.40 |
| Gulf crisis (1990–1) | 0.24 |
| Mt Pinatubo eruption (June 1991) | 0.44 |
| Immediate production losses due to earthquake and eruption | 0.44 |
| Total | 2.30 |

Typhoon-related damage in 1991 is not included: a preliminary figure, however, puts the 1991 damage at over £156 million, thus bringing the total loss to nearly £2.5 billion.

**Table 2.4  Human and economic effects of typhoons: 1988, 1989**

| | Dead | Injured | Missing | Damage (£) | Affected/homeless | Government calamity funds (£) |
|---|---|---|---|---|---|---|
| 1988 | 429 | 468 | 195 | 236 million | 6.3 million | 20 million |
| 1989 | 386 | 903 | 251 | 122 million | 2.5 million | 26 million |

**Table 2.5  Damage due to the disasters of 1990 and 1991**

| Sector | Damage by the 1990 earthquake (£ million) | Damage by the 1991 eruption of Pinatubo (£ million) | Total damage (£ million) |
|---|---|---|---|
| Agriculture (crops, livestock, forestry, fisheries) | 35.60 | 265.30 | 300.90 |
| Private property | 98.87 | 128.20 | 227.07 |
| Infrastructure (roads, water services, schools, hospitals) | 171.10 | 41.56 | 212.66 |
| Industry and commerce | 92.50 | 9.56 | 102.06 |
| Total | 398.07 | 444.62 | 842.69 |

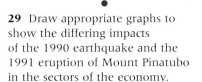

**29** Draw appropriate graphs to show the differing impacts of the 1990 earthquake and the 1991 eruption of Mount Pinatubo in the sectors of the economy.

**30** Compare the impacts of the earthquake, typhoons and Pinatubo eruption on the economy of the Philippines.

**31** Is it appropriate for banks lending money for reconstruction after a disaster to specify hazard-resistant features as part of the agreement – for example, that road rebuilding should include earthquake-proof design?

## Hazard management

### *Hazard assessment*

The government has established several institutions and organisations with responsibility for natural hazard management (Fig. 2.22). There is little systematic hazard mapping which would allow risk to be assessed and planning for disaster mitigation to take place. Hazard data and mapping mainly show past events. High-technology techniques such as aerial photography, remote sensing and Geographical Information Systems are restricted because of cost, although PAGASA has published maps of storm surges,

flooding and typhoon tracks and wind speeds expected over a 100-year period, and there has been some statistical modelling. There has also been a recent study of recurrence intervals of rainfall intensities in the Manila area to allow data to be used in the design of dams and spillways and some risk mapping. Landslide hazards are not mapped, and there is currently no detailed assessment of the impacts of deforestation on natural hazards. The lack of adequate data on disasters makes the assessment of the social and economic impacts difficult.

**National Disaster Co-ordinating Council (NDCC)**
Responsibility for planning, implementation and allocating resources for disaster management. These are established at regional, provincial, municipal, city and *barangay* levels. The aim is to encourage self-reliance among local government units.

There are two key problems – funding, and a lack of power to enforce action. The NDCC is therefore mainly advisory.

**Office of Civil Defence (OCD)**
A co-ordination role and implementing the Calamities and Disaster Preparedness Plan (CDPP) which lays down government and other organisations' responsibilities at all levels. The plan has a pre-, during and post-disaster focus. The work is hampered by a lack of transport and communication facilities, which means that the organisation is ill equipped to disseminate warnings.

**Philippine Atmospheric, Geophysical and Astronomical Services Administration (PAGASA)**
Implements state policy to protect the people against natural hazards and uses scientific knowledge to benefit people's safety, well-being and economic security. This is achieved through environmental monitoring, and providing information on typhoons and floods.

**Philippine Institute of Volcanology and Seismology (PHIVOLCS)**
Management of volcanic and seismic hazards with the aim of detection, forecasting and warning systems, and preparedness plans.

**Department of Social Welfare and Development (DSWD)**
This department provides help to victims.

**National Committees for the International Decade for Natural Disaster Reduction**
The government set up four committees in 1988 to address non-structural measures, structural measures, disaster legislation and disaster research. These are not very active.

**Figure 2.22 Disaster management organisations**

## Forecasting and warning

PAGASA has a typhoon and flood warning system for detecting and monitoring typhoons. Warning bulletins are issued to the mass media, Office of Civil Defence (OCD) and field stations, but this process is hampered by other factors. Only three or four forecasters need to contact over 20 different agencies using a very low-quality telephone system (although in the early 1990s fax machines were introduced). PAGASA also operates a radio station, but this can only be heard within 50 km of Manila. Overall, there is evidence that the loss of life and property damage is increasing from typhoons. Although the typhoon warning system has a high awareness rating, the effectiveness needs to be improved. Major problems are inoperative equipment, inadequate telecommunications and a lack of public education. A key problem is getting the message across. Some warnings are misunderstood and do not convey the need for urgency. Others have proved to be false and result in some complacency by local people. For example, during Typhoon Nitang in 1984, residents in the southern Philippines did not believe the seriousness of the threat because all warnings in the previous 20 years had been false.

PHIVOLCS has responsibility for monitoring and warning for seismic and volcanic hazards, and for preparedness plans. It was established following the disastrous eruption of Hibok-Hibok in 1951. It has 19 seismic stations (the ideal would be 100 stations) and monitors the most active volcanoes in the densely populated areas of the country. The other volcanoes are inspected regularly. Ground deformation studies are undertaken twice a year. When an eruption is detected OCD is informed.

The lack of personnel and equipment resulted in PHIVOLCS establishing its Volunteer Observers Programme (VOP) in 1986. During the eruption of Mayon in 1984, PHIVOLCS personnel were not monitoring the sectors in which precursory activity occurred. Although local people had seen strange events such as crater glow, and abnormal animal behaviour in the days, weeks and even months before the eruption, they did not understand their significance. When the scheme was launched, Mayon residents were very keen to be involved. The scheme aims to enhance public awareness and involvement, and gathering of information at low cost. If volunteers can detect early warning signs, then local people can be informed. Together with education on how to respond, there should be a reduction in the loss of life and property. PHIVOLCS visits the *barangays* to give lectures and workshops. Volunteers are selected and trained in the precursory signs (Fig. 2.23). By the end of 1986, *barangays* near to Mayon and Hibok-Hibok were involved. The hope by the mid-1990s was to cover all active volcanoes and, in the long term, complete coverage of the Philippines.

Paradoxically, the success of PHIVOLCS has added to their difficulties. The Taal volcano in the middle of an island is a high-risk area, and vulcanologists hope to ban people from living on the island. The local people, however, have a different perception. The island has many natural resources and they feel safe in the knowledge that PHIVOLCS has a monitoring station on the island; the population has therefore increased.

Following the tsunami produced by the 1994 Mindoro earthquake, PHIVOLCS launched the Geologic Hazards Information and Education Alliance (GHIEA). This is an alliance of government and other organisations which aimed to spend two years focusing on tsunami hazard information and education campaigns nationwide. This response focuses on educating local people in coastal areas to flee to higher ground on feeling an earthquake. This response is a more practical alternative to tsunami hazard mitigation than hard-engineering structures. The very short warning times also make other methods inappropriate.

**32** Study Figure 2.23. Identify the unusual changes which PHIVOLCS volunteers should respond to most urgently.

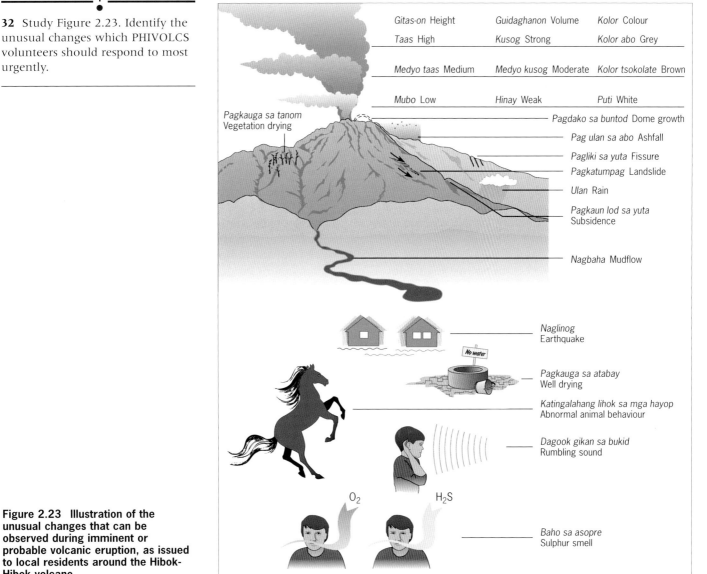

**Figure 2.23 Illustration of the unusual changes that can be observed during imminent or probable volcanic eruption, as issued to local residents around the Hibok-Hibok volcano**

The dissemination of warnings is a major problem, especially outside the Manila area. Mass communications are heavily concentrated in Manila and the large cities. In rural areas, radio is the main source of information and reaches 95 per cent of the population. There are five television networks in the country. Television ownership is about a third in urban areas and a fifth in rural areas. The country's telephone system is inadequate and unreliable. The country has one of the lowest telephone densities in Asia, and the system is generally not available in rural areas.

## Disaster training and education
Members of the National Disaster Co-ordinating Council (NDCC) and civilian workers are trained in disaster management. Within OCD the emphasis is on relief after the event rather than pre-disaster mitigation. Public awareness is raised by OCD using brochures on precautionary measures for fire,

earthquakes, floods and typhoons. Posters for school-children are produced, with some being translated into local dialects. PAGASA is seeking funding to extend its educational activities – for example, using USAid for revising school textbooks to cover the characteristics and causes of natural hazards. Government policy is to increase its disaster control capability and community preparedness. For example, since 1988 the first week of July has been designated as 'National Disaster Consciousness Week'.

## Land-use planning and building codes
Building codes exist but, since the data on hazards is relatively limited and there is no effective assessment made of how buildings perform, these codes are likely to be inadequate. There are land-zoning regulations for areas at risk from flooding, but a lack of funding and enforcement means that these are not as effective as intended.

The vulnerability of housing is high and, after a disaster such as a typhoon, materials will be salvaged to rebuild. There is a clear need for public education on low-cost typhoon-resistant housing, and more government sponsoring of research into alternative types of housing. One such project followed Typhoon Sisang in 1987. Some 450 housing units designed to withstand 180 kph winds were built on a self-help basis with assistance from trained workers. These withstood two typhoons after the trial, and the project has been extended to 14 000 units across the country.

## Structural measures

Most hard-engineering projects are for flood control and involve multi-purpose dams, dykes, revetments and floodgates. During the 1990s there were six ongoing major projects. Coastal towns may have sea walls but these are for protection against high tides and most are only 2 m above mean sea level.

## International aid

The Philippines receives post-disaster relief aid from foreign governments – for example, £1.9 million after the 1990 earthquake. Aid is also provided by charitable organisations such as the Red Cross and Red Crescent. As well as financial aid, post-disaster aid in the form of medicines, clothing and food is received. Aid is also received in the form of technological and information assistance: for example, the assistance to PHIVOLCS from the US Geological Survey at the time of the eruption of Mount Pinatubo, which helped to predict events and thus allowed the government to make decisions about evacuation and other procedures (see Chapter 4). In addition, Japan has helped PAGASA upgrade its geostationary meteorological satellite.

In the early 1990s several foreign-funded projects were relevant to hazards. These included a Disaster Management Programme (UNDP/UK), improvement of telecommunications of the PAGASA (Japan), PAGASA disaster information campaign (USAid) and disaster preparedness programme for Albay in Region V (Italy).

?

**33** Study Figure 2.24.
**a** Identify the key stages in the reporting scheme and suggest guidelines for the responsible person/agency if the system is to be effective.
**b** The last stage in the flow of information is the 'concerned public'. What factors need to be considered if the response they make is to save lives and property?

**34** Why is insurance not much used as a strategy for hazard mitigation in the Philippines?

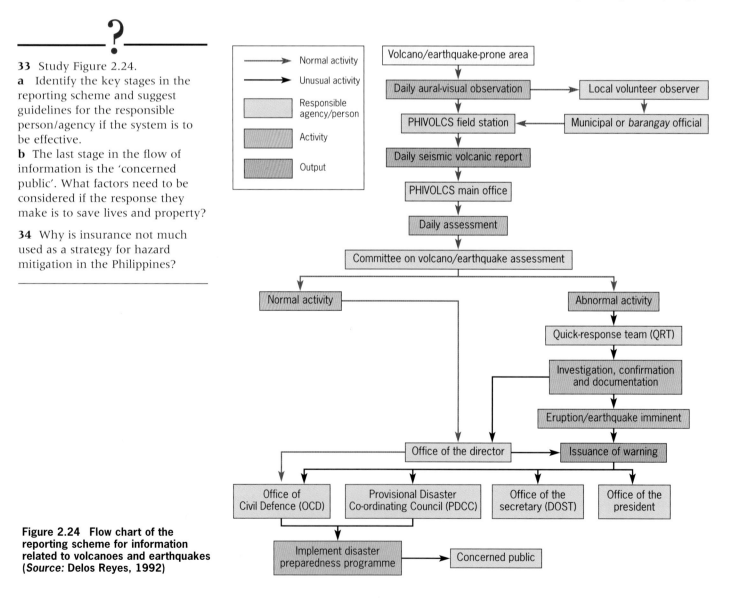

**Figure 2.24 Flow chart of the reporting scheme for information related to volcanoes and earthquakes (*Source:* Delos Reyes, 1992)**

# Recommendations

Hazard management is complex in all countries, and especially for LEDCs where many other considerations are important in raising the quality of life for people.

In its report of 1990, the Asian Development Bank made the following recommendations for hazard management in the Philippines. These concern typhoon hazards but are applicable to all hazards.

**1** Strengthen disaster management capacity at the regional and local level.

**2** The use of loss-reduction techniques, e.g. hazard mapping, risk assessment and land-use planning.

**3** Improving the nature, speed and effectiveness of warnings and communication in the face of a hazardous event.

**4** Increased collection, exchange and dissemination of hazard-related data.

**5** Public education about the nature of hazards and the potential for preventive action.

**6** The use of hazard-reduction techniques in building and low-cost housing, and ensuring their effectiveness.

**7** Strengthening the effectiveness of OCD and establishing an organisation headed by a key cabinet minister.

**8** Consideration of costs and benefits of reconstructing infrastructure at a higher standard or relocation to lower-risk areas after disasters.

**9** Diversification of the economy away from agriculture in vulnerable areas, and consideration of crops grown and cropping patterns.

**35a** Refer to Figure 2.14. Put the nine recommendations in a flow diagram to show the order of priority the Philippines government should adopt.
**b** Justify your choice.
**c** Are any other recommendations to be made?

## Summary

- Risk is the exposure of people to a hazardous event. Hazard impacts have increased in recent decades as a result of more people being placed at risk.

- Vulnerability to hazards has three aspects: people's preparedness, resilience and health which relate to social, economic and political factors.

- People perceive hazards in three main ways: acceptance, adaptation and domination.

- The human response to hazards can be divided into three broad groups: modify the event by environmental control and hazard-resistant design; modify vulnerability by prediction and warning, and community preparation; and modify the loss by aid and insurance.

- The choice of response is related to the nature of the hazard, past experience, economic and technological resources, social and political conditions, and hazard perception.

# 3 Tectonic hazards: earthquakes

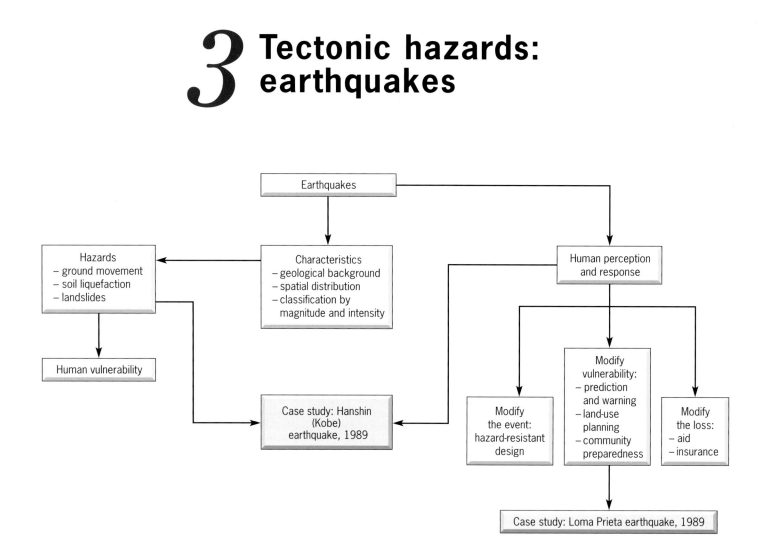

Earthquakes

Hazards
– ground movement
– soil liquefaction
– landslides

Characteristics
– geological background
– spatial distribution
– classification by magnitude and intensity

Human perception and response

Human vulnerability

Case study: Hanshin (Kobe) earthquake, 1989

Modify the event: hazard-resistant design

Modify vulnerability:
– prediction and warning
– land-use planning
– community preparedness

Modify the loss:
– aid
– insurance

Case study: Loma Prieta earthquake, 1989

Figure 3.1 The San Andreas fault crossing the Carrizo Plain some 450 km south of San Francisco and 160 km north of Los Angeles (USA). The fault extends almost the full length of California and is responsible for major earthquakes. The pressure ridges shown are the results of hundreds of fault movements. Here the San Andreas fault is at its most spectacular, though its damage potential (in human terms) is nil.

## 3.1 The geological background

To people living in the UK, the Earth seems to be relatively stable and unchanging, but this is not the case when we look at the global picture. Tectonic processes (from the Greek word *tecton* meaning 'the builder') are the folding, faulting and warping of rocks to form the major features of the Earth's surface such as mountain ranges and ocean basins. Hazards which result from these major geological processes and the release of energy from within the Earth are earthquakes, volcanic eruptions and tsunami (giant sea waves).

The Earth's crust is a relatively thin, rigid outer layer of rock (Fig. 3.1) which moves as a result of heat flow in the denser **mantle** rocks beneath the crust (Fig. 3.2). The lithosphere is not rigid, but is broken into eight major and several minor sections called **lithospheric plates** which move relative to each other (Fig. 3.3) at speeds of between 2 and 15 cm/yr. This is roughly the rate at which your fingernails grow.

The study of these features is called **plate tectonics** and, in terms of understanding the hazards which result from these tectonic processes, it is the three types of boundary between the plates which are most important.

### Constructive margins or divergent plate boundaries
The plates which are moving apart produce tensional stresses in the crust (Fig. 3.2). Molten rock or magma rises from deep magma chambers in the hot **asthenosphere** to form ocean ridges and new oceanic crust. The injection of this new crust moves the lithospheric plates apart in a process called **sea-floor spreading**.

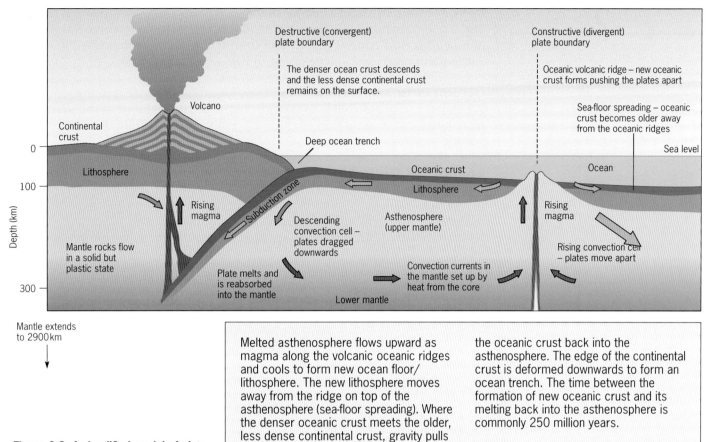

**Figure 3.2  A simplified model of plate tectonics**

Melted asthenosphere flows upward as magma along the volcanic oceanic ridges and cools to form new ocean floor/lithosphere. The new lithosphere moves away from the ridge on top of the asthenosphere (sea-floor spreading). Where the denser oceanic crust meets the older, less dense continental crust, gravity pulls the oceanic crust back into the asthenosphere. The edge of the continental crust is deformed downwards to form an ocean trench. The time between the formation of new oceanic crust and its melting back into the asthenosphere is commonly 250 million years.

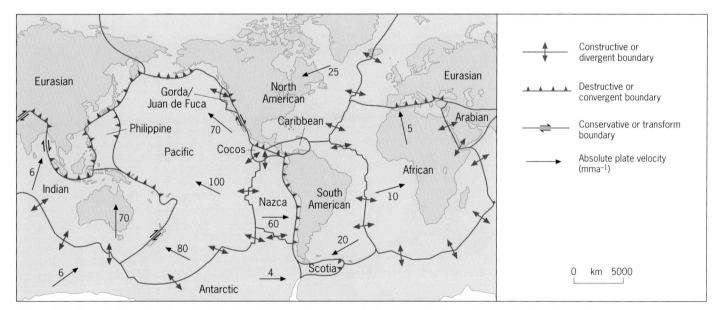

**Figure 3.3  Map of the major lithospheric plates. The various types of plate boundary are shown and the estimated currrent rates and directions of plate movement are indicated by arrows (rates in mma⁻¹). (*Source:* Summerfield, 1991)**

### Destructive margins or convergent plate boundaries

These form by plates colliding: the denser of the two plates moves down through the asthenosphere and is then reassimilated into the mantle. There are three types of destructive plate margins resulting from the collisions of oceanic or continental plates.

1 Study Figure 3.2.
**a** Describe the main features of the upper part of the Earth shown in the diagram.
**b** How do convection cells in the mantle relate to plate movement?
**c** Describe the main features of convergent and divergent plate boundaries.

### Continental plate and oceanic plate

The denser oceanic plate sinks or is subducted beneath the continental plate in a **subduction zone** (Fig.3.2). The continental plate is compressed to form a mountain range and a deep ocean trench, as with the Andes.

### Oceanic crust and oceanic crust

When oceanic plates collide, a volcanic island arc is produced as the denser plate melts and magma rises to the surface. Examples include the Kurile, Aleutian and Tonga Islands.

### Continental crust and continental crust

If the oceanic crust is competely subducted the two remaining continental plates will collide to form mountains as the sediment on the old sea floor is compressed and uplifted. This type of collision has no volcanic activity and earthquakes are mainly shallow in depth. In this category are the Himalayas, formed by the collision of the Indian plate with the Eurasian plate.

### *Conservative or transform plate margins*

Along these boundaries the plates move past each other, resulting in shear stresses, but are not destroyed or constructed (Fig. 3.3). The motion is along a major break in the crust called a **fault**. Large faults with lateral movement are called transform faults. The most well-known example is the San Andreas fault in California (Fig. 3.1).

### *The distribution of earthquakes*

The study of earthquakes is called seismology. Figure 3.4 shows the distribution of 30 000 earthquakes recorded between 1961 and 1967. If you compare this map with Figure 3.3, you can see that the main zones of earthquakes are not randomly distributed but closely mark out the boundaries of the lithospheric plates.

**Figure 3.4 The location of approximately 30 000 earthquakes recorded between 1961 and 1967 (*Source:* Summerfield, 1991)**

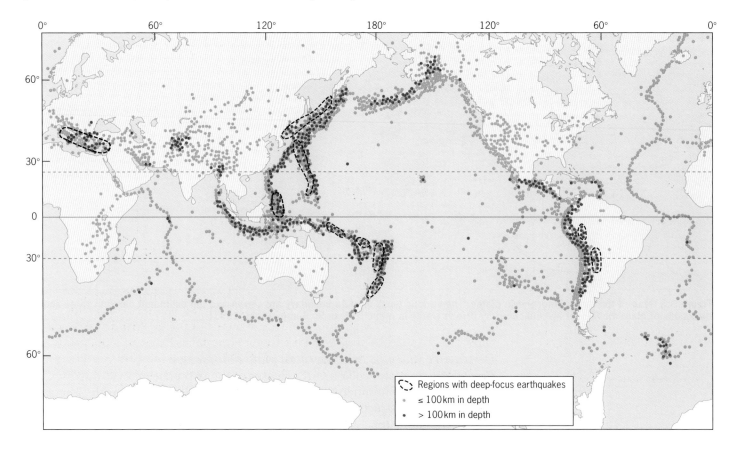

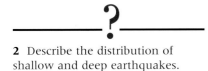

**2** Describe the distribution of shallow and deep earthquakes.

**3** Which two continents have the most and which two the least seismic activity?

**4** Name five countries where the seismic hazard is high.

**5** Describe the depth and spatial distribution of the Benioff zone earthquakes.

**6** Redraw the composite cross-section and label the continental and oceanic plates, and the direction of movement.

Thus plate tectonic theory enables seisomologists to identify the zones of the Earth most at risk from earthquakes. These zones of earthquake or seismic activity can be divided into four.

**1** Constructive boundaries along the oceanic ridges. Earthquakes in this zone are mainly shallow, and result from volcanic activity as magma rises, and tensional forces in the crust. These earthquakes are submarine and pose little hazard to people. However, there are areas of crustal tension on land, e.g. the East African Rift Valley System.

**2** Destructive boundaries where oceanic crust is being subducted into the mantle beneath a continental plate, or where two oceanic plates collide in island arc zones. The compressional force causes crustal stresses, and intermediate and deep earthquakes occur in a narrow zone indicating the subducting plate called a **Benioff zone** (Fig. 3.5). These areas are subject to major earthquakes and represent areas of major hazard: for example, an earthquake off the Pacific coast of Mexico in 1985 killed 10 000 people, injured 50 000, and damaged 35 per cent of the buildings in Mexico City. Tsunami are most commonly generated by these earthquakes (see Chapter 5).

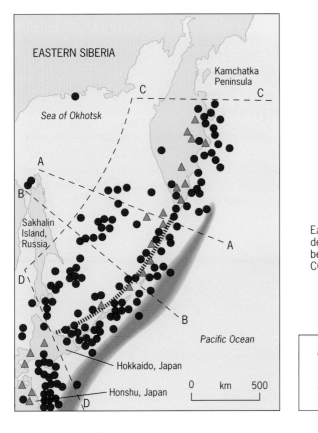

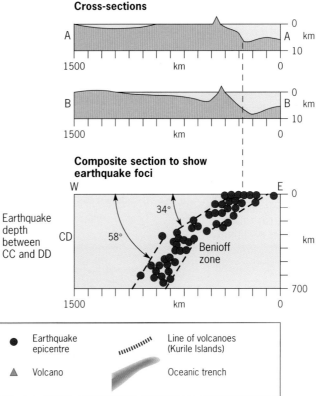

**Figure 3.5 Earthquake epicentres in the Japan–Kurile–Kamchatka region of the north-western Pacific. The composite profile plots the depth of all the earthquakes on the map in relation to their distance from the oceanic trench.**
(*Source:* **Summerfield, 1991**)

**3** Destructive boundaries where continental crust is colliding to produce mountain belts, e.g. the Alpine–Himalayan chain. Since there is no longer any oceanic crust remaining (having been subducted in the geological past), and there is no distinct Benioff zone, shallow earthquakes occur in a relatively broad zone resulting in a high hazard risk. For example, the June 1990 earthquake in Iran was caused by the stresses created as the Arabian plate collided with the Eurasian plate, originally creating the Elburz Mountains. Some 35 000 people were killed, 100 000 injured and 400 000 made homeless. The 1988 Armenian earthquake resulted in 25 000 deaths.

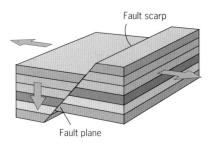

**Normal dip-slip fault.** The fault plane of a normal fault dips away from the uplifted crustal block. Faulting results from tension in the crustal rocks.

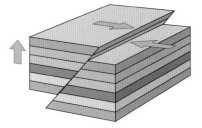

**Reverse dip-slip fault.** The fault plane of a reverse fault dips beneath the uplifted block. Faulting results from compression in the crust. A very low-angled reverse fault is called a thrust fault.

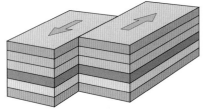

**Strike-slip fault.** The crustal blocks slide past each other. The slip may be left-lateral or right-lateral. This example shows a left-lateral, strike-slip fault. If you stood astride the fault, the left-hand side has moved towards you, whichever way you face.

If the slip on a fault is partly strike-slip and partly dip-slip, the fault is called an oblique-slip fault.

**Figure 3.6 Kinds of faults**

Faults in dashed lines were concealed. The San Andreas fault extends for 800 miles (1287 km) and extends to a depth of 11 miles (17.7 km). Since the fault formed 30 million years ago, there has been 200 miles (322 km) of strike-slip motion. In this region the plate boundary is a broad, complex zone in which the horizontal slip is distributed over the San Andreas, Hayward and Calaveras faults. As a result, the San Andreas takes up only 40 per cent of the relative plate motion, or an average of about one inch (2.54 cm) per year. The 1989 Loma Prieta earthquake occurred as a result of a break on the San Andreas fault in a sparsely inhabited part of the Santa Cruz mountains.

4 Areas of lateral crust movement in the continental regions, producing mainly shallow-depth earthquakes, such as the San Andreas fault system of the western USA.

### Intra-plate earthquakes

Although most earthquakes can be explained by geological activity along plate boundaries, about 15 per cent of earthquakes occur in the relatively stable continental crust. These intra-plate earthquakes are caused by stresses created in the crustal rocks which may be due to plate movement, but they can be caused by other factors which makes their prediction much more difficult. For example, **isostatic recoil** can result in stresses and strains in crustal rocks which may reactivate ancient faults, as with the Boxing Day 1980 earthquake in northern England. An intra-plate earthquake with devastating consequences was the 1976 Tangshan earthquake in China which killed 240 000 and injured 700 000 people.

### Quasi-natural earthquakes?

Human activity has also been blamed by some researchers for intra-plate earthquakes. The September 1993 earthquake at Killari in India resulted in the death of 10 000 people. Killari is in the middle of the Indian subcontinent, well away from the Himalayan collision belt which is responsible for earthquakes in northern India. A reservoir and dam had just been completed 20 km to the west. Some seismologists suggest that the weight of the water in the reservoir and the increase in the pressure of the water in the pores of the rocks can lubricate a fault line so that it can move more easily.

## 3.2 The nature of earthquakes

Most earthquakes result from movement along fractures in rocks called faults (Fig. 3.6). These faults usually occur in groups called a fault zone which can vary in width from a metre to several kilometres. For example, the transform plate boundary of the western USA is not a simple single **fault line**, but a complex zone of faults of different sizes and types (Fig. 3.7).

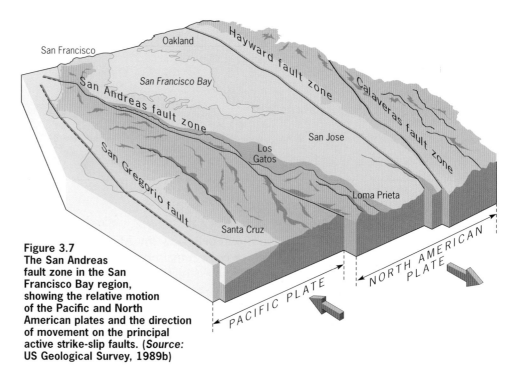

**Figure 3.7**
**The San Andreas fault zone in the San Francisco Bay region, showing the relative motion of the Pacific and North American plates and the direction of movement on the principal active strike-slip faults. (*Source:* US Geological Survey, 1989b)**

Movement occurs along fault planes of all sizes due to the stresses created by crustal movement. The stresses are not usually released gradually, but build up until they become so great that the rocks shift suddenly along the fault (Fig. 3.6). As the fault moves, the shock waves produced are felt as an earthquake. The point of the break is called the **focus** or **hypocentre**. If these stresses are released in small stages there may be a series of small earthquakes. If the stresses build up without being released, the chances of a large earthquake increase. Figure 3.8 shows the motion on the fault during the 1989 Loma Prieta earthquake near San Francisco, USA. The energy released as seismic waves was $10^{22}$ ergs, which is approximately the same as one thermonuclear bomb (500 000 tonnes TNT). The fault segment had been locked since it last moved in the 1906 earthquake (Fig. 3.9). However, the complexity of identifying active faults and the likelihood of movement resulting in earthquakes is immense. The January 1994 Northridge earthquake in the San Fernando Valley severely affected the Los Angeles area. This region of the world is one of the most studied seismic zones but the earthquake occurred on a previously unknown **thrust fault**.

**?**

**7** Use Figure 3.8 to describe the movement on the San Andreas fault during the Loma Prieta earthquake.

Along the Santa Cruz Mountains segment of the fault, the Pacific and North American plates meet along a plane that is inclined to the south-west at 70°. The earthquake produced horizontal movement along the line of the San Andreas fault of 1.89 m and vertical movement along the fault plane of 1.31 m.

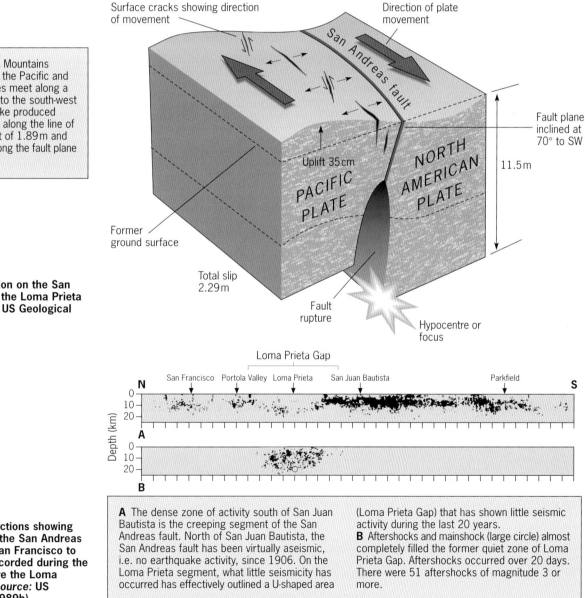

**Figure 3.8  The motion on the San Andreas fault during the Loma Prieta earthquake (*Source:* US Geological Survey, 1989b)**

**Figure 3.9  Cross-sections showing the seismicity along the San Andreas fault from north of San Francisco to south of Parkfield recorded during the 20-year period before the Loma Prieta earthquake (*Source:* US Geological Survey, 1989b)**

**A** The dense zone of activity south of San Juan Bautista is the creeping segment of the San Andreas fault. North of San Juan Bautista, the San Andreas fault has been virtually aseismic, i.e. no earthquake activity, since 1906. On the Loma Prieta segment, what little seismicity has occurred has effectively outlined a U-shaped area (Loma Prieta Gap) that has shown little seismic activity during the last 20 years.
**B** Aftershocks and mainshock (large circle) almost completely filled the former quiet zone of Loma Prieta Gap. Aftershocks occurred over 20 days. There were 51 aftershocks of magnitude 3 or more.

Seismic waves radiate from the focus through the earth rather like the effect of throwing a stone into a pond. There are four types of seismic waves (Fig. 3.10), which travel at different speeds. Sensitive detectors called seismometers are used to record the different intervals of the waves to produce seismograms (Fig. 3.11). The time intervals between the arrival of the waves from different seismograph stations are used to locate the **epicentre** (the point on the Earth's surface directly above the focus) of an earthquake.

The depth of an earthquake's focus may vary from a few kilometres to 700 km. The deepest earthquakes occur along subduction zones. Most earthquakes are relatively shallow with depths of less than 60 km. In California the majority of earthquakes are shallow at 10–15 km deep

**Body waves** travel through the earth itself.

**P waves** are the fastest and travel through rock such as granite at 5.5 km/sec. P waves can travel through both solids and liquids.

**S waves** are slower at 3 km/sec through granite. They can only travel through solid material.

**Surface waves** are long waves, i.e. they take a longer time to complete one cycle of motion.

**Long waves** are faster than Rayleigh waves and shake the ground at right angles to the direction of movement.

**Rayleigh** waves have a rolling motion producing both horizontal and vertical ground movement which feels like rocking in a boat at sea.

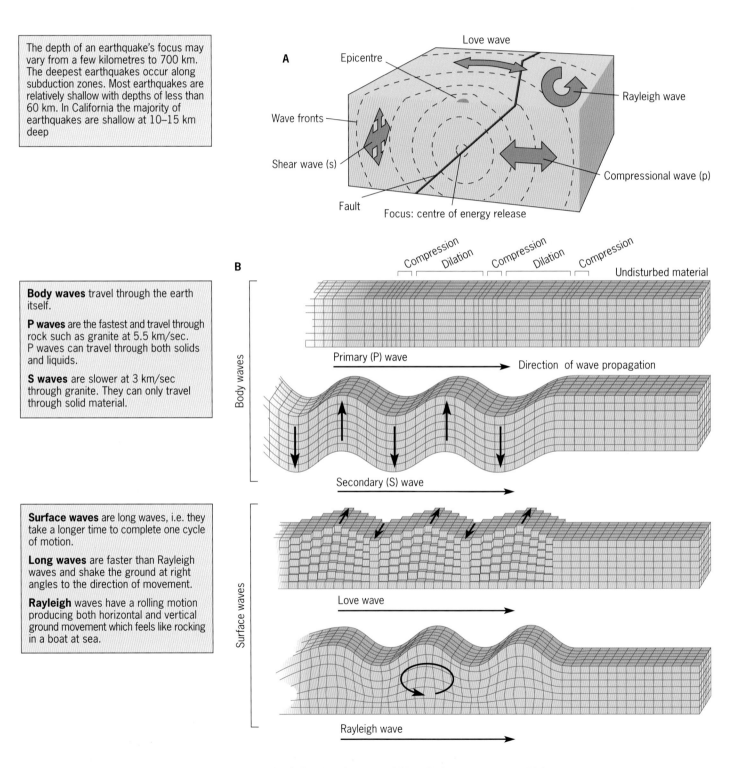

**Figure 3.10 Earthquake waves (*After:* Keller and Pinter, 1996)**

**8a** Tabulate the information in Figure 3.10 and the text to produce a comparison of the wave types and their effects.
**b** Which wave types are most likely to cause damage to buildings and structures? Why?

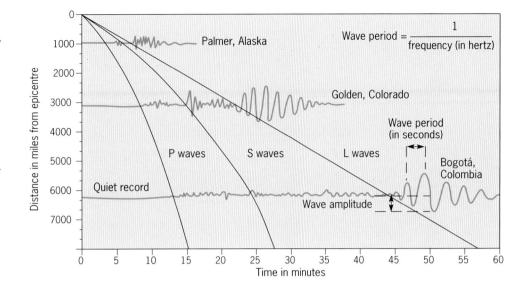

**Figure 3.11 Travel–time curves**
(*After:* US Geological Survey, 1989a)

*Magnitude and intensity of earthquakes*

Seismic waves occur over a broad band of frequencies. The body waves (P and S) are high-frequency waves (0.5 to 20 Hz), i.e. 0.5 to 20 cycles per second. These waves are most energetic close to the epicentre. Surface waves (L and R) are most common at low frequencies (< 1 cycle per second), and these can carry energy for much longer distances.

Earthquake magnitude is measured using the **Richter scale**, which is based upon the amplitude of the lines made on a seismogram using the largest wave amplitude recorded (Fig. 3.11). Thus the bigger the earthquake the greater the shaking of the earth. The Richter scale is logarithmic, so a Richter magnitude 7 earthquake causes a ten times larger amplitude than a magnitude 6 earthquake. The energy released is proportional to the magnitude, but for each one-unit increase in the Richter magnitude the energy released increases about 30 times. This does not mean, however, that a magnitude 8 earthquake would produce 30 times more shaking than a magnitude 7. Instead, the energy is released over a larger area and for a longer time. There are on average a million earthquakes every year at Richter magnitude 3.9 or less, and 19.3 per year of magnitude 7 or above, yet these few major earthquakes release more energy. The largest-magnitude earthquake ever recorded measured 8.9 on the Richter scale. Seismologists are increasingly using a more complex scale called the **moment magnitude** which combines the amount of movement on the fault, rock strength, and the size of the rupture area.

Earthquake intensity measures the degree of surface shaking. This has been used to produce a qualitative or descriptive scale of earthquakes called the **Mercalli scale**, which was modified in 1956 (Table 3.1).

A major earthquake is frequently followed by minor earthquakes called **aftershocks**, which represent the redistribution of stress on the fault plane. The 1994 Northridge, California, earthquake produced 5800 aftershocks between 18 January and 1 July 1994!

## 3.3 Hazards resulting from earthquakes

The primary hazard resulting from an earthquake is ground movement and shaking. Secondary hazards are soil liquefaction, landslides and avalanches, and tsunami (Chapter 5). The impacts of earthquakes on human activity are wide-ranging (see Fig. 1.3).

**Table 3.1  Abridged modified Mercalli intensity scale**

| Average peak velocity (cm/s⁻¹) | Intensity value and description | |
| --- | --- | --- |
| | I | Not felt except by a very few under exceptionally favourable circumstances. |
| | II | Felt only by a few persons at rest, especially on upper floors of buildings. Delicately suspended objects may swing. |
| | III | Felt quite noticeably indoors, especially on upper floors of buildings, but many people do not recognise it as an earthquake. Standing automobiles may rock slightly. Vibration like passing truck. Duration estimated. |
| 1–2 | IV | During day felt indoors by many, outdoors by few. At night some awakened. Dishes, windows, doors disturbed; walls make creaking sound. Sensation like heavy truck striking building. Standing automobiles rocked noticeably. |
| 2–5 | V | Felt by nearly everyone, many awakened. Some dishes, windows and so on broken; cracked plaster in a few places; unstable objects overturned. Disturbance of trees, poles and other tall objects sometimes noticed. Pendulum clocks may stop. |
| 5–8 | VI | Felt by all, many frightened and run outdoors. Some heavy furniture moved; a few instances of fallen plaster and damaged chimneys. Damage slight. |
| 8–12 | VII | Everybody runs outdoors. Damage negligible in buildings of good design and construction; slight to moderate in well-built ordinary structures; considerable in poorly built or badly designed structures; some chimneys broken. Noticed by persons driving cars. |
| 20–30 | VIII | Damage slight in specially designed structures; considerable in ordinary substantial buildings, with partial collapse; great in poorly built structures. Panel walls thrown out of frame structures. Fall of chimneys, factory stacks, columns, walls, monuments. Heavy furniture overturned. Sand and mud ejected in small amounts. Changes in well water. Persons driving cars disturbed. |
| 45–55 | IX | Damage considerable in specially designed structures; well-designed frame structures thrown out of plumb; damage great in substantial buildings, with partial collapse. Buildings shifted off foundations. Ground cracked conspicuously. Underground pipes broken. |
| >60 | X | Some well-built wooden structures destroyed; most masonry and frame structures destroyed with foundations; ground badly cracked. Rails bent. Landslides considerable from river banks and steep slopes. Shifted sand and mud. Water splashed, slopped over banks. |
| | XI | Few, if any (masonry) structures remain standing. Bridges destroyed. Broad fissures in ground. Underground pipelines completely out of service. Earth slumps and landslips in soft ground. Rails bend greatly. |
| | XII | Damage total. Waves seen on ground surface. Lines of sight and level distorted. Objects thrown into the air. |

*Ground movement*

It is the surface seismic waves (Fig. 3.10) which represent the most severe hazard to humans and their activities, since buildings and other structures may collapse and kill or injure their occupants. Underground pipes and power lines may be severed by the ground motion, resulting in fires and explosions, especially from escaping gas. Ruptured water pipes mean that there is often a problem extinguishing these fires. Although the earthquake waves travel at different speeds, near to the epicentre there will be no time for the waves to become separated and so there will be severe and complex ground motion. Different surface materials respond in different ways to the surface waves. Shaking of solid bedrock tends to be less than unconsolidated sediments, which can amplify the shaking. The result is that damage to buildings and other structures will differ according to the surface materials they are built on. The ground waves of the 1985 earthquake which devastated Mexico City were amplified four to five times by the ancient lake sediments on which the city is built. In the Loma Prieta earthquake, California, the earthquake intensities

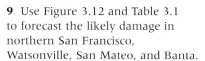

**9** Use Figure 3.12 and Table 3.1 to forecast the likely damage in northern San Francisco, Watsonville, San Mateo, and Banta.

Roman numerals represent the modified Mercalli intensity levels between the isoseismal lines (lines joining places of equal intensity). Refer to Table 3.1 for details of these. The earthquake epicentre is shown by a circled star.

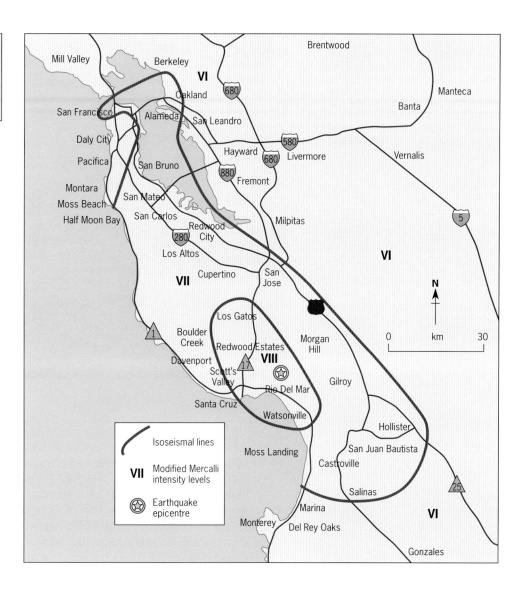

**Figure 3.12 Modified Mercalli intensity levels for the Loma Prieta earthquake (*Source:* US Geological Survey, 1989b)**

varied according to the surface materials as well as with distance from the epicentre (Fig. 3.12). About 98 per cent of the economic losses were as a result of ground-shaking, and 41 of the 67 deaths which resulted from this earthquake occurred when the upper tier of the Nimitz Freeway in Oakland collapsed. This section of the road was constructed on mud and bay-fill material used to infill San Francisco Bay. Elsewhere the roads survived the shaking. The Marina District of San Francisco was severely damaged during the earthquake. This part of the city was built on bay fill and mud, including some of the debris dumped in the Bay after the 1906 earthquake!

The importance of building design, construction, and the nature of the rocks or sediments they are built on, is clearly shown when earthquake statistics are compared. The 1988 Armenian earthquake (magnitude 6.9) killed 25 000 people, injured 31 000 and made 500 000 homeless. Some 700 000 people lived within a 50 km radius of the earthquake epicentre. Compare this with the 7.1 magnitude Loma Prieta earthquake in California, where 1.5 million people live within a 50 km radius of the epicentre. The Californian earthquake was twice as powerful (remember, the Richter scale is logarithmic), affected more than twice the population, but killed only 0.1 per cent as many people. The building design is crucial in explaining the differences. In Armenia, the

**Figure 3.13  The oil town of Neftegorsk in the far east of Russia after the May 1995 earthquake when 2000 people died. Seven five-storey tenements were built in the 1960s and collapsed as people slept when the earthquake struck at 1.05 a.m. Following the Armenian disaster, this second tragedy called into question former Soviet construction standards in seismically active areas.**

older stone buildings were destroyed by the ground shaking, and the pattern of destruction is as might be expected with 88 per cent destroyed in Spitak, only 5 km from the epicentre, and 38 per cent in Leninakan, 35 km from the epicentre. However, in Leninakan, 95 per cent of the more modern 9–12 storey pre-cast concrete-frame buildings were destroyed. The buildings were constructed on soft sediments, which caused eight times the ground displacement for three times longer. The fact that the buildings had no earthquake-proofing features in their design, combined with the soft foundations, resulted in the high death toll. Unfortunately, history repeated itself in the Russian town of Neftegorsk in May 1995 (Fig. 3.13).

### Soil liquefaction

Liquefaction is when a solid material turns into a liquefied state due to an increase in **pore water pressures** as a result of ground-shaking during an earthquake. It affects unconsolidated sediments at depths of less than 10 m, which are saturated with water. These ground failures can destroy or severely damage building foundations and cause them to sink or collapse (Fig. 3.14). Structures such as bridges, dams and subsurface pipes will also be damaged.

### Landslides

Sudden mass movements can result from causes other than earthquakes (see Chapter 7), but the stress resulting from the ground-shaking of an earthquake can result in slope failure on even gentle slopes. These landslides, rock and snow avalanches, can overrun people and structures, cause building damage or collapse, break underground pipes, and disrupt rescue efforts by blocking roads. In many earthquakes, the landsliding has caused as much or more damage than the ground-shaking. The greatest hazard exists with higher-magnitude events (> 6.0). The 1964 Alaskan earthquake caused an estimated $1.26 billion (1984 costs) in damage, 56 per cent of which was due to landsliding. Landsliding also caused at least 48 of the 130 deaths.

**Figure 3.14  Damage in the San Francisco Marina district from the Loma Prieta earthquake in October 1989. Strong ground-shaking was accompanied by soil liquefaction. The area's artificial landfills and natural coastal deposits underlying the houses amplified the ground-shaking and liquefaction. Buildings were distorted, service pipes snapped, and pavements buckled. Four people died, seven buildings collapsed, and sixty-three buildings were unsafe to enter.**

# 3.4 Managing the earthquake hazard

The severity of an earthquake and its human impact depend upon the interaction of a number of variables. It is these factors which form the basis for successful earthquake hazard management.

**Physical factors**
Location of the epicentre
Depth of the focus
Foundation material (e.g. rock type)
Duration of shaking
Time of day

**Human factors**
Building style and land use
How people react during and just after the earthquake
Community preparedness
Emergency and relief services – efficiency and organisation
Economic and social structures and conditions for preparedness, education, and ability to recover

## *Modify the event*

### Controlling the physical variables

Control of the earthquake event itself and the physical variables listed above is unlikely in the foreseeable future, and is not a realistic form of management. An exception to this are the human-induced earthquakes such as those resulting from dam construction. These could be managed by consideration of the seismic hazard when siting these structures.

### Hazard-resistant design

The collapse of buildings (Table 3.2) and structures is responsible for the majority of deaths, injuries and economic losses resulting from an earthquake. Thus the impact of the hazard can be reduced by incorporating earthquake-resistant (aseismic) design features. Buildings made of mud-brick (adobe) or other materials without any reinforcement collapse easily during an earthquake. In multi-storey buildings or buildings of complex shapes the shaking can be increased with height as the building moves, and the building may twist as well as shake.

Each earthquake event provides engineers with lessons in how buildings perform, so techniques and regulations are constantly being updated and improved. However, this does mean that older buildings may not be as safe as was once thought. In the Kobe (1995) and Northridge, California (1994), earthquakes, buildings constructed in the 1980s and 1990s performed much

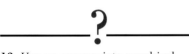

**10** Use an appropriate graphical technique to show the data shown in Table 3.2.

**11** Comment upon the effectiveness of aseismic design in reducing building collapse.

**Table 3.2  Earthquake loss susceptibility for different construction types (*Source:* Dregg, 1993)**

| Construction type | Average damage (%) at intensity (modified Mercalli scale) | | | | |
| --- | --- | --- | --- | --- | --- |
| | VI | VII | VIII | IX | X |
| 1  Adobe (mud-brick) | 8 | 22 | 50 | 100 | 100 |
| 2  Unreinforced masonry, non-seismic design | 3.5 | 14 | 40 | 80 | 100 |
| 3  Reinforced concrete frames, non-seismic design | 2.5 | 11 | 33 | 70 | 100 |
| 4  Steel frames, non-seismic design | 1.8 | 6 | 18 | 40 | 60 |
| 5  Reinforced masonry, medium quality, non-seismic design | 1.5 | 5.5 | 16 | 38 | 66 |
| 6  Reinforced concrete frames, aseismic design | 0.9 | 4 | 13 | 33 | 58 |
| 7  Shear wall structures, aseismic design | 0.6 | 2.3 | 7 | 17 | 30 |
| 8  Wooden structures, aseismic design | 0.5 | 2.8 | 8 | 15 | 23 |
| 9  Steel frames, aseismic design | 0.4 | 2 | 7 | 20 | 40 |
| 10  Reinforced masonry, high quality, aseismic design | 0.3 | 1.5 | 5 | 13 | 25 |

**Figure 3.15  How to design buildings to withstand earthquakes (*Source: Independent*, 20 January 1995)**

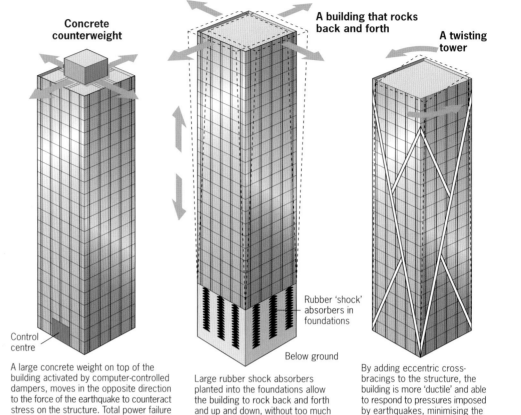

**Concrete counterweight**

**A building that rocks back and forth**

**A twisting tower**

Control centre

Rubber 'shock' absorbers in foundations

Below ground

A large concrete weight on top of the building activated by computer-controlled dampers, moves in the opposite direction to the force of the earthquake to counteract stress on the structure. Total power failure means the block cannot be moved.

Large rubber shock absorbers planted into the foundations allow the building to rock back and forth and up and down, without too much damage to the structure.

By adding eccentric cross-bracings to the structure, the building is more 'ductile' and able to respond to pressures imposed by earthquakes, minimising the damage caused to the structure.

**Figure 3.16  Rescue work in Maharashtra State, India, after an earthquake in September 1993. The death toll was 10 000.**

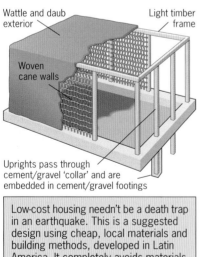

Wattle and daub exterior

Light timber frame

Woven cane walls

Uprights pass through cement/gravel 'collar' and are embedded in cement/gravel footings

Low-cost housing needn't be a death trap in an earthquake. This is a suggested design using cheap, local materials and building methods, developed in Latin America. It completely avoids materials such as breeze blocks, corrugated iron and concrete lintels which cause death and injury in an earthquake.

**Figure 3.17  Low-cost aseismic housing (*Source: Guardian*, 2 October 1993)**

better than those built before this. Currently there are three main types of aseismic building (Fig. 3.15). In the Northridge earthquake, most family homes survived without major structural damage as they were relatively new and subject to building codes that specified aseismic design.

The 'technological fix' of expensive aseismic design provides continued prospects of saving lives during an earthquake, and is particularly important for public buildings and utilities such as hospitals, roads, dams and power stations. However, there are significant drawbacks to this approach. It is not possible to rebuild whole cities using aseismic design, so people's vulnerability remains high. As Dregg (1993) points out, 70 per cent of the world's hundred largest cities (representing 10 per cent of the world's population) are exposed to significant earthquake hazard, i.e. expected earthquake intensities of VI (strong) at least once every 50 years on average. Some 25 per cent can expect intensities of VIII (destructive).

Cities and villages (Fig. 3.16) in LEDCs are the most vulnerable since aseismic designs are too expensive and offer little prospect of reducing the vulnerability of the large number of poor people living in squatter settlements and older housing. The 1976 Guatemalan earthquake was described by a journalist as a 'classquake' since it killed 22 000 people living in unsafe housing in the rural highlands, and those in squatter settlements in Guatemala city. The middle and upper classes were little affected. Attention needs to be given to developing wider use of low-cost housing for rural and urban areas (Fig. 3.17).

Although the more economically developed nations such as Japan and the USA are most able to introduce stricter building codes which can reduce death rates, the poorer members of these societies remain the most vulnerable to the earthquake hazard (see Kobe case study).

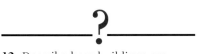

**12** Describe how buildings are adapted to withstand earthquakes (Fig. 3.15).

**13** Explain why the 'technological fix' is not appropriate to most people vulnerable to earthquake hazard.

A final consideration is that an aseismic design means that the building is less likely to collapse on its occupants – it does not mean that the structure is not damaged beyond repair. Economic losses therefore remain high and indeed continue to rise as more expensive techniques are used in the rebuilding programmes.

## Modify vulnerability

The aim is to lessen the impacts of the earthquake by prediction and warning, community preparedness, and land-use planning.

### Prediction and warning

Predicting earthquakes is a seismologist's dream since this would allow people to evacuate the danger areas before the event. Although there have been some advances in earthquake prediction in China, Japan and the USA, the major recent earthquakes in these areas were not forecast. On the global scale, the regions most at risk can be identified using plate tectonic theory. At the regional scale previous magnitude and frequency data can be used to pinpoint areas at risk and predict the probabilities of an earthquake occurring, but not precisely when this will happen. Since an earthquake is the release of strain building up in the crustal rocks, the areas which have 'locked' for some time are likely to move in the future (Fig. 3.9). Seismologists in California have produced earthquake probabilities for the major fault lines such as the San Andreas based upon this 'gap theory'. However, the predictions have a long time-scale and do not allow for movement on minor or unknown faults, as the Northridge earthquake showed.

Attempts to predict earthquakes in the few hours before the event are based upon the observations of earthquake survivors and monitoring equipment, such as changes in ground water levels, release of radon gas, or unusual animal behaviour (Fig. 3.18). These changes are thought to be due to ground

**Figure 3.18 The potential range of monitoring methods which may be used for earthquake prediction along an active fault line. Only a selection of the methods shown would be employed at any one site.** (*After:* Smith, 1996)

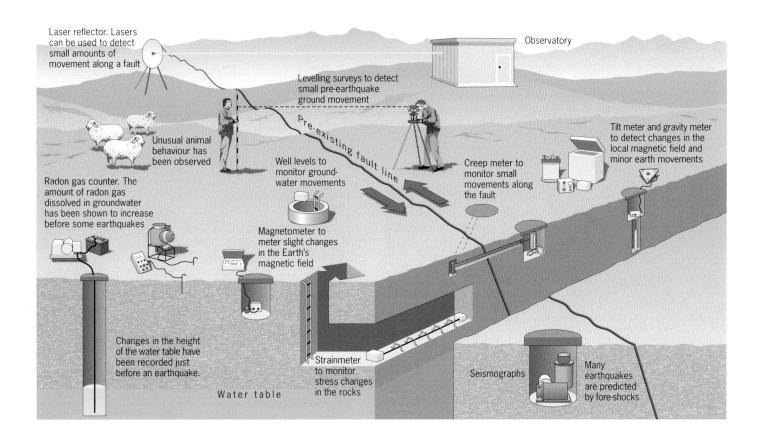

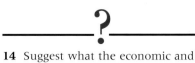

**14** Suggest what the economic and human impacts of a false prediction might be.

**15** Explain fully why each of the variables shown in Figure 3.19 is important in earthquake hazard zoning.

**16a** Evaluate the success of the geologic hazards mapping in the light of the damage resulting from the Loma Prieta earthquake (Fig. 3.20).
**b** How could the system be improved?
**c** What are the constraints in using this as a management technique for all areas of seismic risk?

dilation and rock cracking just before the earthquake. The Chinese successfully forecast the 1975 Haicheng earthquake, 5½ hours before the event. Some 90 000 people were successfully evacuated. The great Tangshan earthquake of 1976, however, was totally unexpected.

Although an earthquake event itself is difficult to predict with present levels of understanding and technology, it is possible to predict the impacts of an earthquake in an area and therefore produce a hazard zone map. This is based upon the known factors regarding ground-shaking and rock types, hillslopes, liquefaction and landslide potential in the area (Fig. 3.19). Computerised geographical information systems (GIS) are now being used to develop this technique further (Fig. 3.20) along with land-use planning (see page 54).

## Community preparedness

This centres on two levels of preparedness: the general public, and the emergency services and government at all levels. Experience of how people behave in earthquakes has helped to devise recommendations on the most appropriate action. The 1976 Tangshan earthquake resulted in 247 419 deaths and 164 581 severely injured. Some 86 per cent of the city's one million people were buried under fallen debris, but only 16 per cent of these were killed instantly by falling structures as they slept, or hit by falling debris as they tried to escape. A further 35 per cent of the victims died by suffocation resulting from the dust produced by the adobe buildings as they awaited rescue, and another 25 per cent from heat, thirst and hunger. However, 250 000 people crawled out of the debris and went on to rescue other victims. About 80 per cent of those buried were eventually rescued. Most survivors had ducked under heavy furniture, and remained calm to conserve their energy while they awaited rescue. However, more injured people died as they awaited medical help on the roadside. Clearly, the key response by the public is to have

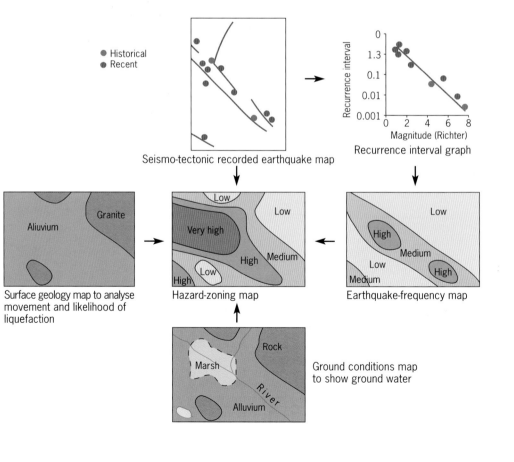

**Figure 3.19 A scheme of earthquake hazard zoning (*Source:* Cooke and Doornkamp, 1990)**

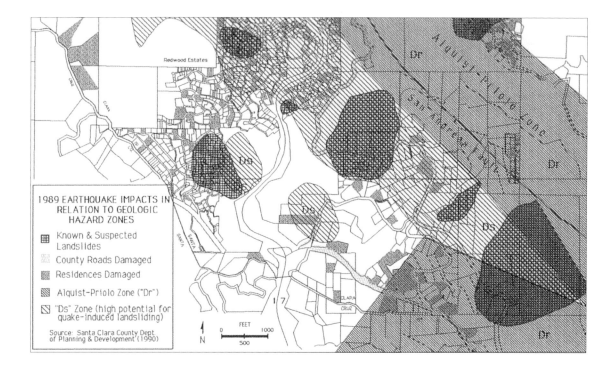

**Figure 3.20 Map of the area near Lexington Reservoir, Santa Clara County, California, showing damage from the 1989 Loma Prieta earthquake with respect to previously defined hazard zones. A GIS was used to prepare the map. The earthquake damaged 384 of the 1243 homes in the area, as well as water pipes and storage tanks. Analysis showed that damage to houses was related to their quality of construction, but the damage to infrastructure correlated with the mapped geologic hazards (the Alquist–Priolo fault zone and landsliding potential). This technique means that building requirements and the suitability of any proposed development can be reviewed quickly and easily. (*Source:* US Geological Survey, 1995)**

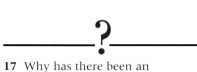

**17** Why has there been an increased focus upon community preparedness rather than earthquake prediction in California?

emergency supplies in stock, move under protective furniture during the earthquake and then await rescue. First-aid training would be valuable, as there is likely to be a delay of several hours or even days before outside help may arrive and essential services are restored. Thus community preparedness in this 'self-help only' period is crucial and needs to be planned at the local level.

The role of emergency services needs careful organisation and planning, with a clear specification of the role of each group of people. Responsibility for decision-making needs to be identified (see the Kobe case study).

One of the key issues confronting the emergency services is where to deploy their people and equipment in an area which may have suffered disruption of transport and communication lines. New computer developments are helping to make emergency response more effective. The Tokyo Gas Company has a seismic network which transmits information to a computer using a radio network. This informs the company about pipeline damage so that gas can be switched off and fires and explosions reduced. Individual houses in Tokyo have 'smart meters' which cut off the gas if an earthquake over magnitude 5 occurs.

In California, there is an increased emphasis upon community preparedness following unpredicted recent earthquakes. Computer systems are being developed to quickly provide the emergency services with vital information. A new seismic computer called 'Earthworm' monitors ground movements in the region, and can detect earthquake activity. A pager system for people working in the emergency services is also linked to 'Earthworm'. A future aim is to use the GIS to plot shaking and liquefaction potential, and service lines such as water, gas and electricity. When this is added to other information using the GIS, such as building type and age, roads, demographic information, and locations of hospitals, schools, etc., the areas most in need of help can be pinpointed. In the near future a new computer called 'Readicube' will use seismometers around California and the GIS to inform emergency teams where to head for within five seconds of an earthquake, and which gas supplies to cut off. After a few more minutes, the combined information can be used to identify which areas the emergency services should be sent to first.

# Experiencing a natural hazard: the Loma Prieta earthquake, California, USA

The Loma Prieta earthquake (Fig. 3.21) was the most costly natural disaster in the USA since the 1906 San Francisco earthquake. This case study summarises research comparing two areas: Santa Cruz near to the epicentre and San Francisco.

## Response during the earthquake

There was little evidence of panic or mass hysteria during the earthquake. The Californian workplace and school earthquake preparedness programme was generally successful, as is shown by the reactions of people during the earthquake (Table 3.3).

## Evacuation behaviour

Whether people evacuated or not depended on how close they were to the epicentre and the amount of damage to their home, but this was not the only reason (Table 3.4).

**Table 3.3 Respondents' actions during the earthquake and where they were at the time of the earthquake for the two areas (*Source:* US Geological Survey, 1992)**

| Action | House (%) | Work/school (%) | In transit (%) | Public places (%) |
|---|---|---|---|---|
| **San Francisco/Oakland** | | | | |
| Could not move | 13.1 | 0.0 | 9.0 | 0.0 |
| Froze | 47.5 | 31.7 | 27.2 | 23.2 |
| Froze, then sought protection | 5.2 | 13.7 | 9.0 | 7.6 |
| Sought protection | 18.4 | 54.6 | 9.0 | 22.9 |
| Ran outside | 7.8 | 0.0 | 0.0 | 46.3 |
| Went to child | 2.6 | 0.0 | 0.0 | 0.0 |
| Pulled car over | 0.0 | 0.0 | 36.9 | 0.0 |
| Continued driving | 0.0 | 0.0 | 9.0 | 0.0 |
| Other | 5.3 | 0.0 | 0.0 | 0.0 |
| **Total** | 37 | 21 | 11 | 13 |
| **Santa Cruz** | | | | |
| Could not move | 7.0 | 0.0 | 0.0 | 0.0 |
| Froze | 31.7 | 7.9 | 36.7 | 16.3 |
| Froze, then sought protection | 17.3 | 7.9 | 22.2 | 26.8 |
| Sought protection | 13.9 | 68.3 | 0.0 | 23.6 |
| Ran outside | 21.8 | 15.8 | 0.0 | 9.8 |
| Went to child | 7.6 | 0.0 | 0.0 | 23.6 |
| Pulled car over | 0.0 | 0.0 | 36.7 | 0.0 |
| Continued driving | 0.0 | 0.0 | 4.4 | 0.0 |
| Other | 0.8 | 0.0 | 0.0 | 0.0 |
| **Total** | 21 | 4 | 4 | 5 |

The sample of residents covered 82 in San Francisco and Oakland, and 122 in Santa Cruz (weighted sample).

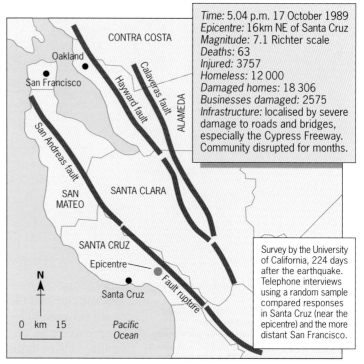

Time: 5.04 p.m. 17 October 1989
*Epicentre:* 16km NE of Santa Cruz
*Magnitude:* 7.1 Richter scale
*Deaths:* 63
*Injured:* 3757
*Homeless:* 12 000
*Damaged homes:* 18 306
*Businesses damaged:* 2575
*Infrastructure:* localised by severe damage to roads and bridges, especially the Cypress Freeway. Community disrupted for months.

Survey by the University of California, 224 days after the earthquake. Telephone interviews using a random sample compared responses in Santa Cruz (near the epicentre) and the more distant San Francisco.

**Figure 3.21 The San Francisco Bay area, including city locations, fault break and earthquake epicentre (*Source:* Palm and Hodgson, 1992)**

**Table 3.4 Percentage evacuated and reason for evacuation by sample strata for earthquake and level of fear (unweighted sample) (*Source:* US Geological Survey, 1992)**

| | Area | | | |
|---|---|---|---|---|
| | San Francisco/Oakland | | Santa Cruz | |
| | Very or somewhat fearful (%) | Not fearful (%) | Very or somewhat fearful (%) | Not fearful (%) |
| **Reason for evacuation** | | | | |
| Did not evacuate | 78.2 | 92.9 | 54.5 | 64.7 |
| Psychological reasons[1] | 12.7 | 3.6 | 10.2 | 11.8 |
| Structure or utilities | 1.8 | 0.0 | 5.7 | 5.9 |
| Both | 7.3 | 3.6 | 29.5 | 17.6 |
| **Total** | 55 | 28 | 88 | 34 |

[1]Includes either alone or in combination: evacuation because too upset to stay, afraid of further damage, concerned about aftershocks, invitation from a friend, or to make contact with others.

## Citizen participation in emergency response

How people respond to a disaster is linked to the concept of **symbolisation** – disasters create an image which is simple, compelling, and shared by those who experience the event. In both Santa Cruz and San Francisco, people helped in the emergency response

(Table 3.5). Those who experienced the most damage and those who had prepared for an earthquake before the event were the most likely groups to help others. An important conclusion was that earthquake victims should be viewed as part of the solution and not just a source of problems. If people are not injured they will help others, and if they are trained in first aid (for example), this help will be more effective.

## Public response to aftershock warnings

The US Geological Survey issued aftershock warnings for the San Francisco and Santa Cruz areas for two months after the earthquake. Both were considered to be at risk from aftershocks. Warnings of risk involve people in going though stages that shape their risk perceptions and behaviour, i.e. hear-confirm-understand-believe-personalise-respond. Each stage is affected by age, gender, education level, the nature of the information in the warning, and how often the warning is repeated.

The research showed that the response to the warnings produced more response in Santa Cruz than in San Francisco (Table 3.6). This was because the mainshock had damaged Santa Cruz more and the perceived risk by Santa Cruz residents was higher. They responded with more action, and in this area gender and ethnic differences were minimised.

**Table 3.5 Public involvement in emergency response activities (*Source:* US Geological Survey, 1992)**

| Emergency response activity | San Francisco (%) | (No.) | Santa Cruz (%) | (No.) |
|---|---|---|---|---|
| No emergency activities performed | 40.1 | 294 | 30.3 | 278 |
| Search and rescue victims | 2.7 | 20 | 4.8 | 44 |
| Provided food and water to others | 14.3 | 105 | 34.6 | 318 |
| Provided shelter to others | 11.6 | 85 | 18.2 | 167 |
| Cleaned/removed debris | 10.6 | 78 | 43.7 | 401 |
| Helped evacuate victims | 3.3 | 24 | 4.0 | 37 |
| Counselled victims | 8.2 | 60 | 16.6 | 152 |
| Put out fires | 0.3 | 2 | 0.7 | 6 |
| Directed traffic | 2.0 | 15 | 1.5 | 14 |
| Provided medical attention to victims | 1.9 | 14 | 3.6 | 33 |
| Totals | | 734 | | 918 |

**Table 3.6 Public response to aftershock warnings in the first 72 hours after the earthquake (*Source:* US Geological Survey, 1992)**

| | San Francisco (%) | (No.) | Santa Cruz (%) | (No.) |
|---|---|---|---|---|
| Sought general earthquake information | 21.1 | 155 | 21.8 | 200 |
| Sought information on what to do about aftershocks | 14.6 | 107 | 18.6 | 171 |
| Read earthquake information in phone book | 21.9 | 161 | 13.4 | 123 |
| Developed an emergency plan | 31.5 | 231 | 43.8 | 402 |
| Made household items safer | 45.2 | 332 | 70.3 | 645 |
| Made dwelling structurally safer | 7.4 | 54 | 17.6 | 162 |

**18** What was the most common response to the earthquake in each of the four places (i.e. house, work, etc.) where people were at the time of the earthquake?

**19** Suggest why the response of people at work was different from those at home.

**20** Which responses are likely to be the most dangerous? Why?

**21** Study Table 3.4. Is there a relationship between the amount of fear shown by people and the rates of evacuation?

**22** What were the reasons for people evacuating, and how did these vary with the location and amount of fear shown?

**23** Compare the type and amount of help given by the public in the two areas (Table 3.5).

**24** Put the list in Table 3.5 into a rank order of priority to save lives. Justify your ranking.

**25** Which tasks would you describe as 'skilled', and which as unskilled and able to be performed by most members of the public?

**26** Create a poster showing the type of training available and encouraging the public to participate.

**27** Suggest how people's socio-economic characteristics may shape their perception and response to the risk warnings given.

**28** Use Table 3.6 to compare the response to the warnings in the two study areas.

**29** How would you expect the response to change after six months and in the longer term?

**30** Summarise the main findings of the Loma Prieta earthquake research, and make a list of the recommendations to be made for future earthquake management.

## Land-use planning

The land use and layout of an area can be crucial in determining the impacts of an earthquake. The most hazardous areas can be identified and regulated and, along with aseismic building design, this can be a very effective hazard-mitigation measure. Lessons learned from major earthquakes can be incorporated into planning new city developments or rebuilding after earthquakes. In the Lunan area of Tangshan, over 120 000 people lived in one-storey brick structures in an area of 800 000 km². The death rate was 45 per cent since the high-density and poor-quality houses made escape difficult. In other parts of the city the death rate averaged 21.3 per cent, and in rural areas 14 per cent. The importance of public open space was shown, since this provides safe areas for people away from fires and aftershock damage to buildings. In addition, it is clear that major city service buildings should not be concentrated together, in order to reduce the chances of total collapse of these services.

Planning can also occur on a national level. In 1990, the Japanese government passed a resolution to transfer some of Tokyo's political and administrative functions to other areas, such as the less seismically active north of Honshu Island. Seismologists expect an earthquake to strike the Tokyo area in the next 40 years. If this were a high-magnitude event, the national economy, administrative and political systems would collapse. This would have major impacts inside Japan, but such an event would also affect the whole global economy.

## *Modify the loss*

### Aid

Disaster aid may help to distribute financial losses on an international scale, but to date this aid has not occurred over the long term to help with rebuilding lives and property. Most international aid has been to help in the few days after the event to provide medical services and other relief goods. Following the 1988 Armenian earthquake, for example, the former USSR accepted over US$200 million of aid from over 67 countries. However, the aid given after the Mexico City earthquake appears to have had only a minor effect. The Mexican government turned down offers of international aid in the first few days after the disaster, believing that it could cope alone.

### Insurance

Insurance is mainly available in the economically richer seismically active nations. The use of insurance as a loss-sharing mechanism is complex (see Californian insurance case study), and the vast majority of people at risk from earthquakes have no realistic access to insurance. Even in the richer parts of the world, it is mainly commercial and industrial property which is insured.

# The great Hanshin (Kobe) earthquake, Japan

The magnitude 7.2 earthquake which devastated the Japanese city of Kobe on 17 January 1995 at 5.46 a.m. had its epicentre only 20 km to the south-west of Kobe in Osaka Bay. Figure 3.22 shows the tectonic background. A 30–50 km long rupture of a strike-slip fault occurred close to and beneath the city of Kobe. In the two weeks after the main shock, 1320 aftershocks were registered, 150 of which were strong enough to be felt by people. The earthquake's shallow depth (14 km) and close proximity to the built-up area meant that buildings and structures were subjected to much ground-shaking and soil liquefaction.

Because of its geological position along a major subduction zone (see page 38) Japan experiences many earthquakes, and before the Kobe disaster the country was considered to be well prepared for a major earthquake striking an urban area, particularly as Japan is one of the richest and most technologically advanced countries in the world. Following the 1923 great Kanto earthquake which killed 140 000 people and destroyed more than 560 000 buildings in the Tokyo and Yokohama areas, the country has introduced several hazard-mitigation measures. The damage sustained during the 1995 earthquake and the shortcomings shown in the emergency response procedures have called into question the effectiveness of these measures.

## Impacts

The city of Kobe is on a narrow strip of land between Osaka Bay and the Rokko Mountains (Fig. 3.23). This heavily built-up strip of land is a major industrial area and port handling 30 per cent of Japan's commercial shipping, and acts as a major transport corridor linking western and north-eastern Japan. All transport routes in the area were severely affected by the collapse of elevated roads and railways (Fig. 3.23). The elevated Hanshin expressway is the main route through Kobe, and this collapsed in several places including one 630 m section (Fig. 3.26). The Sannomiya district suffered a large amount of ground deformation which caused severe damage to buildings, including tilting, collapse of individual storeys, or the collapse of the whole structure. Over 103 500 buildings were destroyed, and only 20 per cent of the buildings in the CBD were usable after the earthquake. The port facilities were severely damaged by soil liquefaction and lateral flow of soil along the quay walls. The city's gas and electricity systems were disrupted by ruptured pipes or collapsed poles, and 70 per cent of the water system was inoperable. Most of the 6300 deaths and 35 000 injuries occurred in the districts such as Nagata ward

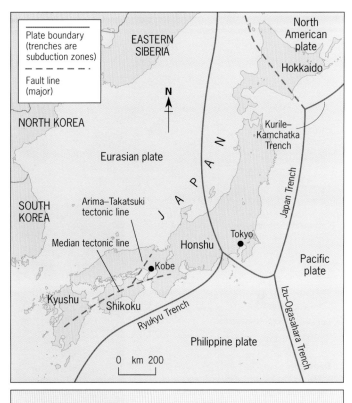

Plate boundary (trenches are subduction zones)

Fault line (major)

The Pacific plate is subducting under the Eurasian plate beneath Japan at about 10 cm per year, creating several deep oceanic trenches with associated earthquake activity. The city of Kobe is located just to the north of where the Philippines plate is subducting beneath the Eurasian plate. These plates meet obliquely, which puts a sideways strain on the Eurasian plate, which has fractured as a result, to produce the median tectonic line. This then puts a strain on the crust behind it which has then fractured to produce a new fault zone, the Arima–Takatsuki tectonic line. Movement in this fault zone resulted in the great Hanshin earthquake.

**Figure 3.22 Japan's tectonic setting and the great Hanshin (Kobe) earthquake**

(Fig. 3.25) where there were a large number of timber-framed houses with heavy tile roofs which collapsed on to their occupants. These older houses were designed to withstand heavy rains and typhoons, but became death-traps during the earthquake. The older and poorer people of Kobe were concentrated in these areas, as more wealthy residents could afford more modern, earthquake-resistant buildings. Over 60 per cent of the deaths were people aged over 60 who had a harder time getting to safety. The ruptured gas pipes resulted in over 300 fires in the city (Fig. 3.24). Immediately after the earthquake, some 300 000 people were homeless, which represented 20 per cent of Kobe's population.

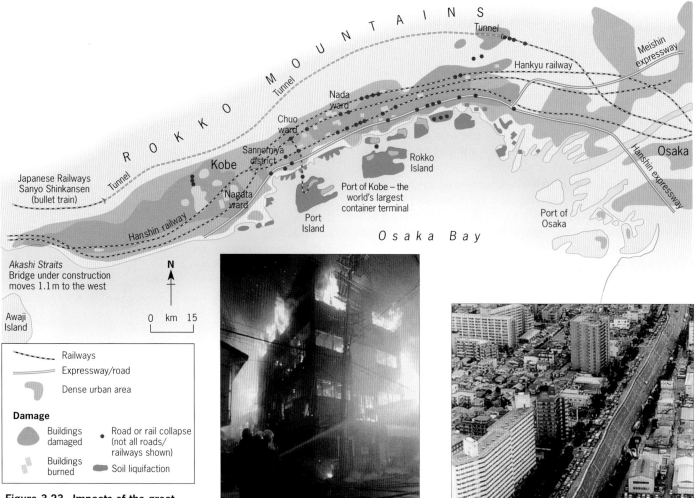

Japanese Railways
Sanyo Shinkansen
(bullet train)

*Akashi Straits*
Bridge under construction
moves 1.1 m to the west

Awaji
Island

N

0    km    15

Railways

Expressway/road

Dense urban area

**Damage**

Buildings
damaged

Road or rail collapse
(not all roads/
railways shown)

Buildings
burned

Soil liquifaction

**Figure 3.23  Impacts of the great
Hanshin (Kobe) earthquake**

**Figure 3.24  Firefighters worked
through the night in an attempt to
contain and extinguish the fires that
raged through Kobe after the
earthquake**

**Figure 3.26  A long section of the Hanshin
expressway lies twisted following the 1995
earthquake.**

**Figure 3.25  Police shovel debris as they continue to search for
bodies in the ruins of the Nagata area of Kobe following the
earthquake**

## The response to the earthquake

'The Kobe earthquake not only destroyed a major city: it also wrecked the nation's confidence in the central government's ability to cope with crises. The state's crisis-management system has been shown to be deeply flawed. We have seen that communications and co-ordination between the politicians and administrators is inadequate and the gears do not intermesh: we have seen also that in the administration of disaster measures the division of labour between central and local government is blurred' (Sassa Atsuyuki in *Japan Echo*, vol. 22, no. 2, 1995).

All schoolchildren in Japan are put through emergency earthquake and fire drills four times a year, and told how to act during an earthquake. Earthquake kits can be bought in department stores or made up by individuals. The kits contain a bucket for putting out fires, bottled water, food, radio, torch, first-aid kit, and protective headgear. The earthquake preparation programme also extends beyond school. Government offices and many companies observe Disaster Prevention Day on 1 September each year, which marks the anniversary of the Kanto (Tokyo) earthquake. Throughout the country, local communities hold drills and department stores organise earthquake-kit promotions.

People's reaction shows that there are flaws in this preparedness system – many were seen running outside buildings and were hit by falling debris or wandering aimlessly through the streets after the earthquake, ignoring small fires. However, it is the response of the local and national government which caused the most concern. The official response was slow. There was a five-hour delay before calling in the Self-defence Force (army), and even then only 200 troops were mobilised. Only by 21 January were there 30 000 troops helping with the rescue. Government officials debated for several days before deciding to designate the area a 'disaster zone' so that it could receive special emergency relief. Three days after the earthquake, the city still had no electricity supplies. There were also delays in accepting international help, e.g. from the US military based in Japan or foreign medical teams and sniffer dogs. Given that the devastation of the city cut off communications and that the few remaining roads were jammed with traffic as people tried to escape the city, the earthquake exposed serious flaws in the Japanese disaster management structure.

A further cause for anger was that Kobe's citizens believed that there was little earthquake risk in the area, although large businesses which had looked more carefully into its geological background had avoided siting expensive plants in the area. What seems to be needed now is a more detailed and open assessment of the risks to urban areas and the ability of the emergency services to react.

## Kobe – the aftermath

Disasters receive considerable media attention at the time that they occur, but what happens to the area and the people involved in the months afterwards? The earthquake caused US$99.3 billion of damage and the price tag for reconstruction has been put at $120 billion. Although the Japanese economy is better placed than most to cope with this huge bill, and jobs will be created in the recovery process, life for the people of Kobe will take many years to return to normal, if ever. Public services were restored between April and June 1995, and the Hanshin expressway by October 1996 (Fig. 3.27). However, in a free economy the economic costs to the city have been high, and 20 000 people lost their jobs. Many businesses and industries, such as Kawasaki shipping and Sumitomo rubber, moved away just after the earthquake and have not returned. Within the CBD, many companies have no plans to locate there again as the office towers are replaced. Of the 269 high-rise commerical buildings in Kobe, 62 were demolished, but there are plans to rebuild only 19 of them.

**Figure 3.27 The new Hanshin expressway**

The earthquake caused many personal tragedies. Unemployment and loss of homes were widespread: 95 000 people were still living in temporary prefabricated housing in January 1996 and could not afford a new permanent home. This figure was still high at 40 000 by October. Citizen groups in Kobe claim that there have been a further 2900 deaths from suicide or neglect. Only 7 per cent of people were covered by earthquake insurance (which is very expensive in Japan), and these are unlikely to be the poorer members of the community who lost their homes. The government has paid for the rebuilding of the public infrastructure, but has given no money for individuals to rebuild their lives.

City planners are re-zoning the city and introducing new regulations for rebuilding. The poorer wards such as Nagata remain devastated while this replanning takes place. The planners are introducing wider thoroughfares and more public open space. Unfortunately, over 200 factories cannot be rebuilt until this re-zoning is finished, delaying people's chances of getting jobs and rebuilding their lives.

**?**

**31** Prepare a brief presentation for your class on the Kobe earthquake to bring out (a) cause, (b) effect, (c) response, (d) problems.

**32** What do you think would have been the impacts if the earthquake had occurred three hours later?

**33** Do you think that the government should give financial aid to individual people? Explain your answer.

**34** Create a list of factors that town planners must consider when rebuilding after an earthquake.

**35** Refer to Figure 1.12. How does the Kobe experience compare with this model? Put a time value on each stage of the model for the Kobe earthquake.

**36a** What were the key flaws identified in the earthquake management structure in Japan?
**b** What recommendations would you make to improve future management of major earthquakes in Japan?

**?**

**37** Essay: Earthquakes represent an example of a natural hazard which cannot be easily predicted. Management of this hazard should centre upon vulnerability modification. Discuss with reference to examples you have studied.

**38** Essay: 'The occurrence of the earthquake hazard and the highest level of vulnerability is centred upon the economically developing nations.' Discuss the truth of this statement and make recommendations concerning how economically developing nations might manage the earthquake hazard.

## Summary

- Earthquakes are the result of stress build-up in crustal rocks, mainly as the result of movement of lithospheric plates.
- The spatial distribution of earthquakes is explained by plate tectonic theory, although some earthquakes are intra-plate or may be quasi-natural.
- Earthquakes represent the release of energy as seismic waves, and are classified by their intensity and magnitude.
- Primary hazards resulting from earthquakes are ground movement and shaking. Secondary hazards are soil liquefaction, landslides, avalanches and tsunami.
- The vulnerability of people to the earthquake hazard is related to social, economic, political and historical factors as well as geophysical factors.
- The earthquake hazard is managed by a range of responses including aid, insurance, hazard-resistant design, land-use planning and community preparedness.
- The nature of people's response to the earthquake hazard is a result of their hazard perception, symbolisation of the event and hazard salience.
- Prediction and warning of earthquakes has been difficult to achieve, but technological developments and better seismic understanding are increasing the likelihood of this in the future.

# 4 Tectonic hazards: volcanoes

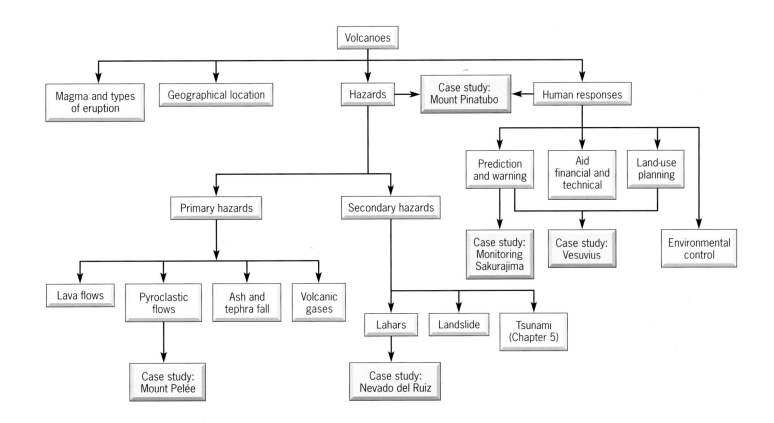

Volcanoes represent spectacular releases of energy (Fig. 4.1) from inside the earth's crust and upper mantle. Today there are about 500 active volcanoes which are closely associated with plate boundaries (Fig. 4.2). These disturbed crustal boundary areas reduce the pressure on the rocks of the asthenosphere beneath, and allow them to melt and become molten. This molten rock or **magma** rises upwards and is injected into the earth's crust or reaches the earth's surface to produce volcanic activity. Only a small number (20–30) of the active volcanoes erupt in any one year. These eruptive events are usually relatively short and are separated by periods of low activity. The dormant periods may last for tens or even thousands of years. A volcano is said to be extinct if it has not erupted in historic time. However, the 1973 eruption of Helgafell on the island of Heimaey, Iceland, after 5000 years, shows that we need to be cautious with so-called extinct volcanoes.

## 4.1 Magmas and types of volcanic eruption

During a volcanic eruption heated rock rises upwards from the asthenosphere to levels with lower overlying pressure. As it melts to form magma, the volume expands and the surrounding rocks become heated and may melt and crack due to the pressure. As the magma moves upwards, the pressure decreases and it becomes even more fluid. The gases at this stage are dissolved in the magma but, as the pressure continues to fall as the magma nears the surface, the gases come out of solution and form bubbles. These expand and help to propel the

**Figure 4.1 Mount St Helens' lateral blast**

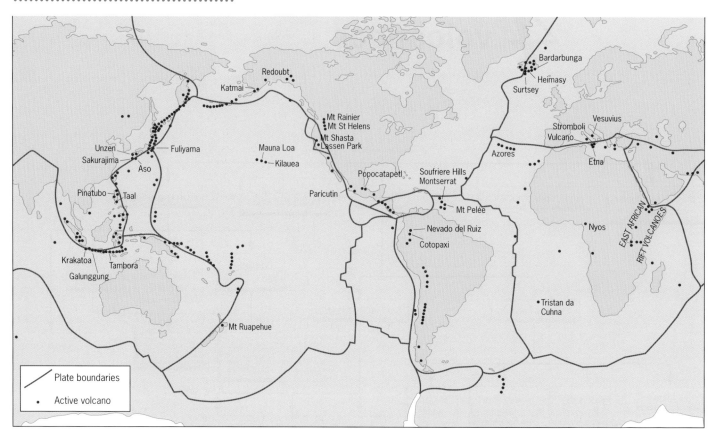

Plate boundaries

• Active volcano

**Figure 4.2 The distribution of active volcanoes (see Figure 3.3 for types of plate boundaries)**

magma on to the surface. Volcanic eruptions can occur through long cracks called fissures in the earth's crust, as a **fissure eruption**, or through a more concentrated area to form a volcano. Magma is called **lava** once it reaches the earth's surface. Most volcanoes are composed of mixtures of solidified magma and ash from broken-up former lava flows and rocks which shatter during the eruption. These build up into a volcanic mountain over time with each eruptive episode. The magma may be ejected through the central vent or from other locations, as shown in Figure 4.3.

This shows possible sites of volcanic activity and volcano structure. A major explosive eruption may blow off the top of the volcano to form a caldera. A composite volcano consist of layers of lava and ash. Other types of volcano are made mainly of lava and cones can build up made mainly of just ash deposits.

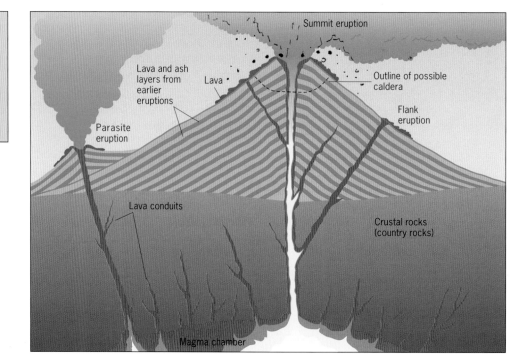

**Figure 4.3 Diagrammatic section through a composite cone**

Not all volcanic eruptions are violent and destructive. In order to understand why this is the case, we need to consider the nature of the material which reaches the earth's surface. Magma is a mixture of molten rock and gases, and a key characteristic is its viscosity. This is a measure of its internal resistance to flow. The lower the viscosity, the more fluid the magma. There are three factors which affect viscosity. Higher temperatures cause atoms to spread out and decrease in density, so magma at a higher temperature is less viscous and will flow more easily. Secondly, dissolved gases make the magma more fluid and buoyant. The higher the temperature, the more the gases remain dissolved and the less viscous the magma. Thirdly, the amount of silica ($SiO_2$) in the magma affects the flow. Silica has close jointing and packing of atoms and makes flow slow, and it is more difficult for gases to escape. Lavas with a high silica content have an acidic chemical composition and form rocks called rhyolites. They are viscous and have relatively low temperatures of 600–1000°C. The lavas flow slowly, the gases do not escape easily, and build up to produce more explosive eruptions. Lavas with a low silica content have a basic chemical composition and form rocks called basalts. They are hotter (1000–1200°C) and have low viscosity. Gases are released more easily and the eruptions tend to be non-explosive. Figure 4.4 shows the main types of eruption resulting from these variations.

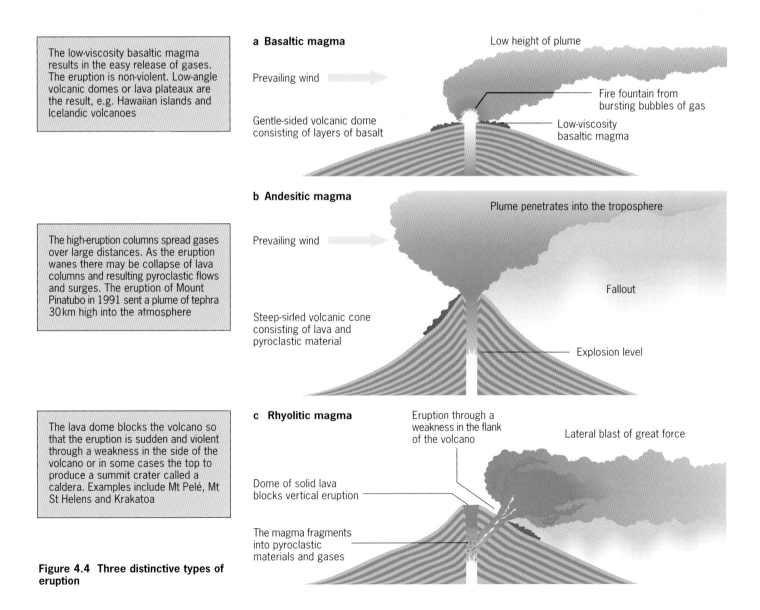

The low-viscosity basaltic magma results in the easy release of gases. The eruption is non-violent. Low-angle volcanic domes or lava plateaux are the result, e.g. Hawaiian islands and Icelandic volcanoes

**a Basaltic magma**

Low height of plume

Prevailing wind

Fire fountain from bursting bubbles of gas

Gentle-sided volcanic dome consisting of layers of basalt

Low-viscosity basaltic magma

The high-eruption columns spread gases over large distances. As the eruption wanes there may be collapse of lava columns and resulting pyroclastic flows and surges. The eruption of Mount Pinatubo in 1991 sent a plume of tephra 30 km high into the atmosphere

**b Andesitic magma**

Plume penetrates into the troposphere

Prevailing wind

Fallout

Steep-sided volcanic cone consisting of lava and pyroclastic material

Explosion level

The lava dome blocks the volcano so that the eruption is sudden and violent through a weakness in the side of the volcano or in some cases the top to produce a summit crater called a caldera. Examples include Mt Pelé, Mt St Helens and Krakatoa

**c Rhyolitic magma**

Eruption through a weakness in the flank of the volcano

Lateral blast of great force

Dome of solid lava blocks vertical eruption

The magma fragments into pyroclastic materials and gases

**Figure 4.4 Three distinctive types of eruption**

**Table 4.1 Classification of volcanic eruptions**

| Type of eruption | Volcanic explosivity index (VEI) | Eruption rate (kg/sec) | Volume of ejecta (m³) | Eruption column height (km) | Duration of continuous blasts in hours | Troposphere/ stratosphere injection | Qualitative description |
|---|---|---|---|---|---|---|---|
| **Hawaiian** | 0 Non-explosive | $10^2$–$10^3$ | $< 10^4$ | 0.8–1.5 | $< 1$ | Negligible/ none | Effusive |
| | 1 Small | $10^3$–$10^4$ | $10^4$–$10^6$ | 1.5–2.8 | $< 1$ | Minor/ none | Gentle |
| **Strombolian** | 2 Moderate | $10^4$–$10^5$ | $10^6$–$10^7$ | 2.8–5.5 | 1–6 | Moderate/ none | Explosive |
| **Vulcanian** | 3 Moderate– large | $10^5$–$10^6$ | $10^7$–$10^8$ | 5.5–10.5 | 1–12 | Great/ possible | Severe |
| | 4 Large | $10^6$–$10^7$ | $10^8$–$10^9$ | 10.5–17.0 | 1–>12 | Great/ definite | Violent |
| **Plinian and ultra-Plinian** Note: Peléean-type eruptions are in this group but the blast is directed laterally, as in Figure 4.4c | 5 Very large | $10^7$–$10^8$ | $10^9$–$10^{10}$ | 17.0–28.0 | 6–>12 | Great/ significant | Cataclysmic |
| | 6 Very large | $10^8$–$10^9$ | $10^{10}$–$10^{11}$ | 28.0–47.0 | >12 | Great/ significant | Paroxysmal |
| | 7 Very large | $>10^9$ | $10^{11}$–$10^{12}$ | >47.0 | >12 | Great/ significant | Colossal |
| Plinian type | 8 Very large | — | $>10^{12}$ | — | >12 | Great/ significant | Terrific |

**Figure 4.5 The volcano Stromboli, Italy, erupts every few minutes. These low level eruptions are not violent and provide opportunities for tourism.**

The visible physical differences in eruptions are the basis of classifying volcanic eruptions. Recent classifications attempt to quantify eruptions as well as the more traditional type of eruption approach (Table 4.1). To date, the intensity of the human impacts of eruptions has not been classified.

## 4.2 Geographical location

The chemical composition of the lava depends on the geological situation in which it has formed. Basaltic lavas (basic) are formed by the melting of oceanic crust and the mantle. Rhyolitic (acidic) lavas with a high silica content are formed from the melting of continental crust. In between these two extremes are several groups of intermediate magmas, the most important of which is andesitic magma. This forms from rising basaltic magma formed in the upper mantle which then mixes with continental crust before it reaches the earth's surface. The resulting volcanic eruptions can be violent. The world's active volcanoes are found in three tectonic situations (Fig. 4.2).

**1** Which continental area has no active volcanoes?

**2a** On a world map devise a colour key to indicate countries as being at high, medium and low risk from volcanoes.
**b** Choose five countries from different continents and tectonic situations and describe the geological reasons for the volcanic activity.

**3** Draw a diagram to show a subduction zone (use the relevant part of Fig. 3.2 to help). Annotate the diagram with details of the formation of the magma and the reasons for the volcanic activity.

**4** Explain why some volcanoes erupt more violently than others.

**5** Study Figure 4.6.
**a** What is the evidence for a change of direction in the movement of the Pacific plate and when did this happen?
**b** Use the dates and the scale to calculate the average rate of movement of the Pacific plate each million years during the last 78 million years.
**c** What will happen to Hawaii in the future? Suggest a time-scale for these events.

## Constructive plate boundaries

Most of the magma which reaches the earth's surface (73 per cent) occurs along these boundaries. The main areas are the mid-ocean ridges where melting of the upper mantle produces basaltic magma (Fig. 3.2). The eruptions tend to be non-violent and, as most occur on the sea floor, they do not represent a major hazard to people except where portions of the ocean ridge emerge above sea level to form inhabited islands such as Iceland in the North Atlantic.

Continental constructive boundaries occur where continental crust is being moved apart, most notably along the East African Rift Valley system stretching from northern Ethiopia to Mozambique. This system has fourteen active volcanoes, with a wide range of magma types depending upon the local geological conditions.

## Destructive plate boundaries

Some 80 per cent of the world's active volcanoes occur along destructive boundaries. As the oceanic plate descends into the mantle and melts, basic magma rises upwards and mixes with continental crust (Fig. 3.2) to produce magma with a higher silica content than along the oceanic ridges. These andesitic and rhyolitic magmas result in the most violent volcanic activity. Volcanic **island arcs** form where two oceanic plates are colliding. The resulting volcanic activity is of andesitic and basaltic magmas.

## Hot spots

Hot spots are small areas of the crust with an unusually high heat flow, and are found away from plate boundaries. Slowly rising mantle rocks create volcanic activity on the surface. The movement of the lithospheric plates over the hot spot produces a chain of what are mainly now extinct volcanoes. The most famous example of an active hot spot is the Hawaiian Islands (Fig. 4.6), but there are thought to have been 125 hot spots active in the last 10 million years. Other examples are the Maldives in the Indian Ocean and the Azores in the Atlantic. Eruptions are usually of low-viscosity basaltic magmas.

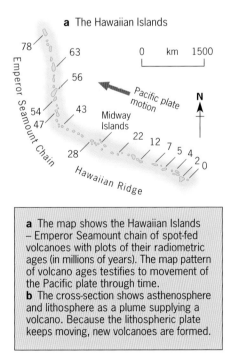

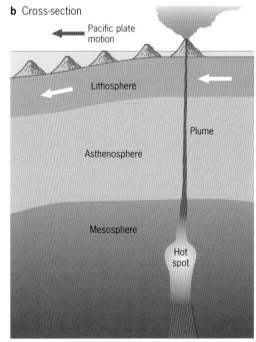

**a** The map shows the Hawaiian Islands – Emperor Seamount chain of spot-fed volcanoes with plots of their radiometric ages (in millions of years). The map pattern of volcano ages testifies to movement of the Pacific plate through time.
**b** The cross-section shows asthenosphere and lithosphere as a plume supplying a volcano. Because the lithospheric plate keeps moving, new volcanoes are formed.

**Figure 4.6 A Hawaiian hot spot and its path (Source: Abbott, 1996)**

**Figure 4.7 The smouldering volcano of Mount Sakurajima (Japan) dominates Kagoshima at its foot, and frequently showers the city with a layer of corrosive ash**

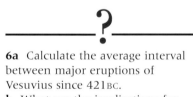

**6a** Calculate the average interval between major eruptions of Vesuvius since 421 BC.
**b** What are the implications for the area today?

## 4.3 Volcanic hazards

Volcanic activity provides both opportunities and risks for people. Volcanic soils are fertile, tectonic activity provides energy sources through geothermal power, lava can be used for building material, and the attractive scenery provides recreational potential, e.g. Etna (Fig. 4.8), Mount St Helens and Fujiyama. In both MEDCs and LEDCs volcano flanks are farmed or developed for housing, exposing the population to the benefits and the risks of such a location (Fig. 4.7). In Indonesia, there are 82 active volcanoes, yet the island of Java is among the most densely populated in the world. Vesuvius in Italy is famous for the AD79 eruption which destroyed the Roman towns of Pompeii and Herculaneum after 500 years of relative inactivity. There were eight large eruptions between 203 and 1138, followed by 500 years of quiet in which the volcano was recolonised and the danger forgotten in people's minds. In 1631, an eruption destroyed 15 towns and killed 4000 people, and there were further major eruptions in 1794, 1861 and 1906. There have also been frequent but minor eruptions in the past 350 years. The flanks of the volcano have become settled, and the modern town of Ercolano lies directly on top of the mudflows which buried Herculaneum (Fig. 4.8)! Settlements are usually sited in lowlands and valleys which are also the routes followed by deadly pyroclastic flows.

It is the often long time-scales of the recurrence intervals of volcanic eruptions, as opposed to human time-scales, which can make the risk involved in such locations seem minimal compared with the day-to-day gains of much-needed land, fertile soils and attractive locations for homes. In the Philippines, Taal volcano, which has erupted 33 times since 1572, has become settled by 6000 households enjoying a relatively prosperous life based upon fishing, agriculture and tourism. This development occurred in spite of objections from volcanologists. Wealthy Filipino families have built houses in this beautiful lakeside area, including the summer palace of former President Marcos. The people have some confidence in the volcano observatory on the site to warn them of any dangers, in spite of the fact that they can only escape by boat.

In contrast to some hazards, volcanoes represent a threat to all property and any person living in the high-risk zone around them, whatever their age, gender, socio-economic or ethnic group. People are equally vulnerable to volcanic hazards, unlike some other hazards where the impacts are often more selective. Housing quality, type, and income provide no protection against the hazards created by an eruption. Tomblin (1987) commented, 'Eruptions differ from other causes of disasters such as earthquakes, hurricanes and floods, in that they cause virtually total destruction of life and property within relatively small areas which can be easily delineated.'

**Figure 4.8 Mount Etna at the start of the July 2001 eruption**

## 4.4 Primary volcanic hazards

### Lava flows

Lava flows are spectacular but they pose more of a threat to property in their path than to human life. The most dangerous are fissure eruptions of basaltic magma which reach speeds of 50 km per hour on steep slopes and can spread tens of kilometres from their source. Andesitic and rhyolitic lavas flow as plastic rather than liquid and move very slowly, rarely reaching more than 8 km from their source. Lava flows are at their most hazardous when large quantities are released quickly. These are rare events, but one example in 1977 killed 72 people. The Nyiragongo volcano, Congo, erupted through five fissures on the volcano's flanks (see Fig. 4.3). This drained the lava lake which had collected in the summit crater in less than one hour. Lavas destroy everything in their path and are likely to result in high but localised economic losses, such as agricultural land, buildings and roads. Kilauea in Hawaii has been erupting lava since 1983, covering 78 km² and destroying 180 houses but with no deaths. The eruptions added 120 km² of new land and are a major tourist attraction.

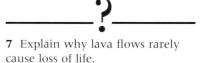

**7** Explain why lava flows rarely cause loss of life.

**Figure 4.9 The Soufriere Hills volcano emits ash and steam just west of St Patrick's, Montserrat, in April 1997. A blanket of ash covered most of the southern half of the island, including the capital city of Plymouth, which had been evacuated for months.**

### Pyroclastic flows and surges

Pyroclastic flows are mixtures of hot rock fragments, lava particles and ash buoyed up by hot gases. They are sometimes known as *nuées ardentes* or 'glowing clouds'. These deadly flows are most commonly associated with subduction-zone volcanoes. The pyroclastic flow moves from the volcanic vent at high speeds and can extend up to 40 km from its source (Fig. 4.9). The pyroclastic material is denser than the surrounding air and moves close to the ground following areas of lower relief, such as river valleys. Pyroclastic surges develop from flows as they move downhill (Fig. 4.10).

Pyroclastic flows develop from a collapsing eruption column, lava dome collapse, or they simply boil out of the crater like soup out of a boiling pot. The most dangerous pyroclastic flows are those directed sideways by a lateral eruption of a volcano where the summit crater is blocked by viscous magma and the gases build up pressure which is released explosively through a weak point in the volcano's flank. These events occur with andesitic or rhyolitic eruptions (see Fig. 4.4c). The force and full volume of the pyroclastic material is projected down the volcano rather than into the atmosphere. The high speed and temperatures of the flow destroy everything in their path (Fig. 4.11).

a Pyroclastic flow

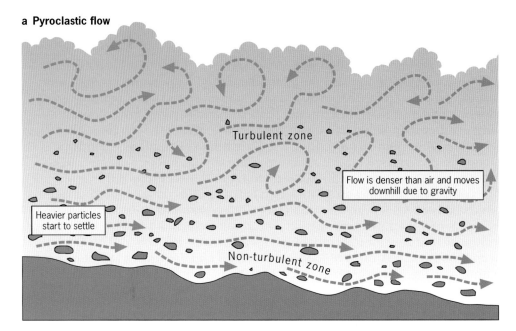

Turbulent zone

Flow is denser than air and moves downhill due to gravity

Heavier particles start to settle

Non-turbulent zone

**Figure 4.10 Pyroclastic flows and surges**

b Pyroclastic surge develops

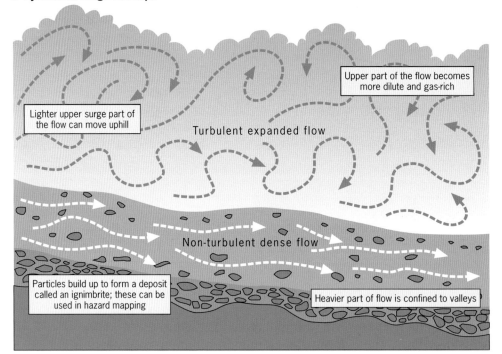

Upper part of the flow becomes more dilute and gas-rich

Lighter upper surge part of the flow can move uphill

Turbulent expanded flow

Non-turbulent dense flow

Particles build up to form a deposit called an ignimbrite; these can be used in hazard mapping

Heavier part of flow is confined to valleys

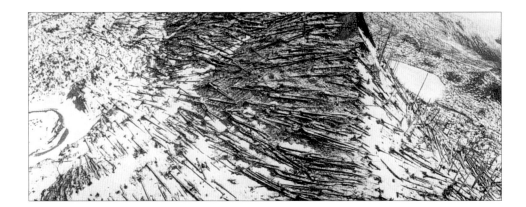

**Figure 4.11 Trees destroyed by the pyroclastic flow after the Mount St Helens eruption, 1980**

# The eruption of Mount Pelée, Martinique

One of the most tragic eruptions was Mount Pelée on the Caribbean island of Martinique in 1902 (Fig. 4.12). A pyroclastic flow killed all but two of the 29 000 inhabitants of the port of St Pierre (Fig. 4.13). In early spring, the crater of Mount Pelée began to fill with very viscous magma which plugged the crater. From 23 April onwards, animals were dying in the surrounding area, suffocated by poisonous gases. On 5 May, a large pyroclastic flow sped down the River Blanche valley and the people of St Pierre became increasingly anxious, with some moving out of the town. However, an election was due on 10 May and the governor did not want the population scattered over the island. Troops were called in to restore order and stop the retreat. On 8 May there were loud explosions as the gas pressure in the volcano reached critical levels. The gases exploded in the crater, disintegrating the magma into a pyroclastic flow which moved at 190 km per hour down the flank of the volcano. The heavier and denser material flowed down the Blanche Valley, but a cloud of hot gases and suspended ash still at a temperature of 700°C or more moved on to St Pierre. This surge was hot enough to melt glass and metal. People were killed quickly by physical impact, inhaling superhot gases, or burns. The cloud continued into the harbour and destroyed seventeen boats. A further *nuée ardente* spread over St Pierre on 20 May, and on 30 August one flowed south-east over four towns killing another 2000 people. The eruption ended with a spine of very viscous magma growing in the summit crater. Today the area is settled once again.

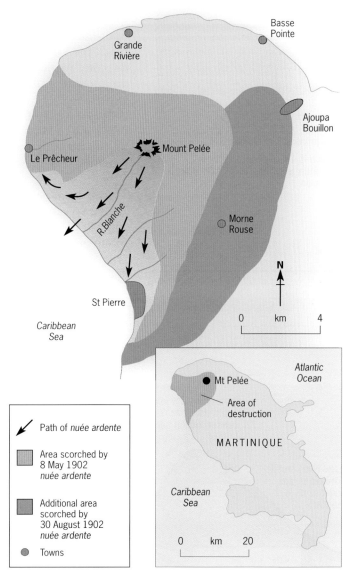

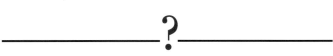

**Figure 4.12. The impacts of the 1902 eruption of Mount Pelée**

**Figure 4.13 St Pierre, following the 1902 destruction**

?

**8** Why are pyroclastic flows so dangerous?

**9** Draw a copy of Figure 4.12. Annotate your map with details of the eruption and its impact.

**10** Write a news broadcast describing the disaster at St Pierre and giving an analysis of why it happened.

**11** What action should have been taken and how might the area prepare for another eruption?

**Figure 4.14 Ash clouds over Missoula after the Mount St Helens eruption**

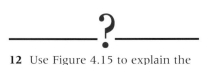

12 Use Figure 4.15 to explain the cause of the Lake Nyos disaster.

*Ash and tephra fall*

Volcanic ash (<2mm diameter) and tephra (>2mm diameter) forms when magma is fragmented by explosions or when solid rocks are broken up by groundwater turning explosively into steam. The finest ash can be carried high into the atmosphere and is carried by prevailing winds over large areas. The finer material is carried the furthest and during very violent eruptions can reach the **stratosphere** and be carried over many thousands of kilometres, affecting world weather patterns and presenting a hazard to aircraft. Ash falls are more of a nuisance (Fig. 4.14) than a cause of death, although people may experience breathing difficulties, and large accumulations may cause building collapse. Agricultural production may be reduced by large ash falls, as occurred following the deposition of 30 kg/m$^2$ on crops in eastern Washington State during the eruption of Mount St Helens. The economic losses from the Pinatubo eruption of 1991 were high as a result of ash fallout (see case study).

*Volcanic gases*

Active volcanoes produce large amounts of water vapour, carbon dioxide, sulphur dioxide, chlorine, hydrogen sulphide, hydrogen, helium, carbon monoxide and hydrogen chloride. They rarely reach lethal levels in populated areas. Carbon dioxide is the most dangerous because it is heavier than air. It collects in depressions where concentrations can become high enough to cause suffocation.

A rare event involving the release of volcanic gases was the Lake Nyos, Cameroon, disaster of August 1986 (Fig. 4.15).

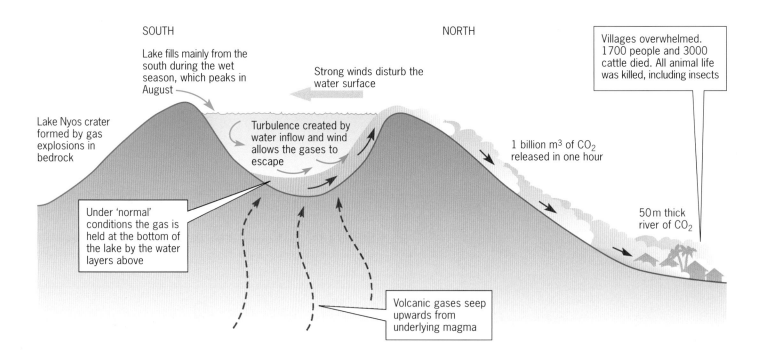

SOUTH

Lake fills mainly from the south during the wet season, which peaks in August

Strong winds disturb the water surface

NORTH

Villages overwhelmed. 1700 people and 3000 cattle died. All animal life was killed, including insects

Lake Nyos crater formed by gas explosions in bedrock

Turbulence created by water inflow and wind allows the gases to escape

1 billion m$^3$ of CO$_2$ released in one hour

Under 'normal' conditions the gas is held at the bottom of the lake by the water layers above

50m thick river of CO$_2$

Volcanic gases seep upwards from underlying magma

**Figure 4.15 The Lake Nyos, Cameroon, disaster of 21 August 1986. The lake lies in an area of ancient volcanic activity associated with continental plate spreading in the past. This event could be repeated.**

# 4.5 Secondary volcanic hazards

There are three main secondary hazards considered here, although more rarely some eruptions can produce other secondary hazards such as acidic rain, or flooding from melting ice-caps and fields. The 1996 eruption of the Bardarbunga volcano under the Vatnajökull ice-cap in south-east Iceland produced the 'flood of the century' which destroyed part of Iceland's southern ring road and three bridges.

## Lahars

Lahars are mudflows of volcanic material and they represent the second greatest threat to people after pyroclastic flows. The huge amount of ash and debris produced by eruptions can mix with water and then move rapidly (up to 22 m per second on steep slopes) over long distances, usually along river valleys and other low-lying areas. The source of the water may be heavy rain, making wet tropical areas such as Indonesia particularly susceptible. Eruption events cause localised heavy rainfall and electrical thunderstorms which can trigger lahars. The 1982–83 eruption of Galunggung, Indonesia, resulted in thunderstorm-generated lahars which made 35 000 people homeless and wiped out the local agricultural economy by burying 94 000 ha of crops and fish farms. Lahars may also be induced by the collapse of a crater lake, or the rapid melting of snow and ice on the volcanic mountain. This was the case with the 13 November 1985 eruption of Nevado del Ruiz in Colombia.

# The Nevado del Ruiz eruption of 1985

The Nevado del Ruiz volcano in Colombia had not erupted since 1845, when lahars killed 1000 people, and in 1595 when 600 were killed. The town of Armero was built on the debris of these earlier events. The volcano started to erupt with small-scale activity in November 1984. By 13 November 1985 eruptive activity had increased, causing melting of the ice-cap as it was showered with hot pyroclastic debris. At 10 p.m. lahars ran down the east slope of the volcano over the town of Chinchina, killing 1800 people. At 11 p.m. lahars travelling westwards at 45 km per hour spread over the town of Armero, burying it in 8 m of mud and killing 22 000 people (Figs 4.16 and 4.17). The hazards had already been mapped by scientists who had gathered once the eruption had started in early 1985. The hazard map (Fig. 4.18) was due to be presented for approval the day after the disaster. The event was devastating for the area and the economy of Colombia (Table 4.2).

**Figure 4.16 Most of the town of Armero, Colombia, and 22 000 of its inhabitants, lie beneath lahars of up to 8 m thick**

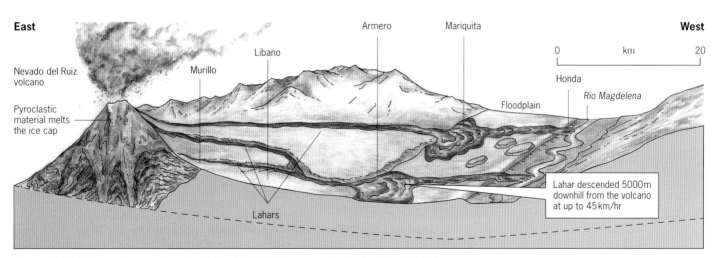

**Figure 4.17 The eruption of Nevado del Ruiz in 1985 dropped hot pyroclastic debris on to the glaciers, resulting in lahars (Source: US Geological Survey, 1989a)**

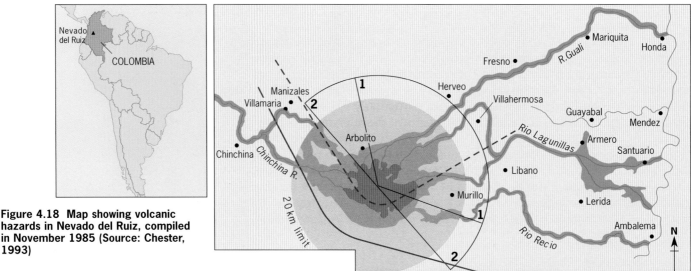

**Figure 4.18 Map showing volcanic hazards in Nevado del Ruiz, compiled in November 1985 (Source: Chester, 1993)**

**Table 4.2 Damage caused by the Nevado del Ruiz eruption in 1985 (*Source:* Chester, 1993)**

| Category of loss | Details |
|---|---|
| Deaths and injuries | Nearly 70 per cent of the population of Armero were killed (~20 000) and a further 5000 (17 per cent) were injured. On the western flanks of the volcano overbank flooding by lahars caused more than 1800 fatalities. |
| Agricultural | 60 per cent of the region's livestock, 30 per cent of the sorghum and rice crop and 500 000 bags of coffee were destroyed.<br>Over 3400 ha of agricultural land was lost from production. |
| Communications | In the vicinity of the volcano virtually all roads, bridges, telephone lines and power supplies were destroyed. The whole region was isolated. |
| Industrial, commercial and civic buildings | 50 schools, two hospitals, 58 industrial plants, 343 commercial establishments and the National Coffee Research Centre were badly damaged or destroyed. |
| Housing | Most of the housing was destroyed and nearly 8000 were rendered homeless. |
| Monetary | The cost of the eruption to the economy of Colombia was estimated at US$7.7 billion. This represented about 20 per cent of the country's GNP for the year in question. |

Legend:

|  | Pyroclastic flow hazard | Ashfall hazard | Low-angle blast hazard |
|---|---|---|---|
| ▨ Lava flow hazard | ▨ High | – – – High | **1** High |
| ▨ Lahar hazard | ▨ Moderate | —— Moderate | **2** Moderate |

**?**

**13** Describe the events which led to the lahar disaster of the Nevado del Ruiz eruption.

**14** Study Figure 4.18.
**a** Compare the distances from the vent of the volcano affected by lava, pyroclastic flow, ashfall, blast and lahar hazards.
**b** Why are lahars and pyroclastic flows the most hazardous?

**15** By using a spider diagram and the information in Table 4.2, devise an information-annotated chart to indicate the impacts of the eruption.

## Volcanic landslides

These are gravity-driven slides of masses of rock and loose volcanic material. They may occur during an eruption, as with Mount St Helens when the side of the volcano collapsed. However, landslides can occur at other times on volcanic craters as a result of heavy rainfall, or earthquakes. If there is a chaotic tumbling flow of material, the term **debris avalanche** is used. **Ground deformation** of volcanic slopes by rising magma may also trigger slope instability and landslides before an eruption.

## Tsunami

Tsunami are giant sea waves and are a secondary hazard of eruptions, especially very violent caldera-forming events (see Chapter 5). The most devastating event is the 1883 eruption of Krakatoa, Indonesia, which produced 30-m high waves which drowned an estimated 36 000 people.

## 4.6 The human response to volcanic hazards

*Modify the event*

### Environmental control

Very little can be done to control a volcanic eruption. Lava flows are the only primary volcanic hazard which people have attempted to control with any success. Two methods have been used – water sprays and explosions. Sea-water sprays were successfully used to cool the lava flows during the 1973 eruption of Eldafell on Haeimaey, Iceland, to protect the harbour of Vestmannaeyjar. Explosives were used with some success in the 1983 eruption of Etna (Fig. 4.19), when 30 per cent of the slow-moving lava flow was diverted from its course. Artificial barriers and blasting were also used in the 1991–2 and 2001 eruptions of Etna.

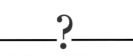

16   Study Figure 4.19.
**a**  What was the property damage resulting from the eruption of Mount Etna?
**b**  Describe the scheme to divert the lava flows.

# Dynamite gang to tame volcano

MOUNT ETNA, Europe's largest volcano, now in full eruption, is to undergo major surgery on Wednesday. In what has been described as 'the first example of volcanic engineering in history', it is hoped to deviate and slow down a torrent of lava threatening villages on the volcano's lower slopes.

The eruption began 42 days ago in the side of the mountain at 2368m. Since then millions of tonnes of lava have gushed out of a small crater and covered the mountainside with immense tongues of molten rock – some of them up to 6km long – which can been seen at night from Catania. So far, one hotel, three restaurants, 25 houses and numerous orange groves have been swallowed up. Last Monday, the main crater of Mount Etna's 3423m summit began to erupt.

There is only one other recorded example of an attempt at volcanic engineering. In 1944, the United States Air Force was called in to bomb the crater of an erupting volcano in Hawaii. It was hoped to open a breach in the crater so that lava threatening an inhabited area would flow out in the opposite direction. The experiment failed totally.

For centuries, Etna's mountain-dwellers tried to divert lava flows from their houses and farms, then in the 19th century this was made illegal. Last week, Orazio Nicoloso, the doyen of Etna's mountaineers, told *The Sunday Times* that during an eruption in 1971 he flouted the law. One night with friends, using bulldozers, he successfully diverted a lava flow that was threatening a cable car station. Nicoloso's achievement became widely known and was probably a factor in convincing the Italian authorities 10 days ago to change the law and take action.

The lava pouring out from the side of the mountain has carved out a channel for itself about 6m wide and 4.5m deep with ridges of solidified lava forming on either side of its course. The lava races along at an average speed of about 16km/hr. After about 0.8km it begins to slow down.

As in an operation to divert a river, the intention is to blow up a section of the solidified ridge and channel the molten lava along a new path. There is frenetic activity at the scene. The technicians spend most of their time at the part to be blown up. There, at a level of about 3m below the molten rock, a section has been dug out for the explosive charges to be placed.

Nearby more than 100 men, using lorries, 15 mechanised shovels and five bulldozers, are working in a biting wind and swirling sulphur clouds, preparing a canal for the lava. It is hoped that the lava will burst into the canal after the explosion, then run into an ancient crater and down the mountainside parallel to the present flows.

The lava wall will be blown up by the Swedish explosives engineer, Lennart Abersten, with an Italian colleague, Giovanni Ripamonte. They will have to place by hand at least 40 high-explosive charges in the wall at a very high temperature.

The danger will be enormous for the two men. They will have only two minutes before the explosion to dash for a shelter 255m away.

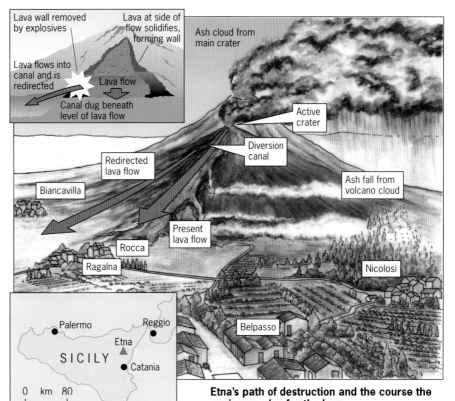

**Etna's path of destruction and the course the engineers plan for the lava**

**Figure 4.19  The dynamiting of Mount Etna, Sicily (*Source: Sunday Times*, 8 May 1983)**

Artificial barriers have been proposed to protect Hilo, Hawaii, from future lava flows. Barriers have also been used to protect against the secondary hazards of lahars, which tend to follow well-defined routes. In Indonesia, some villages have artificial mounds to enable villagers to escape to higher ground, although an adequate warning is needed if this is to be effective. A tunnel through the crater wall of Kelut volcano, Java, has also been tried to drain the crater lake and reduce the risk of lahars forming.

### Hazard-resistant design

Building and structure design can do little to resist lava, pyroclastic flows and lahars, since these volcanic hazards will destroy any structures in their path (Fig. 4.20). Ash fallout has the largest spatial impact, and design may help reduce its impact. The weight of ash on roofs, especially if it is wet, can be enough to cause roof collapse. Roofs need to be strong and designed to shed ash, with steep-sloping sides. In Hawaii, the ultimate hazard-resistant design in timber houses allows residents in high-risk areas from lava flows to move their homes if necessary!

**Figure 4.20 Building destroyed by a lava flow. This example is the old volcano observatory on Mount Etna, Sicily**

*Modify vulnerability*

### Community preparedness

Most volcanic events are preceded by clear warnings of activity from the volcano. If the community at risk is prepared in advance, many lives can be saved. Evacuation is the most important method of hazard management used today. Evacuation of the area at risk can save lives, but advance preparation and management structures to organise the evacuation, temporary housing, food, etc. are needed. The length of time of the evacuation may be long term: for example, 5000 residents of Montserrat were evacuated three times between December 1995 and August 1996 for periods of up to three months, to avoid pyroclastic flows and ashfalls. By November 1996, the disruption was thought likely to continue for a further 18 months. The scale of evacuations can be huge. In 1995, volcanologists and civil defence officials drew up an emergency evacuation plan for the 600 000 people at risk from an eruption of Vesuvius. The operation is large scale and involves removing some people to safety by ship. If the people involved panic, the plan would be useless. People need to be clear about the risk and how to behave during an event.

Evacuations have been very successful in recent years and are the most common hazard-management strategy (Table 4.3). The Galunggung eruption of 1982 in Java, Indonesia, involved the evacuation of 75 000 people, and a relatively small fatality total of 68. Compare this with the 1985 eruption of Nevado del Ruiz (see case study), where the Colombian government did not have a policy in place for monitoring volcanoes or for disaster preparedness. Communications between the scientists monitoring volcanoes and government officials must be clear, consistent and accurate. The eruption was expected, and scientists monitoring the activity had produced a hazard map (Fig. 4.18). However, the lack of clear communication and indecision resulted in the disaster. The Colombian government had more serious and immediate problems – economic crisis, political instability and narcotic cartels – to deal with. Hazard salience is important at the government level.

## Prediction and warning

Knowledge of volcanic processes is incomplete, but there have been great strides made in forecasting eruptions. Various physical processes can be monitored for changes which can signal an impending eruption. The record of past eruptions is also used to help determine what and where the risks are highest. At the present time, only 20 per cent of volcanoes are being monitored. As might be expected, this is mainly in the MEDCs such as Japan and the USA which have the researchers, technology and cash to undertake these activities. Even in these areas, records are not complete. However, satellites may prove useful in the future for a global early warning system (Fig. 4.21). An example of a closely monitored volcano is Sakurajima, in South Kyushu, Japan.

**?**

**17** Use Table 4.3 to evaluate the success of evacuation as a management strategy in preventing loss of life.

**18a** Imagine you have been evacuated. Write a letter to a friend explaining your worries.
**b** Make a list of the human impacts you might see.

**Table 4.3 Major evacuations (1000 people or more) and fatalities arising from volcanic activity between January 1985 and September 1995 (*Source:* Oppenheimer, 1996)**

| Year | Volcano | Evacuees | Fatalities | Causes |
|------|---------|----------|------------|--------|
| 1985 | Sangeang Api (Indonesia) | 1 250 | 0 | |
| | Nevado del Ruiz (Colombia) | 0 | 23 080 | mud flows |
| 1986 | Nevado del Ruiz (Colombia) | 15 000 | 0 | |
| | Lake Nyos (Cameroun) | 0 | 1 700 | release of $CO_2$ gas |
| | Oshima (Japan) | 12 200 | 0 | |
| 1987 | Anak Ranakah (Indonesia) | 4 200 | 0 | |
| 1988 | Gamalama (Indonesia) | 3 500 | 0 | |
| | Banda Api (Indonesia) | 10 000 | 4 | lava bombs |
| | Makian (Indonesia) | 15 000 | 0 | |
| 1989 | Lonquimay (Chile) | 2 000 | 0 | |
| | Galeras (Colombia) | 2 000 | 0 | |
| | Lonquimay (Chile) | 4 600 | 0 | |
| 1990 | Kelut (Indonesia) | 60 000 | 32 | mud flows |
| | Sabancaya (Peru) | 4 000 | 0 | |
| 1991 | Pinatubo (Philippines) | 250 000 | 800 | mud flows; disease |
| | Pacaya (Guatemala) | 1 500 | 0 | |
| | Lokun-Empong (Indonesia) | 10 000 | 1 | pyroclastic flows |
| 1992 | Cerro Negro (Nicaragua) | 28 000 | 2 | ashfall; accidents |
| 1993 | Mayon (Philippines) | 57 000 | 75 | pyroclastic flows |
| 1994 | Rabaul (Papua New Guinea) | 50 000 | 5 | ashfall |
| | Merapi (Indonesia) | 6 000 | 41 | pyroclastic flow |
| | Popocatapetl (Mexico) | 75 000 | 0 | |
| 1995 | Fogo (Cape Verde Islands) | 1 050 | 0 | |
| | Soufriere Hills (Montserrat) | 5 000 | 0 | |

# Satellites spot volcano ready to erupt

A volcanic eruption has been successfully predicted with the use of satellites. Researchers disclosed yesterday that they had detected the impending eruption of Pacaya, in Guatemala, a week before it happened.

The team, using satellites with infra-red detectors, picked up a heat signal on May 13 indicating that hot magma was bubbling towards the surface. The volcano erupted on May 20 sending an ash cloud over Guatemala City and the airport 13 miles away.

Andrew Harris, based at the Department of Earth Sciences at the Open University in Milton Keynes, who was a member of the team, said: 'We saw it coming from space. To date this has not happened before.'

The breakthrough, by British and American scientists, may lead to the establishment of a worldwide automatic forecasting system for the 600 active volcanoes and many others considered potentially active.

The team also detected the eruption of a volcano in the remote Galapagos islands three hours before it began on September 15. The early warning gave experts on the ground time to move wildlife The signals were picked up from the satellites by Chris Okubo, also of the University of Hawaii.

The team also spotted the eruption of Popocatepetl, near Mexico City, from space. The satellites detected a moderate eruption on the morning of November 24 this year. Local ground-based teams recorded the same event and sounded the alarm one minute earlier. But many parts of the world where volcanoes could burst into life are too treacherous to have trained staff in place. Dr Harris said: 'Some places are just too poor and have too many volcanoes.'

The satellite system, even if it spots an eruption only as it occurs, may give emergency services vital hours or days to get people cleared from an impending lava flow.

The breakthrough has been made possible by the recent launch of two geostationary satellites owned by the US National Oceanic and Atmospheric Administration. The craft can provide images of a given volcano or area of land every 15 minutes. Recent computer developments meant that the images can be rapidly analysed for hot spots. The researchers are posting the results on the University of Hawaii's Hot Spot Image Internet site.

Dr Harris said that about seven satellites, able to see heat in the right waveband, would be needed to create a global volcano early-warning system. 'At the moment we are only really covering the Americas and Caribbean.'

Aircraft are also at risk. In 1982 a British Airways Boeing 747 nearly fell from the sky over Java after volcanic dust got into the jet engines.

Some researchers have tried to develop early warning systems that pick up microquakes inside a grumbling volcano. Others have been developing systems that detect land movement and bulges on the Earth's surface in advance of an eruption.

John Murray, also of the Open University, has placed reflectors on Mount Etna that bounce radar beams back to satellites. Any movements caused by an impending eruption would be automatically detected.

Dr Murray said that he believed several different techniques would be needed for a truly accurate early warning system.

'No one method will be 100 per cent reliable. Seismic activity is good on a scale of a few days, and the movement of the ground may give you a warning months in advance. Detecting heat may give you an early warning a few hours or days in advance that the eruption is about to happen,' he said.

**Figure 4.21  The use of technology is aiding hazard-warning systems (*Source: The Times*, 8 December 1998)**

## Monitoring Sakurajima, Japan

The city of Kagoshima, with half a million people, lies close to Sakurajima volcano. The Japanese Meteorological Agency (JMA) and Kyoto University's Sakurajima Volcanological Observatory (SVO) use all the latest technology to monitor events (Fig. 4.22). Below is listed a series of events that appear to herald the build-up to volcanic eruption. While this list applies primarily to Sakurajima, research here and elsewhere indicates that it may be of more general application.

**1** A change from a dormant period to one of likely activity may be signalled by a gradual swelling of land around the volcano, as magma far below the ground starts to build up. At Sakurajima, this is marked by a rise in the seabed of northern Kagoshima Bay, with consequent changes in tide levels on the Sakurajima shore relative to those around Kagoshima city.

**2** As the magma starts to flow, melting and splitting of basement rock will be detectable as volcanic earthquakes. At Sakurajima, they occur two to five kilometres beneath the surface, either directly beneath the crater or south-south-west of it.

**3** With the magma coming closer to the surface, earthquakes will become more frequent, moving ever closer to the surface and to the base of the volcano.

**4** At this time, groundwater levels may change, the temperature of hot spring waters may rise and the chemical composition and the amount of gases released may alter. The ratio of hydrogen chloride to sulphur dioxide in gas emitted from the volcano's active crater increases during earthquake swarms and shortly before an eruption. Remote sensing is used to monitor gases because it is too dangerous to go to Sakurajima's summit.

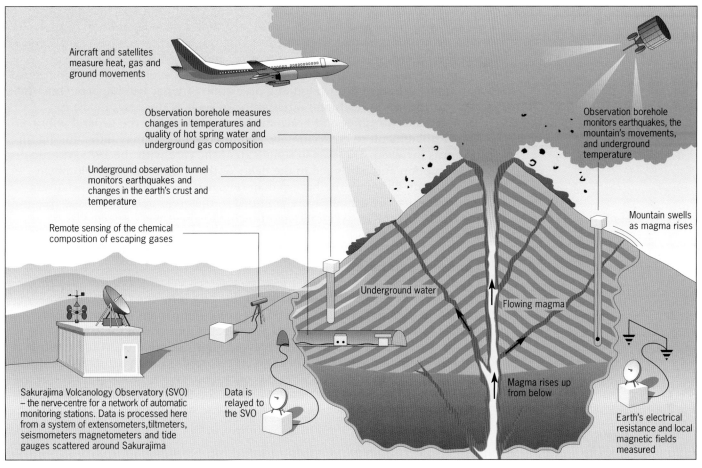

**Figure 4.22 Monitoring the Sakurajima volcano, Japan (*Source: Geographical Magazine*, 1993)**

**5** As an eruption approaches, the extensometer/ tiltmeter system measures minute movements of the mountain. Data is continuously relayed to an automatic monitoring system at the SVO.

**6** Finally, seismometers detect earthquakes which occur immediately beneath the crater, signalling the onset of the eruption. They occur 1 to 1.5 seconds before the explosion at the crater bottom.

**7** The violence of the explosion may correlate with the length of the preceding dormant period, but it is also closely linked with the viscosity of the underground magma. The harder it is for the gases to escape, the more violent it is when the pressure is finally released with the 'uncorking' of the volcano. Magma is blasted skywards, cooling and solidifying as it moves through the air. It can vary in size from a fine dust to boulders as large as houses. Some fragments form 'bombs' that

can fly at speeds of up to 300 kilometres an hour out of the volcano, finally landing several kilometres away. Most of the released magma forms pyroclastic flows of rock, ash and poisonous gases that can sweep down the mountainside at hurricane speeds.

**8** Following the initial explosion there is a general calming down. Lava – essentially magma from which the gases have escaped – may or may not be released, usually flowing from 'parasitic' craters on the side of the volcano or from side fissures opened up by the force of the eruption. Since 1955, Sakurajima has only ever erupted from its summit, with no release of lava.

**9** With the passing of the explosion, the extensometer/tiltmeter system records a settling of the mountain. Subsidence of the surrounding land is detected after either prolonged periods of eruptive activity or the release of large amounts of lava.

**?**

**19** Suggest appropriate land uses for areas at high risk from lava flows.

In countries lacking the financial and technological resources for such monitoring, more basic but still useful techniques have been used. In the Philippines, local people are trained to look out for early-warning signs such as sulphur odours, steam releases, and crater glow (see Chapter 2).

Once scientists have detected signs of activity the events must be interpreted to produce a hazard assessment and prediction of what will happen. Only then can government officials and other agencies such as the news media be informed and warnings and evacuation be introduced to the general public. This is still difficult to do accurately, and interpretations may differ among the scientists involved. This was to some extent the case with the 1985 Nevado del Ruiz eruption and partly led to the delay of the warning to the Colombian government, although the hazard map (Fig. 4.18) eventually produced was very accurate. The ashfalls were confined to the areas delineated as at risk and the Guali, Lagunillas, Azufrado and Cinchina valleys were affected by lahars as predicted. Only the Rio Recio escaped devastating lahars.

## Land-use planning

Land use can be planned once there is an agreed volcanic hazards map to use as a basis. It is still difficult to predict in the long term the timing and scale of volcanic eruptions. Many LEDCs do not possess the maps and past records needed to produce accurate hazard assessments, but where they do exist they can be used to plan land uses which avoid high-risk areas or would result in a reduced economic loss. These need to be enforced through legislation and education. As part of the US hazard programme, lava flow hazards on Hawaii have been mapped and can now be used as the basis for informed land-use planning.

# Hazard forecasting: Vesuvius, Italy

A short-term volcanic hazard forecast aims to predict the nature of an eruptive event based upon measured geophysical and geochemical changes. This is the case with the eruption of Mt Pinatubo (see page 81). In contrast, a long-term volcanic hazard forecast is based upon the volcano's past history and is intended to inform hazard management before an eruption occurs (Fig. 4.23). Thus in defining hazardous areas, knowledge of the distribution and depth of the volcanic deposits is needed to identify the dates and nature of eruption events which have characterised the volcano in the past.

The area around the volcano, Vesuvius, has some of the highest densities of population in Europe (Fig. 4.24). In September 1995, the Italian Department of Civil Defence presented an emergency Management Plan to local governments of the towns around Vesuvius. The plan was based upon the volcano's 1631 eruption. This was a subplinian eruption with tephra fall, pyroclastic flow and surge deposits. There have been several major eruptions of the volcano in recorded history and recent research has tried to provide further data for use in hazard management. Some geologists felt that to base a management plan only on the 1631 event was not as accurate as possible.

Figure 4.23 The crater of Vesuvius, Italy, looks quiet (July 2001). There is little sign that this is an active volcano. However, a recent geophysical survey shows that the vent has a huge rock plug which is likely to be erupted violently when pressure builds up again

## Defining volcanic hazard

Past activity has been plinian events alternating with subplinian–strombolian eruptions. Deposits show evidence of two major hazards:

- ash falls and pumice falls
- pyroclastic flows and surges.

The area covered varies in extent and the direction of the fall deposits has also varied. The areas affected by pyroclastic fall have been plotted using data from eight past explosive eruptions, between 8000 years ago and 1906. The hazard presented by pyroclastic ash fall deposits is based upon the pressure the ash would cause on a roof. The possible damage is related to thickness and density of the fall deposits plus the quality of the roofs. The maximum load for roofs defined by the Civil Defence Department as 300 kg/m$^2$ was used as the critical level to produce a frequency map of how often the loads were exceeded (Fig. 4.26).

**Figure 4.24  The densely populated area at the base of the Vesuvius volcano, Italy**

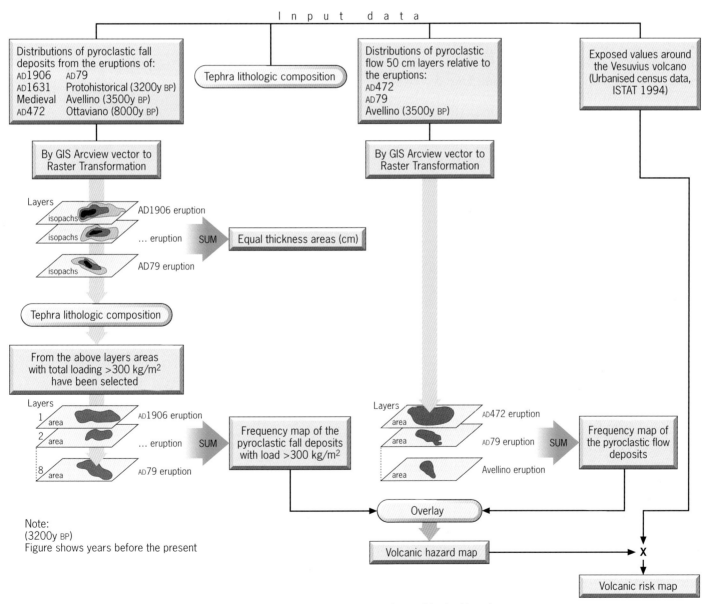

**Figure 4.25  Flow chart showing the modalities used to define the volcanic hazard in the Vesuvius area**

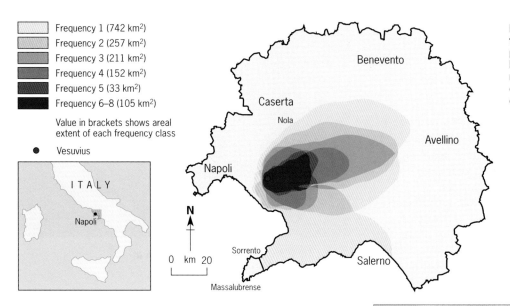

Frequency 1 (742 km²)
Frequency 2 (257 km²)
Frequency 3 (211 km²)
Frequency 4 (152 km²)
Frequency 5 (33 km²)
Frequency 6–8 (105 km²)

Value in brackets shows areal extent of each frequency class

● Vesuvius

ITALY

Napoli

0  km  20

**Figure 4.26 Frequency map deduced from superimposing the thickness of pyroclastic fall deposits on critical roof loading values. A frequency of one means that only one of the eight eruptions generated deposits exceeding the critical roof loading**

Quantifying the impacts of a pyroclastic flow or surge is more difficult. The AD79 eruption has left a 50 cm thick pyroclastic deposit at the ancient town of Ercolano (Fig. 4.27). The event completely destroyed the town. Therefore a flow thickness of 50 cm represents the limit above which buildings would be completely destroyed. From this data a frequency map was produced based upon three eruptions. (Fig. 4.28).

The result is a volcanic hazard map (Fig. 4.29) based upon this ashfall and flow–surge data. However, the volcanic hazard is only part of the assessment if a volcanic risk map is to be produced; it only shows the physical events. To produce the hazard map the population also needs to be considered. (Table 4.4). In this example, population density was used. The result is the volcanic risk map combining physical process and an assessment of human vulnerability (Fig. 4.30). The research also considered the possibility of lahars (mudflows) from heavy rain saturating the unconsolidated deposits. Such an event was described from an account of the 1632 eruption.

**Figure 4.27 Part of the city of Pompeii buried by ash during AD79 eruption. A much smaller Vesuvius can be seen. The top was blown off in the AD79 eruption**

**Figure 4.28 Frequency map deduced from the pyroclastic flow data**

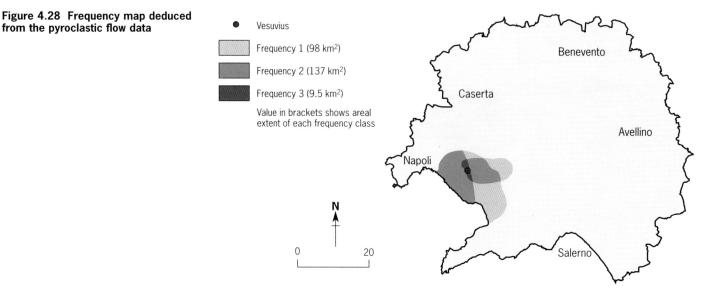

● Vesuvius

Frequency 1 (98 km²)

Frequency 2 (137 km²)

Frequency 3 (9.5 km²)

Value in brackets shows areal extent of each frequency class

0        20

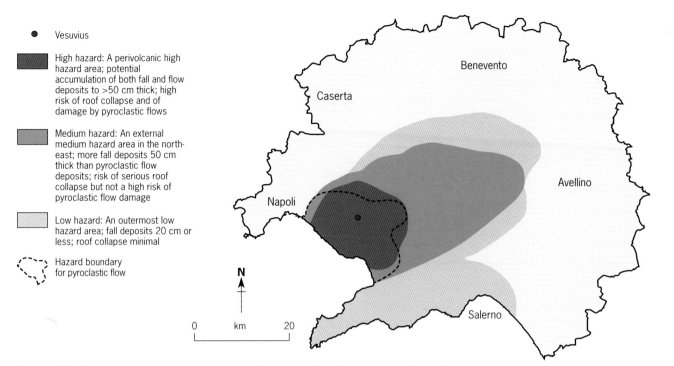

Figure 4.29 Volcanic hazard map for the Vesuvius area, using three grades of hazard

**Table 4.4  Area of extent and main urbanisation parameters for each region of risk**

|  | Inhabitants | Total area (km²) | Urban area (km²) | Urban area/Total area (km²) | Population density (inhabitants/urban area) |
|---|---|---|---|---|---|
| High hazard area | 984 954 | 274 | 86 | 31 | 11 453 |
| Medium hazard area | 520 308 | 610 | 102 | 17 | 5 101 |
| Low hazard area | 398 427 | 679 | 100 | 15 | 3 984 |
| Total | 1 903 689 | 1 563 | 288 |  |  |

Urban area, ISTAT 1994

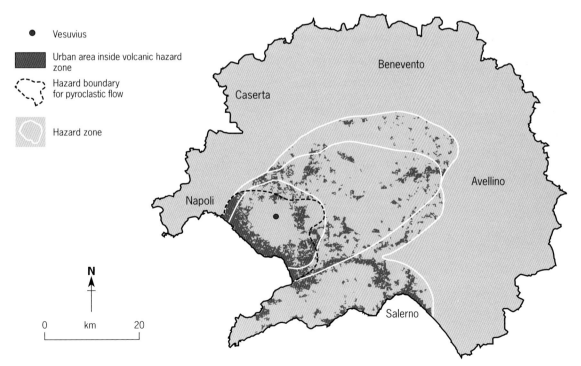

Figure 4.30  Volcanic risk map based on volcanic hazard zones and population data

The researchers concluded their long-term eruption hazard forecast as:
- a perivolcanic high hazard area with potential ash falls and pyroclastic flows
- an external medium hazard area in the north-east where fall deposits are the main risk; the main risk is of roof collapse, but not a high risk of pyroclastic flows
- an outermost low hazard area where there is likely to be ash fall but the risk of roof collapse is low.

**?**

**20** Lava flows are not used to construct the hazard map. Suggest why this is the case.

**21** The researchers suggest that this map (Fig. 4.30) is more accurate than earlier version since it considers more than one eruption (earlier maps had only used the 1631 eruption). Explain why this is likely to be the case.

**22** What other socio-economic data would be useful in assessing human vulnerability in the area?

**23** Suggest the response needed for the people living in (a) the high risk hazard and (b) the medium risk hazard area. How will they be similar and how different?

*Modify the loss*

Aid for volcanic hazards comes in two main forms: technical aid for monitoring and forecasting, and financial/goods aid. Technical aid is usually supplied by MEDCs experienced in volcanic eruptions. This involves the use of high-cost monitoring equipment and expertise to try to forecast events. Financial and other aid is used as a strategy during and after the event. This may need to occur over a long period compared with other natural hazards, since eruptions may continue for months at varying levels of activity. For aid to be an effective management approach, governments must be willing to ask for and receive help from other nations. Indonesia has much experience with volcanic eruptions and has developed a high level of hazard mitigation within its financial resources. This involves monitoring of volcanoes and planning for how aid will be used (Table 4.5).

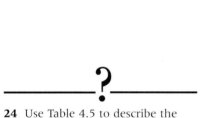

**24** Use Table 4.5 to describe the sources and use for aid following the Galunggung eruption.

**Table 4.5 Aid donors and the use made of monetary and non-monetary assistances following the Galunggung eruption of 1982–3 (*Source:* Chester, 1993)**

| Principal aid donors | Aid received and action taken |
| --- | --- |
| **1** United Nations agencies<br>**a** Disaster Relief Organisation<br>**b** Development programme<br>**c** Children's Fund<br>**d** World Health Organisation<br>**e** World Food Programme<br>**f** International Labour Organisation | Monetary aid and non-monetary assistance (e.g. medicine, sanitation facilities, food, clothing, emergency shelters and technical assistance) was valued at over US$4.4 million.<br>The money was spent on:<br>**1** 18 emergency shelters at Garut and 334 at Tasikmalaya |
| **2** Bilateral aid provided by: Australia, Canada, Japan, Netherlands, New Zealand, Sweden, Switzerland and the USA | **2** Equipping, clothing and feeding refugees and evacuees. A rice ration was the initial response to hunger and this was followed by field kitchens and a coupon system to discourage the sale of food. |
| **3** International agencies<br>**a** Association of South East Asian Nations<br>**b** Catholic Relief Services<br>**c** Church World Service | **3** Following a survey of refugees and evacuees, it was found that 45 per cent (nearly 8000) could be resettled in other villages in Java, while over 9000 (mostly poor and unskilled) were encouraged to migrate to other Indonesian islands. Clearing the shelters meant there was room in the event of secondary lahars. |

# The eruption of Mount Pinatubo, Philippines, 1991

The eruption of Mount Pinatubo is the largest volcanic eruption to occur in over 50 years. It is an example of the events associated with the eruption of andesitic magma, and shows clearly how eruption prediction and effective response can be a successful hazard-management strategy.

Pinatubo is a subduction-zone volcano (Fig. 4.31) with no activity in the 600 years before the 1991 eruption. On 2 April, steam explosions and a smell like rotten eggs (due to hydrogen sulphide gas) surprised the villagers of Patal Pinto. A team from PHIVOLCS (Philippine Institute of Volcanology and Seismology) began to monitor seismic and other activity on the volcano. By late April they were joined by a team from the USGS (United States Geological Survey) who together set up the Pinatubo Volcano Observatory (PVO). Using the geological evidence of past eruptions they were aware that the volcano had erupted violently in the past, and PVO produced a volcanic hazards map (Fig. 4.32). This map, along with monitoring of the events, enabled the PVO team to inform civil defence officials and military commanders of the potential hazards the area faced. To simplify communication in an area with no eruption experience, the volcanologists devised a six-point scale ranging from 0 (quiet) to 5 (eruption in progress). A video showing pyroclastic flows and lahars was used to reinforce the message and illustrate the serious hazards the area faced. Table 4.6 shows the events and the human response which undoubtedly saved many lives. Figure 4.33 shows the impacts of the eruption.

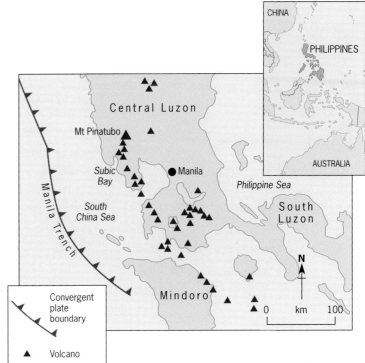

**Figure 4.31  The location of Mount Pinatubo within the Luzon volcanic zone (*Source:* Wolfe, 1992)**

The death toll from the eruption was 350 people, 300 of whom were killed by collapsing roofs. However, the secondary impacts of the eruption increased the death toll to over 800. Lahars (Fig. 4.35) killed 77 people, and continued for several years after the eruption. However, most deaths occurred in evacuation centres. The most vulnerable were the tribal Aetas people who lived on the slopes of Mount Pinatubo by slash-and-burn agriculture and collecting forest products. Some of the Aetas refused to leave their holy mountain, and died during the eruption. Their isolated lifestyle before the eruption meant that many died in the evacuation camps in the following months. They became susceptible to diseases such as measles, and were reluctant to take medicines. Malnutrition due to unfamiliar diet added to the death toll. Some 94 per cent of the camp deaths were of Aetas, mainly children.

It is estimated that 2 million people were affected by the eruption. About 80 000 ha of farmland were buried under ash, disrupting the livelihoods of 500 000 farmers. The total losses were US$711.4 million (Table 4.7).

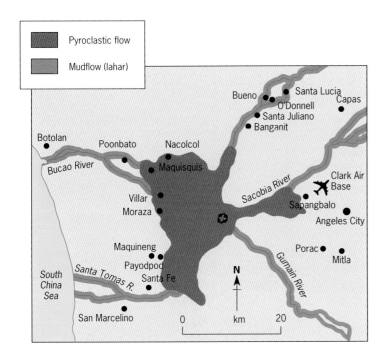

**Figure 4.32  Pinatubo hazards map, compiled in May 1991 (*Source:* Wolfe, 1992)**

**Table 4.6 The timing of events and responses during the Mount Pinatubo eruption, 1991 (*Source:* US Geological Survey, 1992b)**

| Date (1991) | Volcanic activity | Monitoring | Alert level | Response |
|---|---|---|---|---|
| 2/4 | Small steam explosions; earthquakes began. | | | PHIVOLCS alerted. |
| 5/4 | | PHIVOLCS installed portable seismometers. | | |
| 23/4 | | USGS joined PHIVOLCS' efforts in monitoring and hazard assessment. | | Villages within 10 km of the summit were evacuated. |
| 30/4–10/5 | | PHIVOLCS–USGS radio-telemetered seismic network installed. Earthquakes located on north-east side of summit. | | |
| 13/5 | Continued earthquakes and steam emission. | Correlation spectrometer (COSPEC) measurements began. $SO_2$ emission equalled 500 tons a day. | 2 | Alert system in place. |
| 23/5 | | Hazard map completed. | | Information distributed to local officials. |
| 28/5 | | $SO_2$ emission equalled 5000 tons a day. | | |
| 5/6 | Greatly increased earthquake activity; volcanic tremor identified. | Continued seismic and other monitoring provided basis for eruption forecast and setting of alert levels. | 3 | Villages on north-west slope were evacuated again. |
| 8/6 | Dome of viscous magma extruded; further increase in number of earthquakes and increased volcanic tremor; beginning of continuous ash emission. | | | |
| 9/6 | | | 5 | Radius of evacuation extended to 20 km. 25 000 people now evacuated. |
| 10/6 | | | | Near-total evacuation of Clark Air Base. |
| 12/6 | First large explosive eruption reached 20 km high: pyroclastic flows moved down northwest valleys. Ash spread as far as Vietnam and Cambodia. | | | Evacuation radius extended to 30 km. 58 000 people now evacuated, 200 000 people relocated. |
| 15/6 | Climactic (caldera-forming) eruption. Dome collapse; widespread ashfall; large pyroclastic flows and lahars. Typhoon Yunya produced heavy rainfall and saturated the ash. | | | Buildings collapsed from loading by water-saturated ash combined with felt earthquakes. Manila International Airport closed. |
| Ongoing from 16/6 | Continuous ash emission punctuated by larger ash eruptions all smaller than 15 June event; continued small pyroclastic flows to northwest and lahars in all directions. | Continuing PHIVOLCS–USGS monitoring. | | Continuing PHIVOLCS–USGS hazard evaluation. Houses, bridges and roads destroyed by the lahars. |

**?**

**25** Use Table 4.6 to identify the key volcanic events and the human response.

**26a** From Figure 4.33 measure the radius of the area affected by pyroclastic flows.
**b** What was the possible death toll in this area if evacuation had not occurred (Table 4.6)?

**27** Evaluate the success of the hazard zone map (Fig. 4.32) compared with the actual events (Fig. 4.33).

**28** Suggest the direction of the dominant wind during the eruption from the ashfall thickness (Fig. 4.33). Give precise evidence to support your answer.

**29** Why was monitoring seismic activity and gas emissions so important to the PVO team (refer to Fig. 4.22)?

**30** Compare the number of deaths resulting from the direct impacts from the eruption and those from secondary impacts. Suggest ways in which these impacts could be further reduced.

**31** Essay: Discuss the assertion that volcanic hazards are predictable and any loss of life is the result of human error or inactivity, using examples from this chapter.

**Table 4.7 The economic impacts of the Mount Pinatubo eruption**

|  | US$ (millions) |
|---|---|
| Agriculture (mainly crops and forestry) | 424.5 |
| Industry | 15.3 |
| Infrastructure | 66.5 |
| Private property | 205.1 |

Figure 4.34 Ash fall from Pinatubo

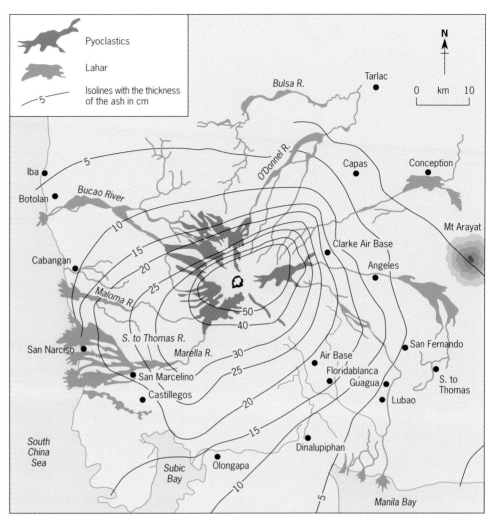

Figure 4.33 The distribution of volcanic impacts (Source: Rantucci, 1994)

Figure 4.35 A Pinatubo lahar

# Summary

- The nature of volcanic activity is largely determined by the type of magma and gas behaviour. Eruptions may be through fissures or a volcano.

- The spatial distribution of volcanoes is related to plate tectonic theory, especially destructive plate boundaries, constructive plate boundaries and hot spots.

- Volcanoes are classified by the visual manifestations of eruption style, and the type and amount of material ejected.

- Volcanic hazards include lava flows, pyroclastic flows and surges, ash and tephra fall and volcanic gases. Secondary hazards include lahars, volcanic landslides, and tsunami.

- Primary volcanic hazards are destructive of all human life and, unlike some other hazards, are not selective of social, economic and cultural differences.

- People respond to volcanic hazards mainly by monitoring, warning, and evacuation. Less commonly used strategies are environmental control, hazard-resistant design and land-use planning. Aid is given in terms of financial, knowledge and technological resources.

# 5 Tectonic hazards: tsunami

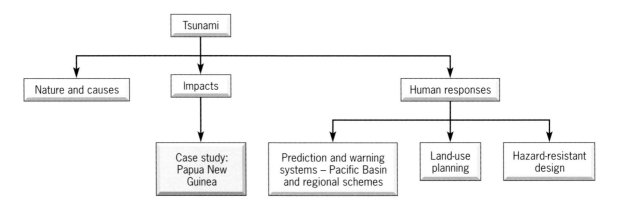

Tsunami
- Nature and causes
- Impacts
  - Case study: Papua New Guinea
- Human responses
  - Prediction and warning systems – Pacific Basin and regional schemes
  - Land-use planning
  - Hazard-resistant design

## 5.1 The nature and causes of tsunami

"Jason, what's a tsunami?"

**Figure 5.1 Tsunami – a little-known hazard**

Tsunami are giant sea waves caused by large-scale and sudden disturbance of the seawater. The popular name for tsunami is tidal waves, but this is technically incorrect since they have nothing to do with tides. The word tsunami is from the Japanese word meaning 'harbour wave'. Most tsunami are secondary hazards from earthquakes (see Chapter 3), and nearly all large tsunami result from large and rapid vertical movements of the sea floor covering an area of many hundreds of square kilometres. Although there have been large tsunami resulting from volcanic activity, especially the explosion of volcanic islands and landslides or rockfalls, these causes are much less common. The association of tsunami and seismic activity explains their spatial distribution. Most are generated at subduction-convergent plate boundaries (see Fig. 3.2) around the Pacific Ocean. Some 90 per cent of damaging tsunami occur in the Pacific Basin although there are notable exceptions, such as the eruption of the Mediterranean volcanic island of Santorini in about 1450BC, and the earthquake near Lisbon, Portugal, in 1755. Within the Pacific Basin itself, the spatial distribution of tsunami is not even: one-third of all major tsunami are generated in the deep sea trenches bordering Japan, the Aleutians and South America. The most active source area is the Japan–Taiwan island arc (over 25 per cent of tsunami), with Japan being affected by four or five large tsunami per century. Between 1900 and 1980, 370 tsunami were observed in the Pacific Basin. In the 1990s, 11 tsunami affected the Pacific coastline with 4000 victims.

Tsunami are generated by large-scale disturbance of the ocean, but not all earthquakes will result in tsunami. Most result from earthquakes of magnitude 6.5 or more with a focus depth of less than 50 km. The key is the amount of displacement of the sea floor. The larger the earthquake and the shallower the focus, the larger the tsunami. This relationship has been used to classify tsunami by intensity and frequency (Table 5.1).

Due to the nature of tsunami they are very difficult to detect in the open ocean (Fig. 5.2). However, as with wind-generated waves, as they approach the shore the wave changes in nature due to **wave refraction**. Where the wave fronts converge, the energy is concentrated and wave height increases. Where the wave fronts diverge, the energy is spread out and the wave height decreases. Detection of tsunami formed by seismic activity in the ocean mainly relies upon earthquake monitoring in areas of likely tsunami formation.

**Table 5.1 The scale of tsunami intensity (*Source:* Soloviev, 1978)**

| Intensity | Run-up height (m) | Description of tsunami | Frequency in Pacific Ocean |
|---|---|---|---|
| I | 0.5 | *Very slight.* Wave so weak as to be perceptible only on tide gauge records | |
| II | 1 | *Slight.* Waves noticed by people living along the shore and familiar with the sea. On very flat shores waves generally noticed. | One per four months |
| III | 1 | *Rather large.* Generally noticed. Flooding of gently sloping coasts. Light sailing vessels carried away on shore. Slight damage to light structures situated near the coast. In estuaries, reversal of river flow for some distance upstream. | One per eight months |
| IV | 4 | *Large.* Flooding of the shore to some depth. Light scouring on made ground. Embankments and dykes damaged. Light structures near the coast damaged. Solid structures on the coast lightly damaged. Large sailing vessels and small ships swept inland or carried out to sea. Coasts littered with floating debris. | One per year |
| V | 8 | *Very large.* General flooding of the shore to some depth. Quays and other heavy structures near the sea damaged. Light structures destroyed. Severe scouring of cultivated land and littering of the coast with floating objects, fish and other sea animals. With the exception of large ships, all vessels carried inland or out to sea. Large bores in estuaries. Harbour works damaged. People drowned, waves accompanied by a strong roar. | Once in three years |
| ≥VI | 16 | *Disastrous.* Partial or complete destruction of man-made structures for some distance from the shore. Flooding of coasts to great depths. Large ships severely damaged. Trees uprooted or broken by the waves. Many casualties. | Once in ten years |

## 1 Generation of a tsunami in deep ocean (tsunamigenesis)

Tsunami are difficult to detect by ships due to small waveheight and long wavelength

## 2 Tsunami run-up

Nature of the waves will depend upon:
- cause of the wave, e.g. eruption or earthquake
- distance travelled from source, as energy is lost as they travel
- water depth over route affects energy loss through friction
- offshore topography and coastline orientation

## 3 Landfall

Death and destruction will depend upon land uses, population density and any warning given, as well as the physical geography or relief of coastal areas

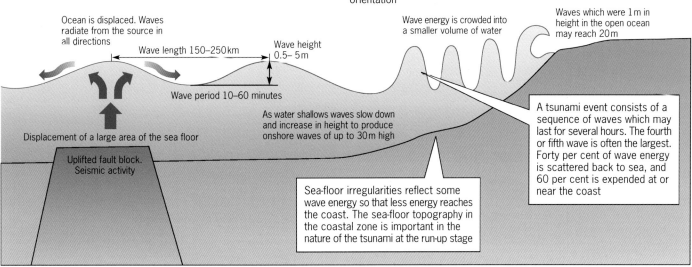

Ocean is displaced. Waves radiate from the source in all directions

Wave length 150–250 km

Wave height 0.5– 5 m

Wave period 10–60 minutes

Displacement of a large area of the sea floor

Uplifted fault block. Seismic activity

As water shallows waves slow down and increase in height to produce onshore waves of up to 30 m high

Wave energy is crowded into a smaller volume of water

Waves which were 1 m in height in the open ocean may reach 20 m

Sea-floor irregularities reflect some wave energy so that less energy reaches the coast. The sea-floor topography in the coastal zone is important in the nature of the tsunami at the run-up stage

A tsunami event consists of a sequence of waves which may last for several hours. The fourth or fifth wave is often the largest. Forty per cent of wave energy is scattered back to sea, and 60 per cent is expended at or near the coast

**Figure 5.2 The formation and key features of a tsunami (not to scale)**

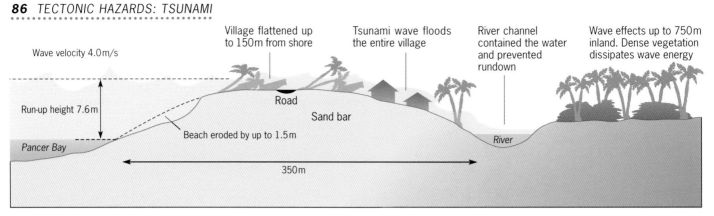

Wave velocity 4.0m/s

Run-up height 7.6m

Pancer Bay

Beach eroded by up to 1.5m

Road

Sand bar

350m

River

Village flattened up to 150m from shore

Tsunami wave floods the entire village

River channel contained the water and prevented rundown

Wave effects up to 750m inland. Dense vegetation dissipates wave energy

**Figure 5.3 The village of Pancer, eastern Java, showing how the village was sandwiched between the ocean and a small river during the 1994 tsunami**

Tsunami generated in one part of the Pacific can travel to the other side of the Pacific Basin. One of the worst tsunami occurred in 1960. Displacement of the sea floor over an area the size of California followed a major earthquake off the coast of Chile (a subduction zone). Two tsunami killed 2500 in Chile. Fifteen hours later, 61 died at Hilo, Hawaii, and 22 hours after the earthquake, 150 died in Japan as the wave crossed the Pacific Ocean. The travel time of these waves makes warnings more feasible (see below). Tsunami generated in the ocean near to the land are potentially much more destructive, since there is little warning time. Waves can travel at 800–950 km/hr in deep ocean water. This means that they can reach the coast in a matter of minutes. Locally generated tsunami are responsible for 99 per cent of the deaths resulting from this hazard. Indeed, most deaths occur within 100 km of the point of wave generation. The Japanese islands are particularly vulnerable to these locally generated tsunami.

In the **run-up stage** the wave changes dramatically (Fig. 5.2). If the first part of the wave to reach the coastline is a wave trough, there may be a lowering of sea level below normal levels, called a **drawdown.** In the 1960 Chilean tsunami, the local people were aware of this warning and moved to higher ground. If this drawdown is not recognised then the resulting loss of life can be high. In the 1964 Alaskan earthquake, at the small fishing village of Chenega, on Chenega Island in Prince William Sound, the drawdown moved the water 40 m below mean sea level. The following tsunami was 12 m high and killed one-third of the population (23 people), who did not recognise the warning; some tsunami give no warning at all. The 1994 Java tsunami gave no

**Figure 5.4 Schematic cross-section showing waves generated by a submarine landslide (*Source:* McCulloch, 1985)**

Bedrock     Deltaic deposits     Bottom deposits

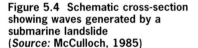

**a Pre-slide conditions**

Drawdown of water – sea retreats temporarily
Earthquake triggers landslide

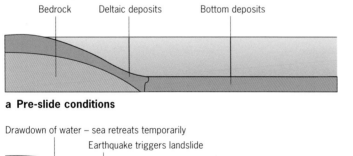

**b Start of sliding**

Water rushes to fill the void left by the slide
Slide moves on to the sea bed

**c Wave overtopping**

Slide toe displaces the water upwards

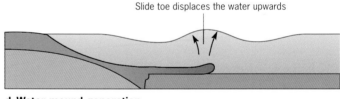

**d Water mound generation**

Waves radiate from the source area

Mound sinks

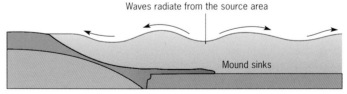

**e Waves radiate from source area**

The 1964 Alaska submarine slides generated waves with run-up heights of at least 10m. Seaward, Valdez and Whittier experienced the two phases of waves shown in stages **c** and **e** above. At Kenai lake, the waves broke off spruce trees as much as 0.5m in diameter. These trees were driven like battering rams up to 100m ashore. Large blocks of frozen sediment, some weighing 50 tonnes, were pulled from the sinking slide mass and carried ashore with the trees.

warning to the east coastline, 250 km away from the earthquake epicentre. The impact was greatest on low-lying coastal villages (Fig. 5.3).

Landslides can result in highly destructive localised tsunami. The slides are usually the result of earthquakes causing rapid movement of material on the sea floor or into the sea from the land. The largest tsunami ever recorded resulted from a rock slide in July 1958 in Alaska's Lituya Bay. The confined shape of the fiord funnelled the water into a surge which reached an incredible maximum 540 m in height. A boat and its two occupants were swept above the treetops and out to sea about 30 m high over the spit of the bay. They survived to tell the tale! This destructive force can have disastrous consequences in populated areas.

Slide-generated tsunami may show a double-event pattern, as shown by the Alaskan tsunami in 1964. A magnitude 7.4 earthquake in the Gulf of Alaska caused delta fans to slide into the deeper ocean which triggered a chain of events (Fig. 5.4) resulting in 119 deaths.

### The effects of tsunami

The destructive effects of tsunami (Fig. 5.5) are related to the run-up height of the waves as they reach landfall. The effects are of three main types:

**1** *Hydrostatic effects*: objects such as boats and vehicles, and structures like wooden buildings, are lifted and carried inland by the wave. The backwash, or rundown, of the wave may have a similar effect, carrying objects offshore.

**2** *Hydrodynamic effects*: tearing buildings apart, washing away soil, undermining foundations of buildings, bridges and harbour structures.

**3** *Shock effects:* battering by debris carried in the wave.

The human deaths result from the victims being drowned, by impact as they are lifted and battered, or hit by moving debris.

**Figure 5.5 Tuna fish lie in the streets of Maumere, on Indonesia's Flores Island, which bore the brunt of a tsunami in December 1992**

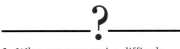

**1** Why are tsunami a difficult hazard to predict?

**2a** Write a report for a newspaper on the 1994 tsunami in the village of Pancer to explain the impacts and why the village was so vulnerable (Fig. 5.3).
**b** What prevented the damage from being even worse?

**3a** Use Figure 5.6 to describe the events of July 1993.
**b** Why was there so much loss of life and destruction?
**c** How did the local people respond to the tsunami event?

**Figure 5.6 A tsunami hits northern Japan (*Source: Time*, 26 July 1993)**

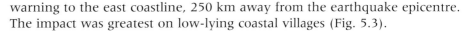

# Tsunami horror

## The worst tidal wave in 45 years hits a northern island, leaving more than 100 dead and nearly as many missing

NAMIKO KANI, 53, WAS ABOUT to settle down for a late-night soap opera on television when she felt the sudden jolt all too familiar to Japanese: an earthquake. Cupboards crashed to the floor, and the lights went out. Kani, a widow, groped for the flashlight she kept on top of the refrigerator and stepped outside to inspect the damage to her shoreline home on Okushiri, a tiny island off the southwestern coast of Hokkaido. Then she remembered a terrifying fact: earthquakes often trigger tidal waves. 'I rushed back inside to collect my husband's memorial tablet,' she recalls. 'When I came back outside, the water was up to my waist.'

Kani survived by scrambling up a nearby hill, but scores of her neighbours were not so fortunate. A wall of water, at one point 30 m high, swept across Okushiri, triggered by an earthquake measuring 7.8 on the Richter scale. In terms of casualties, it was the worst quake-related disaster in Japan since 1948: at week's end, 166 were dead and 95 were listed as missing.

Most of the fatalities occurred on Okushiri, 700 km north of Tokyo and only 60 km from the quake's epicentre in the Japan Sea. Minutes after the tremblor struck, Aonae, a small fishing village on the southern tip of the island, was engulfed by a tsunami roaring at 500 km/h. 'Waves came from two directions, and houses started drifting towards me,' said Gunji Sekiguchi, 64, an abalone fisherman who ran uphill to safety. Sushi chef Jun Nishimoto, 30, saw refrigerators and television sets floating around him as he drove amid the waves looking for his sister's car. Then he raced to higher ground – and safety. Koji Suehiro, 55, a squid fisherman who lived close to the shoreline, ran to high ground with his wife. 'A minute later and I would have been gone,' he said. After the flood came the fire, as kerosene storage tanks and fuel depots erupted in flame. On the eastern coast of the island a landslide buried a two-storey hotel, trapping nearly 40 guests; at least 15 were killed.

Once the waters receded, Aonae looked as if it had been systematically bombed. Barely a building in the settlement was left standing; smoking embers sizzled alongside the torn-up earth. Soldiers pulled away debris and searched the harbour for bodies.

# 5.2 The human response to tsunami

*Modifying vulnerability*

People respond to the tsunami hazard mainly by modifying their vulnerability. This is achieved in two ways.

## Prediction and warning

Scientists are able to predict a possible tsunami by monitoring earthquake activity which may result in disturbance of the sea floor. The aim is to issue warnings to the vulnerable population and evacuate the area. Warning systems, of which there are two scales, are relatively well developed.

PACIFIC BASIN

In 1948, the Pacific Warning System for the 24 nations of the Pacific Basin was established with its centre near Honolulu, Hawaii. The system consists of 30 seismic and 70 tidal stations throughout the Pacific Basin (Fig. 5.7). The seismic stations detect all earthquakes in the area, and the events are interpreted to see if there is a risk of tsunami. Remember that shallow, high-magnitude earthquakes in subduction zones are the main suspects. The tidal gauges can give little or no warning of the tsunami since they are close to shore and can really only record details of the event. The aim is to alert all areas at risk within one hour. The time it takes for a wave to travel across the Pacific (Fig. 5.7) allows ample time to warn shipping and evacuate low-lying coasts. However, issuing tsunami warnings is problematic. Not all earthquakes will result in tsunami, and it is a difficult decision whether or not to issue a warning. At the Hawaiian headquarters of the Pacific Tsunami Warning Centre an automatic alarm goes off if an earthquake is detected by one of the seismic stations. If it is larger than 7.5 (Richter scale), all locations within three hours' travel time of possible tsunami are put on warning, and coastal areas will be evacuated. Those three to six hours away are put on 'standby' or 'watch'. A false warning results in a high financial loss – for example, the cost is $30 million in Hawaii alone for each false warning. In addition, there is the

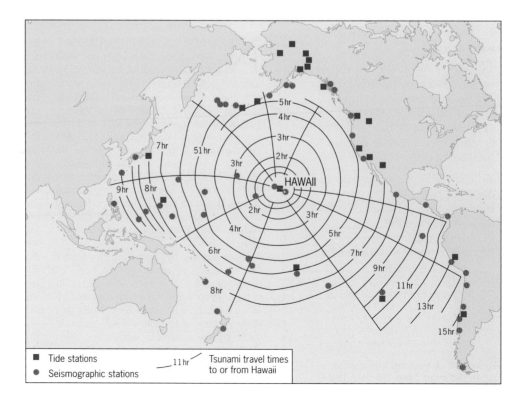

**Figure 5.7 Pacific tsunami travel times and warning system (*Source:* Alexander, 1993)**

■ Tide stations
● Seismographic stations

11 hr — Tsunami travel times to or from Hawaii

problem that if there are too many false warnings people will become complacent and ignore them.

The nature of the warning can also be important, and there is a need for clear warnings and education of people in the hazard areas concerning the nature of tsunami.

REGIONAL LEVEL

Regional warning systems aim to respond to the locally generated tsunami, which pose a much greater threat due to the short warning time. About 99 per cent of tsunami deaths occur within 400 km of the source area, and there may be less than 30 minutes between the tsunami's formation and landfall.

As might be expected, the Japanese have the most developed system, which has been in operation since 1952. The system aims to issue a warning within 20 minutes of a tsunamigenic earthquake within 600 km of the Japanese coastline. In 1994, a new network of 150 seismic detectors was set up by the Japanese Meteorological Agency (JMA) in Tokyo. The main control computer can calculate the size of a tsunami which may be generated by an earthquake and issue a warning using television.

However, there are two main difficulties to overcome. Firstly, the earthquake may destroy power and communication lines and make a warning message impossible to get through, or the events may be too quick to issue a warning.

THE FUTURE

Many coastal areas remain unprotected by warning systems, especially in the economically less developed countries of the Pacific Basin. Work is under way to develop a cheap warning system which could be adopted by all countries. Project THRUST (Tsunami Hazards Reduction Utilising Systems Technology) is based upon rapid warning via satellite communication links. This is relatively low cost, has great potential, and has been trialled in Valparaiso, Chile.

For locally generated tsunami, the degree of hazard in coastal areas can be mapped using land-use, coastal relief and offshore topography. Using this information, tsunami run-up heights can be projected and the degree of risk identified. Public education programmes have been shown to be effective.

The future aim by scientists is to detect a tsunami in the open ocean by a better understanding of tsunami formation. Recent research suggests that it is the long-wavelength seismic waves which are important in tsunami generation. These are not picked up by most conventional seismometers. Work is also under way to develop deep ocean sensors which can detect changes in water pressure as a tsunami passes. These would be more reliable for the Pacific-wide warning system to use, and they would also help to give some short warning of locally generated tsunami. The hope is for independently powered, offshore tsunami detectors in all areas prone to the hazard. One system called DART (Deep Ocean Assessment and Reporting of Tsunami) is using receptors on the sea bed and buoys on the surface to detect a passing tsunami. The aim is for the data to be transmitted via satellite as part

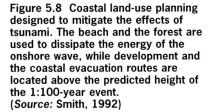

**4** What are the advantages and problems with the tsunami warning systems in operation today?

**5a** How can land-use planning be used to mitigate tsunami (Fig. 5.8)?
**b** What are the problems with this approach?

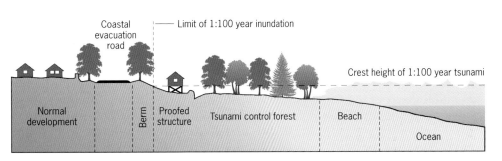

**Figure 5.8 Coastal land-use planning designed to mitigate the effects of tsunami. The beach and the forest are used to dissipate the energy of the onshore wave, while development and the coastal evacuation routes are located above the predicted height of the 1:100-year event.**
(*Source:* **Smith, 1992**)

?

**6a** How do people try to modify the tsunami event (Fig. 5.9)?
**b** What are the likely advantages and disadvantages of this approach?
**c** Comment upon the environmental/visual impacts.

**7** Tabulate volcanic eruptions and tsunami to compare them in terms of:
**a** the nature of the hazard to people
**b** monitoring and prediction
**c** the management strategies used.

of an early warning system. However, the costs involved are likely to be high, especially for less economically developed nations.

### Land-use planning

Re-zoning of low-lying coastal land can be an effective defence against the effects of tsunami. Following the tsunami damage to Crescent City, California, from the 1964 Alaskan earthquake, the waterfront has been turned into public parks and the beach has been re-zoned so that businesses have been moved to higher ground back from the shore. Figure 5.8 is an example of tsunami hazard land-use planning.

### *Modify the event*

A less-common response to the tsunami hazard is to try to modify the tsunami event by hazard-resistant design. Defensive engineering works can provide some protection, and the trend nowadays is towards onshore walls and coastal redevelopment (Fig. 5.9). Building design aims to resist the passage of the waves, for example by open ground floors that allow the wave to pass through between concrete piles. Positioning the buildings at right angles to the coast, rather than parallel, will lessen the impact of the wave upon the structure. Coastal power stations, especially nuclear reactors, receive most engineering protection.

Protection for rural areas in LEDCs is more difficult due to the large area involved and the lack of capital for hard-engineering structures. Measures recommended following the 1994 tsunami in eastern Java include reinforcing houses near to the shore so that they stay tethered to the ground, and planting large trees to dissipate the wave energy.

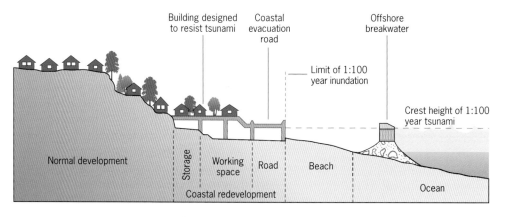

**Figure 5.9 Tsunami engineering works, including offshore breakwaters and some coastal redevelopment, as employed in parts of Japan (*Source:* Smith, 1992)**

## Papua New Guinea tsunami, 1998

On Friday 17 July 1998, a remote part of the coast of north-west Papua New Guinea was hit by a major tsunami (Fig. 5.10). The area affected was a low-lying spit of land sandwiched between the Bismarck Sea and Sissano Lagoon. The affected area had a population of 10 000 in seven villages. A magnitude 7 earthquake struck the area at 6.49 p.m. The tsunami hit the coast 20 minutes later following further aftershocks.

Researchers flew into the area to try to establish the size and impacts of the tsunami. Evidence from eyewitnesses indicated that there was a drawdown of the sea before the wave arrived. Debris and damage to trees shows that the wave reached 10 m high. The

large size of the wave was a puzzle to the researchers. A magnitude 7 earthquake is unlikely to have produced a tsunami and certainly not one as big as this. Later research revealed that what was originally thought to be an aftershock of the main earthquake was probably sound waves picked up by a massive undersea landslide. This was on the continental shelf off the coast and resulted from the earthquake. Thus this event probably resulted from a mass movement displacing huge amounts of seawater (Fig. 5.4). However, the trigger was an earthquake.

In the low-lying area between the sea and the lagoon, there was no escape. The death toll was over 2000,

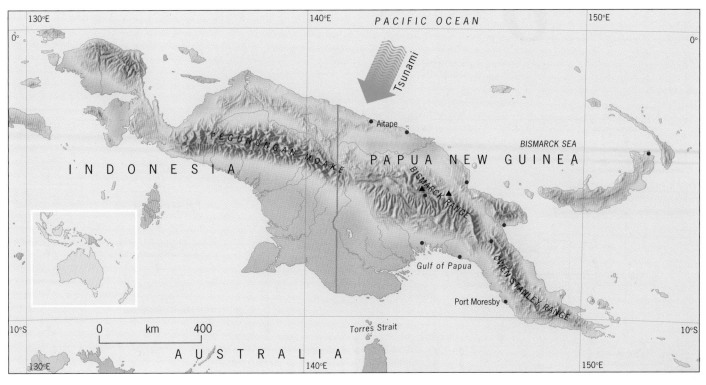

**Figure 5.10  Location of Papua New Guinea**

with 500 deaths from the village of Warpu alone. Over 6000 were made homeless as their homes were smashed to pieces by the wave. Survivors suffered from broken bones as they were tossed about in the water with the debris from smashed homes, vegetation and uprooted trees (Fig. 5.11). In this remote area, disease quickly became a problem, as clearing away the bodies was slow. Dysentery and pneumonia were common from swallowing too much sea water. Mass cremations were needed. It is a measure of the high vulnerability of the local people that at the end of the twentieth century and near the end of the International Decade for Hazard Reduction, that the use of international aid was the only management option available. Most of this help came from nearby Australia in the form of medicine, engineering equipment, and army and medical personnel.

**Figure 5.11  Villagers search amid the ruins of their home, which was devastated, like many others in Papua New Guinea, when the tidal wave swept in**

## Summary

- Tsunami are the result of large-scale disturbances of the ocean floor as a result of seismic or volcanic activity and mass movements. Subduction zones are key locations for their development.

- Tsunami are classified by magnitude and frequency of events and their human impacts.

- People respond to tsunami hazards by prediction and warning systems, community preparedness, land-use planning and hazard-resistant design.

# 6 Atmospheric hazards

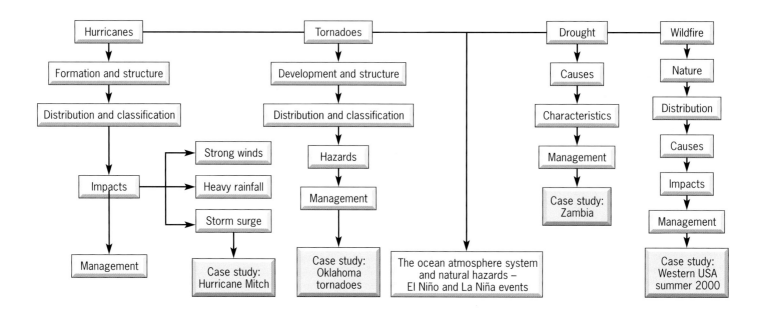

Atmospheric hazards are widespread in occurrence and range in scale from large storms with strong winds, and drought-causing atmospheric conditions, to more localised events such as tornadoes and hail storms. Globally, atmospheric hazards result in large-scale human suffering, especially as a result of droughts and tropical cyclones (Figs 1.5 and 1.6). Atmospheric processes can affect a range of other geophysical systems, causing secondary hazards such as wildfire, landsliding and flooding.

## 6.1 El Niño and natural hazards

In recent years our understanding of atmospheric processes has increased dramatically. The oceans and atmosphere are closely linked, and the heat supply in the oceans has a major effect on world climate. The oceans store large amounts of heat when warmed which is released back to the atmosphere on cooling. The Hadley Cell circulations between the subtropical high pressures and the equatorial trough transfer heat energy north–south across the Tropics. There are also east–west circulations called Walker Circulations (Fig. 6.1a).

Every few years this Walker Circulation breaks down. The easterly trade winds decline, and warm water moves eastwards across the Pacific (Fig. 6.2) to produce a warm-water ocean current off the coast of South America called El Niño. This change has an impact on the circulation, to produce an El Niño–Southern Oscillation event (ENSO) (Fig. 6.1b). The impacts on the general atmospheric circulation can extend into the northern hemisphere as the jet stream path is changed.

The effects of these El Niño events are widespread and can be related to an increase in the occurrence of natural hazards, especially droughts and flooding (Fig. 6.3). The 1982–3 El Niño event was one of the twentieth-century's worst (Fig. 6.5). Work in Australia has shown a correlation between flooding, drought, beach erosion, heavy rainfall and landslide hazards and ENSO events.

• Heat sources over Africa, South America and Indonesia–Australia set up pressure differences and heat is transferred as the Walker Circulation.
• Rainfall is produced in low-pressure areas of rising air over land masses.
• Trade winds move warm water westwards in the Pacific Ocean.
• Storm and cyclone activity occurs which brings seasonal rainfall to east Australia and Indonesia.

A warm-water ocean current moves eastwards across the Pacific off the South American coast (El Niño). This changes circulation to shift rainbelts and areas of high pressure. Drought may occur over eastern South America, East Africa, Indonesia and Australia.

H – High pressure
L – Low pressure

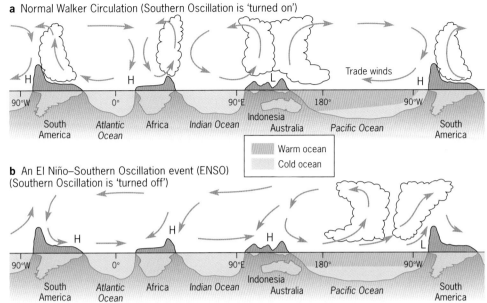

**a** Normal Walker Circulation (Southern Oscillation is 'turned on')

**b** An El Niño–Southern Oscillation event (ENSO) (Southern Oscillation is 'turned off')

Warm ocean
Cold ocean

**Figure 6.1  Walker Circulations**

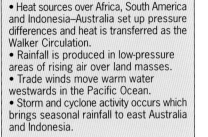

−2 −1.5 −1 −0.5 0.5 1 1.5 2 3 4 5
7-day average centred on 17 September 1997

**Figure 6.2  The El Niño event of 1997–8: observed sea-surface temperature anomaly (0°C)**

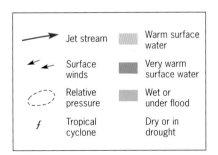

→ Jet stream
↖ ↘ Surface winds
⌁ Relative pressure
*f* Tropical cyclone

Warm surface water
Very warm surface water
Wet or under flood
Dry or in drought

**Figure 6.3  The evolution and effects of an El Niño–Southern Oscillation event**

• Summer heating of the Indonesian–northern Australian land masses produces low pressure.
• Off the coast of Peru, the Hadley Cell circulation together with the cold ocean produces intense high pressure.
• Winds blow eastwards across the Pacific as an easterly trade wind to the Indo-Australia low pressure.
• Warm surface water piles up in the Coral Sea, east of Australia.
• This easterly trade wind is called the Walker Circulation.

• Cyclones which usually form in the Coral Sea now affect Tahiti, Tonga and the Hawaiian islands.
• Westerly winds become dominant over the easterlies and the west coast of South America is swamped by a layer of warm water.
• The high pressure which had existed because of the cold ocean is now replaced by low pressure. The ocean is 4–6°C above normal.
• The warm water results in heavy rainfall on the usually arid coastline and drought elsewhere.

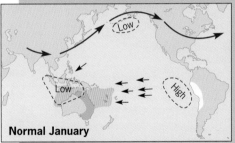

**Normal January**

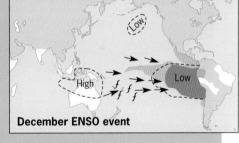

**December ENSO event**

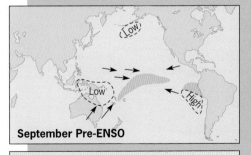

**September Pre-ENSO**

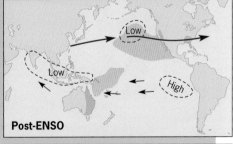

**Post-ENSO**

This Walker Circulation is variable (called the Southern Oscillation). It weakens and breaks down every 2–7 years. This occurs as the Indo–Australian low-pressure centre moves eastwards and warm ocean water moves eastwards. As the Walker Circulation collapses, low pressure and rainfall move to the central Pacific.

• Warm water spreads slowly north, causing intense low pressure in the north Pacific. The heat released by the moist air in the low pressure causes the westerly jet stream to move south, resulting in dramatic climatic events in North America, e.g. flooding and heavy snow. As the warm water spreads out in the Pacific, the Walker Circulation re-establishes itself.

# Global warning boosts El Niño

Global warming is increasing the frequency of El Niño, the vast climatic cycle that can wreak havoc on much of the world's weather systems, scientists have found.

Scientists studying corals in the central Pacific have found that the phenomenon, which in strong years can trigger powerful hurricanes in the Atlantic and devastating droughts in southern Africa and Indonesia, sparking famine and fires, has increased over the past 150 years from once every ten years to once every four.

Scientists have speculated that rising global temperatures, caused by a build-up of greenhouse gases, may be intensifying and increasing the frequency of El Niño years. Measurements by instruments date back only to the 1950s, however, so a team from the University of Colorado have turned to coral records stretching back to 1840.

Tiny cores, taken form the Mariana Atoll, near Kiribati, have different isotope balances at different levels or rainfall and temperatures affecting the corals. These in turn reflect the arrival and disappearance of El Niño The coral cores show that in the nineteenth century El Niño happened every ten to 15 years. Since the late 1970s it has shifted to a four-year cycle.

The researchers suspect that the more frequent El Niños are being triggered by higher surface sea temperatures since the late 1970s, which in turn have been linked to the build-up of greenhouse gases.

'The warming and freshening of the central Pacific since the late 1970s is unique over the coral record. It seems likely that El Niño will respond to further global warming,' he states.

The findings came as researchers predicted that 2000 will have been one of the hottest years on record across the globe. Phil Jones, of the University of East Anglia's climate research unit, said: 'It looks like it will be similar to 1999, making 2000 the fifth or sixth warmest since 1856.'

In non-El Niño years sea temperatures off South America are cooler than those in the western Pacific. Cold, nutrient-rich waters come to the surface off countries such as Peru and are responsible for a thriving anchovy fishery. The eastern Pacific is relatively dry and the western Pacific relatively rainy. In El Niño years there is a sharp and disruptive shift in ocean and atmospheric patterns. Trade winds relax and warm waters spread east to South America, leading to a collapse of fisheries.

Heavy rainfall can also push far into the eastern Pacific triggering deluges and mudslides in South America and droughts and bushfires on the other side of the Pacific in Indonesia through to Australia.

El Niño can be followed by La Niña, or the Little Girl, in which conditions switch to a colder than normal eastern Pacific. It can trigger colder than normal winter temperatures in northwest America.

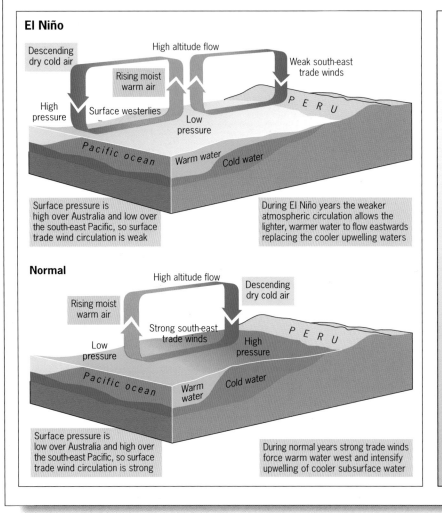

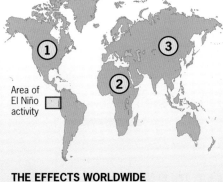

## THE EFFECTS WORLDWIDE

### 1 Americas
El Niño is already making itself felt in the Americas with the worst drought in Brazil since 1926. Winds, rainfall and mountain snow are expected to exceed those of the last extreme El Niño event in 1997–98.

### 2 Africa
The effect of the 1997–98 El Niño in Africa was a drought which reduced maize production across southern Africa, putting millions of people at risk of starvation. This time Africa's wheat, sugar and other crops could be similarly affected.

### 3 Asia
El Niño has already wreaked havoc with weather patterns throughout Asia. It is being blamed for the drought in the region which is threatening to claim the lives of up to one million people. Rice crops are failing across the Asia-Pacific region.

**Figure 6.4  El Niño is increasing in frequency (*Source: The Times*, 26 October 2000)**

Research suggests that some hazards are reduced during ENSO years – for example, Atlantic tropical cyclones (hurricanes) are fewer and less intense.

Recent evidence suggests that a very well-developed Walker Circulation can also cause atmospheric extremes. The cool water off South America can move northwards and across the central Pacific, lowering the ocean temperature. This is called a La Niña event. In 1988–90 there were record-breaking floods in Bangladesh, Thailand and Sudan, and an exceptionally late cyclone in Bangladesh. Australia experienced large rainfall quantities and record flooding. The **jet stream** shifted northwards over North America, deflecting rain-producing depressions from the Great Plains to Canada. The result was a severe drought in the Midwest.

It is hoped that greater understanding and early detection of ENSO events will provide advance warning of drought, heavy rainfall, and other hazards in large parts of the world. El Niño events seem to be occurring more regularly in recent years, with several in a row in the early 1990s, dying down in 1995–6, and intense activity in 1997–8. Global warming may cause more frequent events (Fig. 6.4).

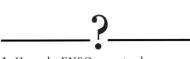

**1** How do ENSO events change the global circulation?

**2** Use Figure 6.5 to produce an annotated map of the 1982–3 El Niño-induced natural hazards.

---

Monsoon rains fell over the central Pacific Ocean instead of to the west. Consequently, droughts plagued the Pacific Rim countries. Forest fires in eastern Borneo burned a total area greater than that of Switzerland. Eastern Australia suffered its worst drought in recorded history; Melbourne choked on thousands of tonnes of earth blown in by a vast dust storm. Killing droughts also afflicted Indonesia, India, Sri Lanka, China, Africa and Brazil.

Meanwhile, heavy rainfall caused freak tropical storms on central Pacific islands. Typhoons hit Hawaii and Tahiti. Island bird populations were decimated as their nests in sand bars were flooded by heavy rains. Along the western coast of South America

El Niño suppressed the normal upwelling of cold, nutrient-rich water that feeds phytoplankton production. Deprived of their food, anchovies that teem off the Peruvian coast perished. The anchovy catch in 1983 was 1 per cent of what it had been 10 years before. Sardines swam south into Chilean waters. Without fish to eat, seabird populations were decimated. Hunger also claimed one-quarter of the year's fur seal and sea lion adults and all the pups.

Meanwhile coastal Peru received up to 3 metres of rain within six months, transforming arid desert into a lush land where water washed away bridges and roads. Rainfall soaked other areas as well, among them southern Brazil, parts of the US

bordering the Gulf of Mexico, and southern China, where floods crippled the wheat crop. Winter storms smashed into coastal California, causing $1 billion worth of damage.

Accurate forecasting of El Niño can help farmers decide on what crops to plant, and give policy-makers time to adjust plans. Australia, Peru, Ecuador, Brazil, India, China and Ethiopia all use El Niño forecasts to aid critical decision-making.

One example of the potential use of El Niño forecasts came last year. It was reported in Nature that from 1973 to 1990 maize yield in Zimbabwe fluctuated almost exactly in step with El Niño and the Southern Oscillation.

**Figure 6.5  El Niño's global signature** (*Source: New Scientist*, 4 February 1995)

## 6.2 Tropical cyclones

*The formation of tropical cyclones*

Tropical cyclones are violent storms between 200 and 650 km in diameter and are the most significant atmospheric hazard in terms of loss of life and damage. Disturbances in the tropical atmospheric circulation (Fig. 6.6) are common and cause most of the rainfall experienced in the tropics. These disturbances may develop into low-pressure systems called tropical depressions and storms, and a few into mature tropical cyclones. These intense storms are given local names including hurricanes, cyclones, typhoons and willy willies.

There are two main areas where these disturbances start. About 80 per cent of tropical cyclones originate in or just poleward of the **Intertropical Convergence Zone** (ITCZ) in latitudes 5–15°N and S (Fig. 6.6). The disturbances can develop into storms of varying intensities, measured using sustained wind speeds (of 10 minutes' duration). Tropical depressions (wind speeds average 17 m/s) and tropical storms (17–33 m/s) are lower intensity but can still cause widespread damage. The storm becomes a tropical cyclone if wind speeds exceed 33 m/s.

These storms are important in transferring excess heat from the tropics to higher latitudes, but the trigger that makes an atmospheric disturbance develop into a tropical cyclone is not fully understood. It is known that certain conditions are needed if this is to happen. Musk (1988) has identified seven conditions needed to produce a tropical cyclone.

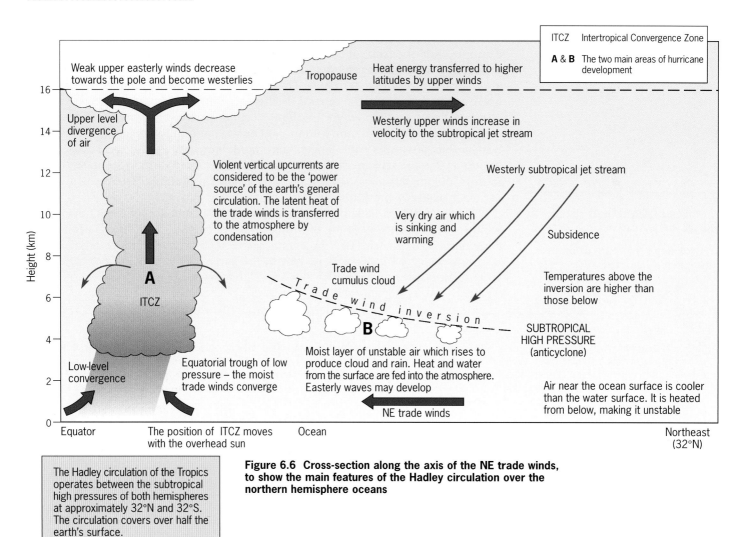

**Figure 6.6 Cross-section along the axis of the NE trade winds, to show the main features of the Hadley circulation over the northern hemisphere oceans**

The Hadley circulation of the Tropics operates between the subtropical high pressures of both hemispheres at approximately 32°N and 32°S. The circulation covers over half the earth's surface.

1 Ocean with surface temperatures over 26°C with warm water to a depth of 70 m
2 A disturbance in lower atmospheric circulation
3 A large-enough Coriolis force to produce a circular pattern of winds
4 Winds at all levels in the same direction
5 A rapid outflow of air from the upper troposphere is replaced by an inflow at ground level
6 Excess heat is transported away from the storm by upper-troposphere winds
7 Unstable air with high humidity.

However, all of these occurring together will not necessarily mean that a tropical cyclone will develop.

*Structure of a tropical cyclone*
Figure 6.7 shows the structure of a mature tropical cyclone after it has developed from an initial disturbance with a tropical storm stage lasting 4–5 days, to form a fully developed hurricane lasting 2–3 days.

The tropical cyclone exists while there is a supply of latent heat and moisture to provide energy and low frictional drag on the ocean surface. When the storm moves over a colder ocean surface or land area that reduces the heat and/or moisture supply that sustained the convection, it will start to decay. If the storm moves over the land, the increased friction with the ground surface reduces the speed of sustained winds but gusting may be stronger due to the more variable surface conditions.

## Spatial and temporal distribution

Figure 6.7 shows the main zones of tropical cyclone formation, local names and the tracks taken by the storms. Worldwide, their spatial distribution is not even. Tropical cyclones do not occur all year round, but in distinctive seasons when the conditions necessary for their formation occur.

**Figure 6.7 The structure of a tropical cyclone (*Source:* Buckle, 1996)**

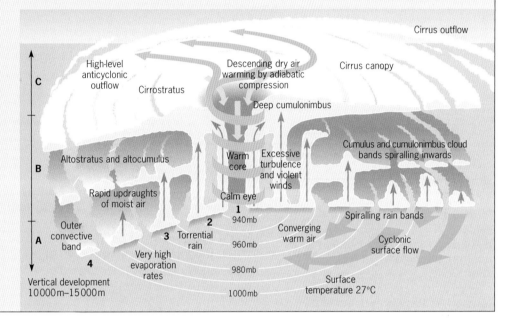

### Hurricane Structure
#### Cross-section

**1** The 'eye' in the middle of the storm between 5 and 50 km in diameter. Wind speeds are low, with clear skies due to subsidence of air and **adiabatic** warming. In Hurricane Anita (September 1977) wind speeds of 10 m/sec were recorded. Very low pressure (about 965 mb). Formation is not fully understood.

**2** The main 'throat' of the storm 10–20 km wide. Towering cumulonimbus clouds form a wall around the eye as a result of intense **convection**. Wind speeds are very high (gusts over 50 m/sec) and torrential rainfall. Up to 200 towers of cumulonimbus cloud release latent heat of condensation to drive the storm.

**3** Main storm cloudiness with intense connective cloud and heavy rainfall forming rainbands which spiral towards the storm centre. There may be six cloud cells in a typical cyclone.

**4** Outer convective band of deep convective cloud around the main cloudmass. This results from the convergence of the subsidiary outflow of air with the main surface inflow into the low-pressure centre. This triggers off small-scale instability.

#### Vertical

**A** The inflow layer from the ocean surface up to 3 km. Water is evaporated into the air in large quantities from the warm ocean surface and is carried into the storm centre. The water vapour condenses in the convection cell to liberate latent heat which provides the energy to drive the storm.

**B** The main cyclonic circulation of the storm between 3 to 7 km.

**C** The outflow layer above 7 km to the **tropopause**. Maximum outflow occurs at 12 km and above. The air motion moves out to higher latitudes via the upper westerly flow, transferring heat energy surplus from the tropics to temperate latitudes.

**Figure 6.8  Areas of tropical cyclone formation**

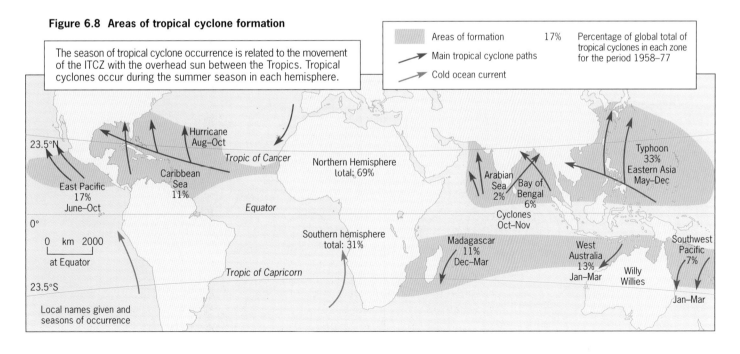

**Table 6.1 The Saffir–Simpson hurricane disaster-potential scale**

| Scale number | Central pressure (mb) | Wind speed (ms⁻¹) | Storm surge (m) | Damage potential. The amount of damage increases exponentially with the scale: a category 5 is likely to cause 250 times more damage than a category 1 |
|---|---|---|---|---|
| 1 | >980 | 33–42 | 1.2–1.6 | **Minimal:** Damage to vegetation and poorly anchored mobile homes. Some low-lying coasts flooded. Solid buildings and structures unlikely to be damaged. |
| 2 | 965–979 | 43–49 | 1.7–2.5 | **Moderate:** Trees stripped of foliage and some blown down. Major damage to mobile homes. Damage to some roofing materials. Coastal roads and escape routes flooded 2–4 hours before the cyclone centre arrives. Piers damaged and small unprotected craft torn loose. Some evacuation of coastal areas is necessary. |
| 3 | 945–964 | 50–58 | 2.6–3.8 | **Extensive:** Foliage stripped from trees and many blown down. Great damage to roofing materials, doors and windows. Some small buildings structurally damaged. Larger structures may be damaged by floating debris. Serious coastal flooding and escape routes cut off 3–5 hours before cyclone centre arrives. Evacuation of coastal residents for several blocks inland may be necessary. |
| 4 | 920–944 | 59–69 | 3.9–5.5 | **Extreme:** Trees and signs all blown down. Extensive damage to roofing, doors and windows. Many roofs of smaller buildings ripped off and mobile homes destroyed. Extensive damage to lower floors of buildings near the coast. Evacuation of areas within 500 m of coast may be necessary and low-lying areas up to 10 km inland. Major erosion of beaches. |
| 5 | <920 | >69 | >5.5 | **Catastrophic:** Complete roof failure of many residential and industrial buildings. Major damage to lower floors of all structures lower than 3 m above sea level. Evacuation of all residential areas on low ground within 16–24 km of coast likely. |

This scale describes the meteorological characteristics of the storm based on the intensity of the low pressure, its disaster potential and the likely damage. This is useful for governments and emergency services in areas at risk.

---

**?**

**3a** Why do tropical cyclones not form near to or move across the equator?
**b** Suggest why tropical cyclones do not form off the coast of western South America.
**c** Explain the temporal pattern (seasons) of tropical cyclones in the main regions.

---

*Classifying tropical cyclones*

The magnitude of tropical cyclones is measured using the five-category Saffir–Simpson scale (Table 6.1). The physical size of the storm has no relationship to intensity measures.

Tropical cyclones are a relatively frequent hazard. Globally between 1968 and 1989, the largest number recorded in one year was 65 and the smallest 34, with an average of 45 per year. These variations are less in El Niño years and more in La Niña events.

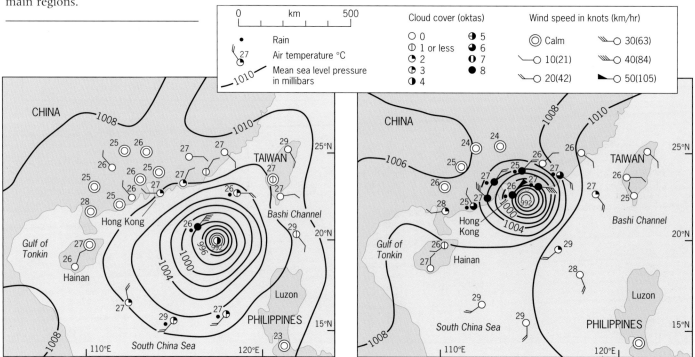

**Figure 6.9  Typhoon Ellen: the synoptic situation at 10 a.m. on 8 September 1983**

**Figure 6.10  Typhoon Ellen: the synoptic situation at 10 a.m. on 9 September 1983**

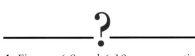

**?**

**4** Figures 6.9 and 6.10 are synoptic charts of the Hong Kong area during Typhoon Ellen, September 1983.
**a** Describe and explain the changes in weather over Hong Kong between 10 a.m. on 8 September 1983 and 10 a.m. on 9 September 1983.
**b** Assuming that Typhoon Ellen continued to travel in the same direction at the same rate, suggest a weather forecast for Hong Kong for the 24 hours between 10 a.m. on 9 September 1983 and 10 a.m. on 10 September 1983. Give reasons for your answer.

# 6.3 The impacts of tropical cyclones

Tropical cyclones are one of the most destructive natural hazards in terms of frequency and number of deaths (see Fig. 1.6). They are a major threat to coastal areas, especially in densely populated low-lying delta areas, most notably Bangladesh; isolated island groups including the Japanese, Philippine and Caribbean islands; and densely populated coastlines such as the Gulf of Mexico, the Atlantic coastline of the USA, and the Queensland Gold Coast of Australia. Globally, the deaths and damage resulting from tropical cyclones reflect the often-found pattern of highest death rates in the LEDCs and the highest economic losses in MEDCs. Financial losses in LEDCs are mainly as a result of damage to cash crops. Additionally, the threat of disease is much higher owing to decaying bodies of livestock, and lack of immediate emergency aid and supplies.

Tropical cyclones are a multiple hazard since loss of life and property damage can result from the three main hazards of winds, heavy rainfall and storm surge (Fig. 6.11).

*Winds*
The strong winds associated with very low atmospheric pressure cause structural damage to buildings, roads and bridges, and crops, especially tree crops, may be damaged. Wind speeds of up to 320 km/hr have been observed. All of the deaths and most of the damage from Hurricane Andrew resulted from the wind hazard as buildings collapsed and large debris particles were hurled around (Fig. 6.12).

**Figure 6.11 The impacts of tropical cyclones (Source: Chapman, 1994)**

**Figure 6.12 Florida City, Florida, USA, was devastated by Hurricane Andrew in August 1992**

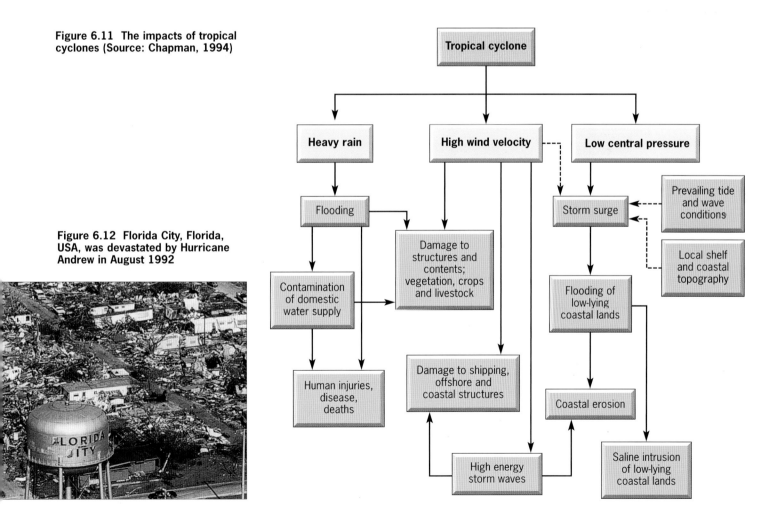

## Heavy rainfall

Rainfall figures are variable but can be extremely high and result in secondary hazards such as flooding and landsliding. On average, tropical cyclones result in rainfall events of 100 mm per day within 200 km of the eye, and 40 mm per day between 200 and 400 km. The largest rainfall total was recorded in Réunion Island in the southern Indian Ocean with 1144 mm in 12 hours (Cyclone Denise in 1966).

## Storm surge

Storm surges cause 90 per cent of deaths resulting from tropical cyclones, and extensive damage to agricultural land by salt contamination from the inflowing sea water. The storm surge results from the piling up of water by wind-driven waves, with their greatest effect on low-lying coasts (Fig. 6.13).

**Figure 6.13 A storm surge (shown above mean sea level, although its height can be higher or lower depending on the tide level)**

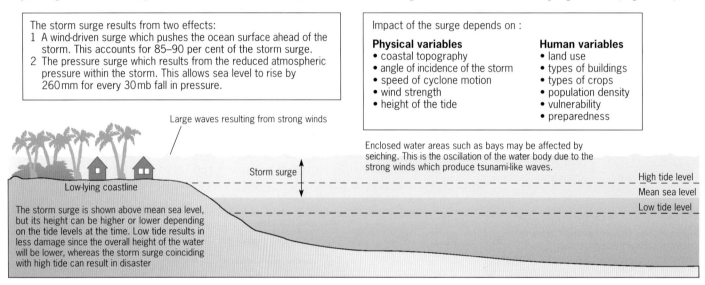

The storm surge results from two effects:
1 A wind-driven surge which pushes the ocean surface ahead of the storm. This accounts for 85–90 per cent of the storm surge.
2 The pressure surge which results from the reduced atmospheric pressure within the storm. This allows sea level to rise by 260 mm for every 30 mb fall in pressure.

Impact of the surge depends on :

**Physical variables**
• coastal topography
• angle of incidence of the storm
• speed of cyclone motion
• wind strength
• height of the tide

**Human variables**
• land use
• types of buildings
• types of crops
• population density
• vulnerability
• preparedness

Large waves resulting from strong winds

Enclosed water areas such as bays may be affected by seiching. This is the oscillation of the water body due to the strong winds which produce tsunami-like waves.

Storm surge

Low-lying coastline

High tide level
Mean sea level
Low tide level

The storm surge is shown above mean sea level, but its height can be higher or lower depending on the tide levels at the time. Low tide results in less damage since the overall height of the water will be lower, whereas the storm surge coinciding with high tide can result in disaster

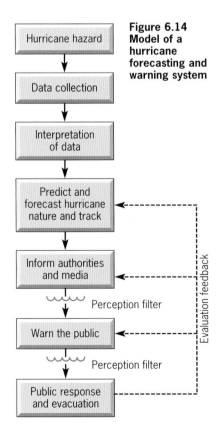

**Figure 6.14 Model of a hurricane forecasting and warning system**

Hurricane hazard → Data collection → Interpretation of data → Predict and forecast hurricane nature and track → Inform authorities and media → Perception filter → Warn the public → Perception filter → Public response and evacuation

Evaluation feedback

# 6.4 Managing the tropical cyclone hazard

## Modify vulnerability

### Prediction and warning

Coastal areas at risk from tropical cyclones are protected by warning systems. These aim to monitor tropical cyclone development and forecast their intensity and tracks so that the population can prepare themselves by moving to shelters or evacuating their property from the danger area. The MEDCs are most protected because of the availability of financial, technological and communication resources.

One of the most-developed warning services is the US government-funded National Hurricane Centre (NHC) in Miami, Florida. Data from **geostationary satellites** and land- and sea-based recording centres are constantly provided so that meteorologists can look for developing circulations between 0° and 140°W. If a storm develops, more detailed and accurate data are collected by reconnaissance flights. The data are then beamed via satellite to NHC to be analysed by super-computers.

Predictions and forecasts are based upon computer models of atmospheric processes and statistical models of hurricane activity and tracks in previous years. Research at Colorado State University and University College, London, uses global climatic data and ocean surface temperatures to make hurricane activity predictions. The difficult part of the process is interpreting the data for warning purposes. If the population at risk are warned and evacuated, then lives will be saved. However, if the warning proves wrong, there are high

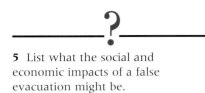

**5** List what the social and economic impacts of a false evacuation might be.

economic losses from evacuation. There are also the impacts on the population and their reaction to future warnings. Too many wrong warnings may produce complacency, and warnings must be issued in a way which will not cause panic.

A key element in the future of hurricane forecasting is time. As population densities along the coastline increase, it takes longer for an evacuation to be implemented, and exit roads are put under increasing strain (Fig. 6.15). For example, the Lower Florida Keys are over 100 km from the closest mainland. Estimates suggest that it could take over 31 hours to evacuate the area along the only highway. This is longer than forecasters can currently predict the landfall of a hurricane with accuracy. As the hurricane approaches the forecasts become more accurate, but specific hurricane warnings are rarely issued more than 12–18 hours before landfall. Once the forecast has been made this then has to be disseminated to a wider audience (Fig. 6.14).

Figure 6.15 Residents of Cocoa, Florida, forced to move out of the path of Hurricane Floyd in September 1999

Figure 6.16 Overall wind effects on building surfaces (*Source:* Chapman, 1994). The 'explosion' effect can be reduced by roof design and materials which are more secure. Glass is a high-risk part of the building and breaks as a result of the pressure effect or impact from wind-borne debris. External shutters will reduce this effect.

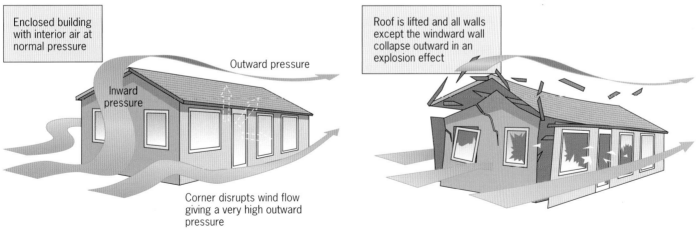

### Community preparedness

If warnings are to be effective, the authorities and public must be aware of the specific actions to take. Dissemination of information to the public and evacuation procedures need to be planned in advance. The public needs to know how to prepare themselves and their property. People may still not evacuate the area or move to shelters due to personal perceptions, cultural or economic factors (see case study, pages 19–23).

**?**

**6** Do you consider that legislation to prohibit coastal development is justified or should people have freedom of choice? Explain your answer.

The Pan-Caribbean Disaster Preparedness and Prevention Project, established in 1980, concentrated on technical help, the training of local people in emergency health care, and preparing training materials. The scheme had some success regarding the potential loss of life, though the economic losses remain large.

### Land-use planning

Land-use planning is most effective in the coastal zone at risk from the storm surge. Past tropical cyclone data and coastal topography can be used to identify areas at high risk. The aim is to limit development in these areas to uses more compatible with flooding such as beaches and parkland. This is a difficult aim to achieve. In LEDCs the need for land, and in MEDCs the desire for a beach-front location, are likely to outweigh the risks involved, even if people are aware of them. The US Growth Management Act of 1985 requires local governments to address natural hazards by limiting public expenditure on developments in high-risk areas, directing population away from these areas, maintaining or reducing evacuation times, and having post-disaster redevelopment plans.

*Modifying the event*

### Environmental control

Hurricanes are powered by the condensation and precipitation process, and it was hoped that they could be weakened by seeding clouds with dry ice or silver iodide crystals acting as **condensation nuclei**. The unpredictable consequences on global energy transfer and the inconclusive results, however, led to the abandonment of research.

### Hazard-resistant design

This focuses on protection against both the storm surge and wind hazards. The storm surge hazard can be reduced by engineering structures such as sea walls, breakwaters and flood barriers. The most comprehensive engineering scheme took place at Galveston, Texas, following the storm surge of September 1900 when 6000 people died. The whole city was elevated by 3.5 m and is now protected by a huge sea wall. The scheme took seven years to complete and is unlikely to be repeated elsewhere because of the huge costs involved.

Building design can protect against the storm surge by raising the building on stilts, and using concrete/brick rather than wood which is more easily swept away. Building design can do much to reduce the wind hazard (Fig. 6.16).

### Modifying the loss

Hurricanes often result in state and international aid provision in terms of cash and technical help, for example to restore electricity supplies. Insurance is an important management strategy, especially in MEDCs. The availability of insurance cover may encourage people to locate in high-risk areas, however, and the withdrawal of this would assist land-use-planning approaches.

**Figure 6.17 Part of the original sea wall at Galveston, Texas**

# Hurricane Mitch, October 1998

Hurricane Mitch struck Central America in October 1998, resulting in 11 000 deaths and over $10 billion damage. The worst affected countries were Nicaragua and Honduras. Mitch was the second most destructive Atlantic hurricane ever (Table 6.2). In a meteorological sense, Mitch reached category 5 on the Saffir-Simpson scale (Table 6.1) in the Caribbean Sea on 26 October, and it ranks in the the top five Atlantic hurricanes on record (Table 6.3). As Mitch approached the coast of Honduras it became stationary for 24 hours and then weakened to a tropical storm by 29 October (Fig. 6.18).

The most destructive aspect of Mitch was the huge amounts of rainfall due to the storm's slow movement and the orographic effects of the Central American mountains. Rainfall duration and intensities were exceptional. This information is gained from a few surviving rain gauges and satellite information. In southern Honduras, away from the main centre of the stationary storm, the rain gauge recorded 896 mm rainfall between 18.00 hours on 27 October and 21.00 hours on 31 October. Mitch made landfall on 29 October and when rainfall began at 09.00 hours, it rained continuously for 61 hours, until 21.00 hours on 31 October; 787 mm rain were recorded. Compare this with London's total annual rainfall of 582 mm. During this time there were three distinct periods of very intense rainfall with maximum intensities ranging from 138 mm/hour to 584 mm/hour. Data for northern Honduras is based on satellite information and estimate rainfall amounts at 1270–1905 mm.

The high rainfall intensities and total amounts resulted in widespread flooding, rivers changing course, and landslides (Fig. 6.19). These impacts were made worse by the high amounts of rainfall already experienced in the region as this was the end of the wet season. The mountainous terrain encouraged hillslope instability and agricultural practices had left hillsides eroded and soils exposed. Floods and landslides were the causes of most death and damage to crops (Fig. 6.18). The worst single event was the collapse of the volcanic crater; the crater lake of Casitas volcano burst, sending an avalanche of mud which buried 80 km$^2$ and killed 2000 people.

The main management approach was international aid, totalling over $100 million. The USA spent $3.5 million and the EU $7.7 million. Personnel were also sent to help, including Japanese soldiers, Dutch engineers, American airforce and doctors, and British medical help. The International Red Cross launched an appeal for $7.4 million (£4.5 million).

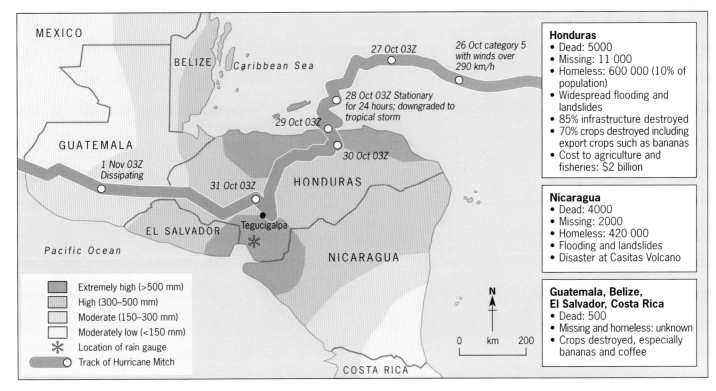

**Figure 6.18** Track information from the national Hurricane Centre, Miami, USA, and rainfall estimates from 25 October to 17 November 1998, as determined by the US National Oceanic and Atmospheric Administration / Climate Prediction Centre. Also shown is the location of the rain gauge at 13°17'N, 87°04'W. Times are GMT (Honduran time is GMT –6h)

**Table 6.2  Most destructive western hemisphere hurricanes on record**

| Hurricane | Date | Areas struck | Deaths |
|---|---|---|---|
| Great Hurricane | 10–16 Oct 1780 | Martinique, St Eustatius, Barbados, ships | 22 000 |
| Hurricane Mitch | 21 Oct–4 Nov 1998 | Honduras, Nicaragua | 11 000+ |
| Galveston, Texas | 8 Sept 1900 | Galveston Island | 8 000 |
| Hurricane Fifi | 14–19 Sept 1974 | Honduras | 8 000 |
| Dominican Republic | 1–6 Sept 1930 | Dominican Republic | 8 000 |
| Hurricane Flora | 30 Sept–8 Ot 1963 | Haiti, Cuba | 7 200 |
| Martinique | 6 Sept 1776 | Pont Petre Bay | >6 000 |

(*Source:* McCown, et al, 1998)

**Table 6.3  Strongest Atlantic hurricanes on record**

| Hurricane | Date | Pressure (mbar) | Peak winds (km) | Total time at category 5 (h) | Total time winds 155+ km (h) |
|---|---|---|---|---|---|
| Gilbert | 13 Sept 1988 | 888 | 160 | 18 | 6 |
| Florida Keys | 3 Sept 1935 | 892 | 140 | 3 | 0 |
| Allen | 7 Aug 1980 | 899 | 165 | 24/24/12* | 3/12/3* |
| Mitch | 26 Oct 1998 | 905 | 155 | 33 | 15 |
| Camille | 17 Aug 1969 | 905 | 165 | 24 | 18 |

*Hurricane Allen attained category 5 status three times during its duration
(*Source:* McCown, et al, 1998)

**Figure 6.19 Flood damage caused by Hurricane Mitch in the Honduran capital, Tegucigalpa**

# 6.5 Tornadoes

Tornadoes are the most violent atmospheric storms. They are usually more intense than hurricanes but are much smaller in size and short-lived, so although the damage is high, the area affected is much smaller.

## *The development and structure of a tornado*

A tornado is a rapidly rotating vortex of air which extends from a **cumulonimbus** cloud to the ground (Fig. 6.19). Research in the USA shows that tornadoes result from the interaction of air streams with different characteristics of temperature, density, humidity and wind flow (Fig. 6.20). Once these conditions exist, tornadoes may develop from the thunderstorm cell which is the result of this interaction (Fig. 6.21).

## *Geographical and temporal distribution*

Since tornadoes result from the interaction of contrasting air masses, they are mainly found in mid-latitude regions where tropical and polar air meet as part of the global atmospheric circulation. They can also develop from the cumulonimbus cloud development around hurricanes, or in other situations where there are strong vertical contrasts of temperature, winds and moisture.

Tornadoes are a constant hazard in the USA, with 80 per cent of the world's reported occurrences and almost all of the violent tornadoes. The hazard is widespread (Fig. 6.19), with the area of the Great Plains (which has five or more tornadoes per year) being called 'Tornado Alley'. In this area, contrasting air masses often with temperature differences of 20–30°C meet along cold

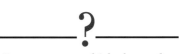

**7** Draw a poster which shows the safe areas of a building during a tropical cyclone and explain why these areas are safest.

**8** Is insurance an appropriate management strategy for the hurricane hazard?

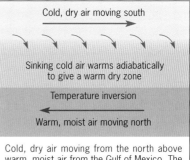

Cold, dry air moving from the north above warm, moist air from the Gulf of Mexico. The cold air sinks and warms adiabatically to give a band of warm, dry air sandwiched between the two air streams. A temperature inversion forms above the warm, moist air.

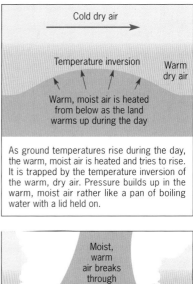

As ground temperatures rise during the day, the warm, moist air is heated and tries to rise. It is trapped by the temperature inversion of the warm, dry air. Pressure builds up in the warm, moist air rather like a pan of boiling water with a lid held on.

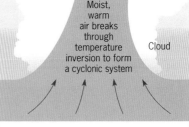

A trigger mechanism, usually a cold front, breaks the temperature inversion and the warm, moist air rushes through the cold air streams creating a low-pressure (cyclone) centre. There will be rapid and large cumulonimbus cloud development often up to the tropopause.

**Figure 6.21 Conditions for storm and tornado development in the USA**

**Figure 6.20 A tornado funnel-cloud touches down north of Jarrell in Texas, USA, May 1997. At least 29 people died and hundreds were made homeless in the small town.**

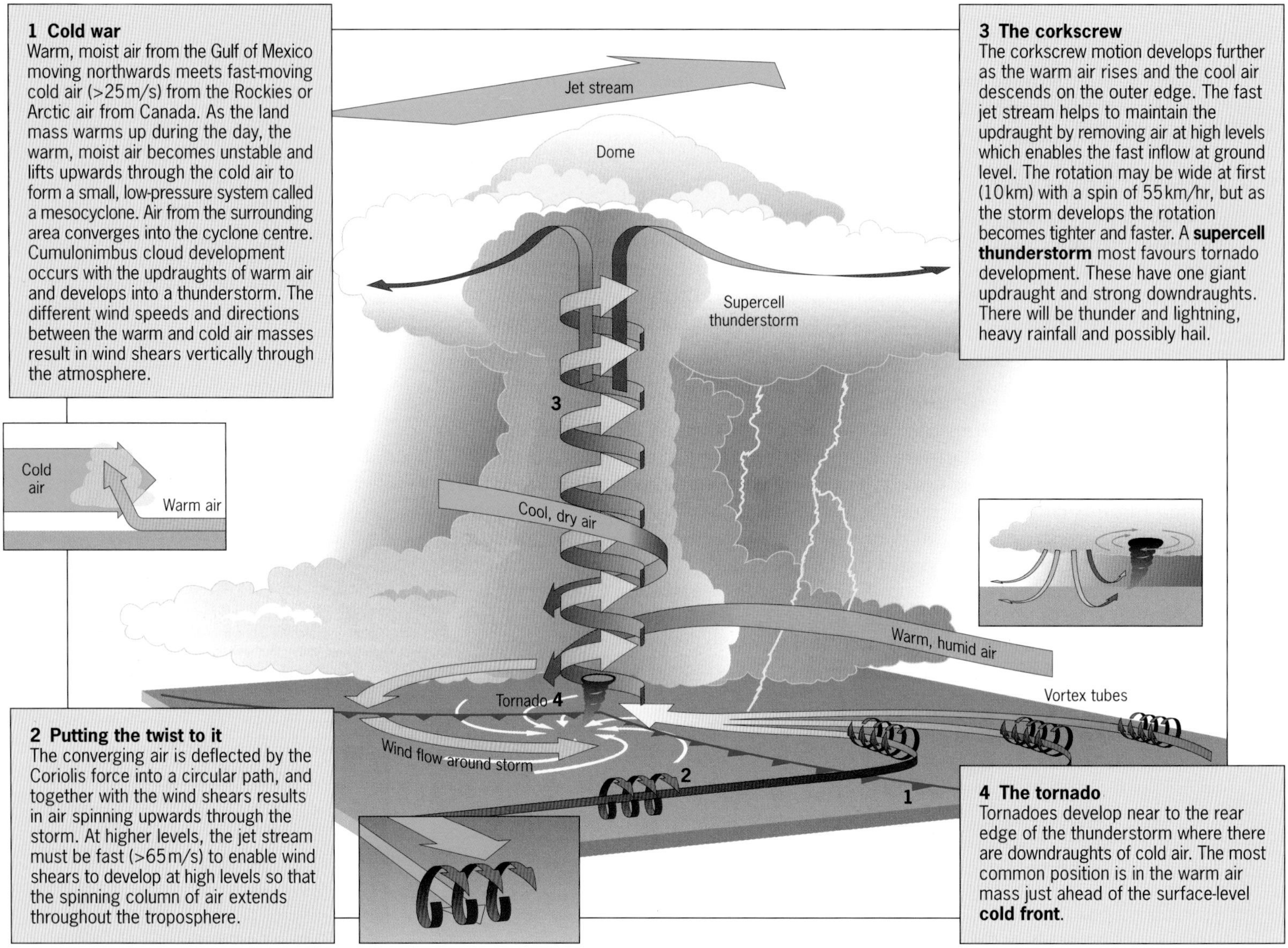

**1 Cold war**
Warm, moist air from the Gulf of Mexico moving northwards meets fast-moving cold air (>25m/s) from the Rockies or Arctic air from Canada. As the land mass warms up during the day, the warm, moist air becomes unstable and lifts upwards through the cold air to form a small, low-pressure system called a mesocyclone. Air from the surrounding area converges into the cyclone centre. Cumulonimbus cloud development occurs with the updraughts of warm air and develops into a thunderstorm. The different wind speeds and directions between the warm and cold air masses result in wind shears vertically through the atmosphere.

**3 The corkscrew**
The corkscrew motion develops further as the warm air rises and the cool air descends on the outer edge. The fast jet stream helps to maintain the updraught by removing air at high levels which enables the fast inflow at ground level. The rotation may be wide at first (10km) with a spin of 55km/hr, but as the storm develops the rotation becomes tighter and faster. A **supercell thunderstorm** most favours tornado development. These have one giant updraught and strong downdraughts. There will be thunder and lightning, heavy rainfall and possibly hail.

Jet stream

Dome

Supercell thunderstorm

Cool, dry air

3

Cold air

Warm air

Warm, humid air

Tornado 4

Vortex tubes

Wind flow around storm

2

1

**2 Putting the twist to it**
The converging air is deflected by the Coriolis force into a circular path, and together with the wind shears results in air spinning upwards through the storm. At higher levels, the jet stream must be fast (>65m/s) to enable wind shears to develop at high levels so that the spinning column of air extends throughout the troposphere.

**4 The tornado**
Tornadoes develop near to the rear edge of the thunderstorm where there are downdraughts of cold air. The most common position is in the warm air mass just ahead of the surface-level **cold front**.

**Figure 6.22 Tornado formation (*Source: Time*, 20 May 1996). Tornadoes can occur singly or in families, where several funnels occur together or in sequence from one thunderstorm. Funnel diameters range from 300 to 400 m. The path over the ground can vary, but is usually between 15 and 65 km. In exceptional cases they can exceed 75 km.**

**?**

**9** Explain why the late afternoon is the most likely time for tornadoes to develop (refer to Figs 6.20 and 21).

**10** Produce an annotated world map to show the distribution of the tornado hazard. Add notes to give the reasons for their formation in each area.

fronts (Fig. 6.21). The flat land of the plains encourages the rapid movement of the cold air and the necessary **wind shears** to develop.

Large numbers of weak tornadoes are reported from Australia and the UK. In the UK about 32 small, low-intensity tornadoes occur each year, mainly in lowland England. In Australia, tornadoes develop mostly in the east where cold fronts pass over the area. Other countries with significant tornado reports are other European countries, India, Bangladesh, Uruguay, China and Japan. Equatorial regions lack the contrasting air masses for their development and insufficient Coriolis force for a circulation to develop. Polar regions lack the warm, moist air necessary for their formation. Thus tornado reports are concentrated between latitudes 20° and 60° N and S.

Tornadoes can occur at any time of the day or year. In the USA most occur between mid-March and August, while in the UK the most likely time is between September and January when the contrasts between air masses are most marked.

*Classifying and measuring tornadoes*
Tornadoes are classified by their path length and width, and wind speed. The Fujita Intensity Scale used in the USA classifies tornadoes by the damage they cause. In 1972, the UK-based Tornado and Storm Research Organisation

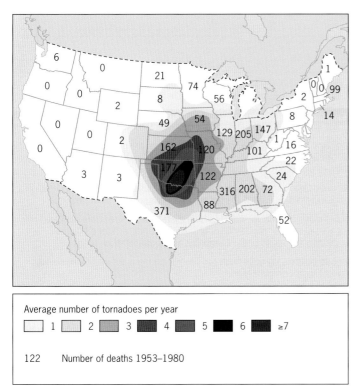

**Figure 6.23 The average annual occurrence of major tornadoes and tornado deaths in the USA (1954–80). The general direction of travel is towards the north-east. (*Source:* Abbott, 1996)**

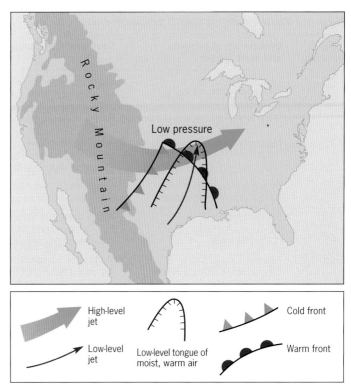

**Figure 6.24 The atmospheric conditions governing severe storms and tornadoes over the Great Plains, USA (*After:* Berry and Chorley, 1992)**

speed (based upon the Beaufort wind scale) and damage observed.

## Hazards resulting from tornadoes

The destructive effects of tornadoes are due to the high wind speeds, the lifting force of the funnel wall, and to the abrupt change in atmospheric pressure. The lifting force can be considerable, with reports of train carriages being moved hundreds of metres. The rapid and large change in pressure is very damaging. As a tornado passes over a building the outside pressure is up to 200 mb lower than that inside, resulting in an explosion effect on the building. People and animals can appear to be burnt by a tornado due to the rapid dehydration resulting from the pressure fall. There is also damage from high wind speeds (may exceed 60 m/sec) and the resultant flying objects and debris (Table 6.4).

## Managing the tornado hazard

It is not possible at present to modify the tornado event itself. Hazard-resistant design can help to reduce deaths by requiring solid construction of buildings and using basements as part of the structure. As with the hurricane hazard, the key approach to managing tornadoes is to modify people's vulnerability by prediction and warning, and preparedness.

The atmospheric conditions and thunderstorm weather which produces tornadoes is predicted by using radar and satellite technology. These technologies have helped to reduce the rate of false warnings from 73 to 24 per cent. It is not possible to predict whether a tornado will occur, its path, or how intense it will be. In many cases, the vortex does not reach the ground and will not be destructive. At other times the vortex may only reach the ground briefly, or it may stay in contact with the ground for many kilometres moving along an irregular path.

**Table 6.4 The international TORRO tornado intensity scale**

| TORRO intensity | Description of tornado and wind speeds | Description of damage |
| --- | --- | --- |
| T0 | Light tornado 17–24 ms$^{-1}$ (39–54 mph) | Loose light litter raised from ground level in spirals. Tents, marquees seriously disturbed; most exposed tiles, slates on roofs dislodged. Twigs snapped; trail visible through crops. |
| T1 | Mild tornado 25–32 ms$^{-1}$ (55–72 mph) | Deckchairs, small plants, heavy litter made airborne; minor damage to sheds, more serious dislodging of tiles, slates, chimney pots. Wooden fences flattened. Slight damage to hedges and trees. |
| T2 | Moderate tornado 33–41ms$^{-1}$ (73–92 mph) | Heavy mobile homes displaced, light caravans blown over, garden sheds destroyed, garage roofs torn away, much damage to tiled roofs and chimney stacks. General damage to trees, some big branches twisted or snapped off, small trees uprooted. |
| T3 | Strong tornado 42–51 ms$^{-1}$ (93–114 mph) | Mobile homes overturned/badly damaged; light caravans destroyed; garages, outbuildings destroyed; house roof timbers considerably exposed. Some of the bigger trees snapped or uprooted. |
| T4 | Severe tornado 52–61 ms$^{-1}$ (115–136 mph) | Mobile homes destroyed; some sheds airborne for considerable distances; entire roofs removed from some houses or prefabricated buildings; roof timbers of stronger brick or stone houses completely exposed; possible collapse of gable ends. Numerous trees uprooted or snapped. |
| T5 | Intense tornado 62–72 ms$^{-1}$ (137–16 0 mph) | Motor cars levitated; more serious building damage than for T4, yet house walls usually remaining; the weakest, old buildings may collapse completely. |
| T6 | Moderately devastating tornado 73–83 ms$^{-1}$ (161–186 mph) | Heavy motor vehicles levitated; strong houses lose entire roofs and perhaps also a wall; more of the less-strong buildings collapse. |
| T7 | Strongly devastating tornado 84–95 ms$^{-1}$ (197–212 mph) | Frame house completely demolished; some walls of stone or brick houses beaten down or collapsed; steel-framed warehouse-type buildings may buckle slightly. Locomotives thrown over. Noticeable debarking of any standing trees by flying debris. |
| T8 | Severely devastating tornado 96–107 ms$^{-1}$ (213–240 mph) | Frame houses and their contents dispersed over big distances; most other stone or brick houses irreparably damaged; steel-framed buildings buckled; motor cars hurled great distances. |
| T9 | Intensely devastating tornado 108–120 ms$^{-1}$ (241–269 mph) | Many steel-framed buildings badly damaged; locomotives or trains hurled some distances. Complete de-barking of any standing tree-trunks. |
| T10 | Super tornado 121–134 ms$^{-1}$ or more (270–299 mph or more) | Entire frame houses and similar buildings lifted bodily from foundations and carried some distances. Steel-reinforced concrete buildings may be severely damaged. |

**?**

**11** Using the data in Figure 6.23 draw a choropleth map of tornado deaths in the USA by state. Compare your map with the distribution of tornadoes and suggest why some states have more deaths than others.

**12** Draw up a table to contrast tornadoes and hurricanes under the following headings: size; duration; area affected; nature of the hazard; damage caused; onset time and warning; management strategies used.

Currently only the USA has a formal tornado forecasting and warning system. This has a similar structure to that for hurricanes (Fig. 6.14). However, warning times to the public are much shorter and unreliable. The warnings are of possible tornado activity, not that a tornado will affect a specific area at a specific time and be of a known intensity.

As with all prediction and warning systems, community preparedness is important if they are to be effective. People need to be aware of the threats and the safest place to be. In buildings, underground shelters should be used if they are available, or a central room away from windows. In the open, lying flat on the ground or in a ditch and abandoning vehicles are the best tactics to survive the hazard.

The number of deaths from tornadoes shows a different distribution from the occurrence of the hazard (Fig. 6.23). These can be explained to some extent by differing perceptions and responses to the hazard. Tornado deaths are being reduced by warning systems and preparation. The differing degrees of preparedness can result from varying attitudes and experience.

# The Oklahoma tornadoes, May 1999

In May 1999 a swarm of 65 tornadoes occurred along a 150-mile belt running from the south-west of Oklahoma State towards Kansas (Fig. 6.25). The events left 45 people dead and widespread damage, including 8000 buildings ruined or damaged. A large tornado, 1–2 km wide, that touched down for a track over 61 km long including parts of Oklahoma City was the first tornado to cause one billion dollars worth of damage (Fig. 6.24). At times it reached the rare top level F5 of the US-based Fujita Scale (Fig. 6.26) with winds of 117–142 kph (261–318 mph). It damaged three times as many structures (1000 buildings) as any other tornado, and 22 homes were completely lifted off their foundations. Another huge tornado touched down in Mulhall 64.5 km north of Oklahoma City. This reached F4 and measured 1.93 km across. Luckily it did not cross a populated area. These rare F4 and F5 tornadoes account for only two per cent of US tornadoes but they have caused 66 per cent of all deaths. Even following all guidelines and sheltering in an inner 'safe room' may not ensure survival.

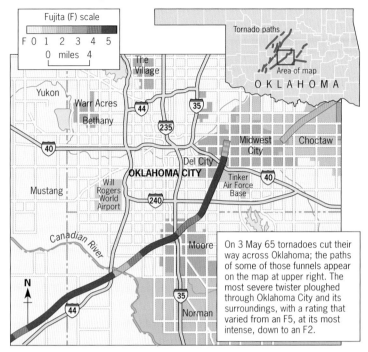

On 3 May 65 tornadoes cut their way across Oklahoma; the paths of some of those funnels appear on the map at upper right. The most severe twister ploughed through Oklahoma City and its surroundings, with a rating that varied from an F5, at its most intense, down to an F2.

**Figure 6.25 Path of destruction created by the Oklahoma tornadoes**

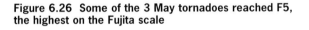

**Figure 6.26 Some of the 3 May tornadoes reached F5, the highest on the Fujita scale**

**Figure 6.27 The Fujita Scale**

| Fujita | Wind speed (mph) | (mps) | Damage scale |
|---|---|---|---|
| F-0 | Under 72 | 32 | light |
| F-1 | 73–112 | 32.6–50 | moderate |
| F-2 | 113–157 | 50.5–70 | considerable |
| F-3 | 158–206 | 70.6–92 | severe |
| F-4 | 207–260 | 92.5–116 | devastating |
| F-5 | over 261 | 116.7 | incredible |

Ideal conditions in the Great Plains for tornado formation
- warm moist air from Gulf of Mexico
- cool drier air on top of the warm air, leading to instability
- separation layer of warm dry air so that the two main layers do not mix
- wind shear at upper levels
- a clear frontal boundary between two contrasting air masses
- rotation in the jet stream.

At 6.30 a.m. on 3 May the Storm Prediction Centre (SPC) based in Norman thought that there was a slight risk of tornadoes. Upper winds were not strong and the front between the moist Gulf air and the dry desert air was not moving much. By early afternoon upper level conditions had caused a kink in the jet stream and winds of 100 mph. Unfortunately the changing upper level conditions were small enough geographically to be missed by the 100 weather balloons launched at 7.00 a.m. However, wind profilers (upward-pointing radars) picked up the increased wind speed at upper levels by mid-day. By mid-afternoon the SPC were convinced there was a high risk of tornadoes, especially as clearing skies would allow the region to heat up and generate convection storms. At 3.49 p.m. the area was placed under 'high risk' of tornadoes but it was still not possible to say exactly if and where tornadoes would strike. The storms were relatively severe and long-lived super cell storms and almost all of the them produced tornadoes.

The tornadoes folded the garage doors of most homes inwards and shattered windows. Roofs were lifted and walls caved in (Fig. 6.28). Even homes built to withstand 80-mph winds could not stand up to this. Paths of damage were also found at right angles to the tornadoes' path as the result of large items of debris such as weak roofs being sucked into the vortex. Mobile homes were the most vulnerable. An F1 would overturn a mobile home and an F2 would demolish it. In this event, mobile homes accounted for less than two per cent of the damaged structures but 25 per cent of the deaths were in these homes.

Considering the severity of this tornado swarm, the number of deaths were relatively few. There were no deaths at all in the 4–24 age group. Reasons for the low death toll include:

- The tornadoes were huge, visible and audible.
- Local radio and television gave huge coverage.
- Warnings from the National Weather Service (NWS) gave an average lead time of Oklahoma City of 32 minutes. This is twice the normal time.
- Warnings have improved with the use of doplar radar which can detect wind changes.
- The SPC gave early alerts.

**13** Use Figure 6.27 to measure the track distance at the different Fujita intensities as the tornado touched down in Oklahoma City.

**14** Suggest why there were no deaths in the 4–24 age group.

**15** How has hazard management by the use of technology and community preparedness reduced death tolls in the USA?

**Figure 6.28 The spring tornadoes that hit Oklahoma and Kansas damaged thousands of buildings, including these homes at Dell City, Oklahoma**

# 6.6 Drought

## What is drought?

Drought is a temporary shortfall of water supply which has hydrological and agricultural impacts. It differs from most other hazards in that it develops slowly as a creeping hazard, is longer term (usually weeks to months) and affects a larger geographical area. It is difficult to identify when a drought actually starts and ends. Drought is often linked with aridity and desertification, but they are not the same. Aridity is a permanent and natural condition, and desertification is associated with human activity in degrading ecosystems (Table 6.5).

Drought is characterised by moisture deficiency below normal levels for the environment affected. Human systems are adapted to the average conditions and therefore they will be affected by this deficit. The impact will depend not only on the lack of rainfall but also on the amount of evapotranspiration, runoff and infiltration. For a drought to develop the lack of rainfall must be enough to cause the soil and groundwater stores to decline, and result in a reduction in hydrological processes producing streamflow. A drought may therefore exist in a humid environment such as the UK after only a few weeks without rain, but in semi-arid parts of the world with seasonal rainfall, the onset of drought is much slower.

## The causes of drought

A drought has hydrological impacts, but the initial cause is a change in 'average' conditions in atmospheric processes. Drought is associated with three main situations:

### Persistent sub-tropical high-pressure systems

If sub-tropical high-pressure cells (Fig. 6.6) increase in area and persistence, drought may result. The Sahel in Africa has suffered recurring droughts which have been associated with an expansion of the Azores high pressure to the east and south that blocks the rain-bearing monsoon winds (Fig. 6.29).

**Figure 6.29 Seasonal migration of the ITCZ in West Africa**

• The Sahel countries are situated in semi-arid parts of Africa.
• Seasonal rainfall occurs after the ITCZ has migrated northwards.
• Drought occurs because rains are unreliable and in some years the ITCZ may not move so far north. Thus hot, dry tropical continental air dominates for the whole year.
• Natural and human systems come under increasing pressure when drought occurs over several years.

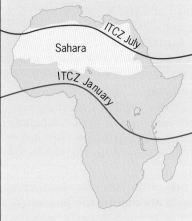

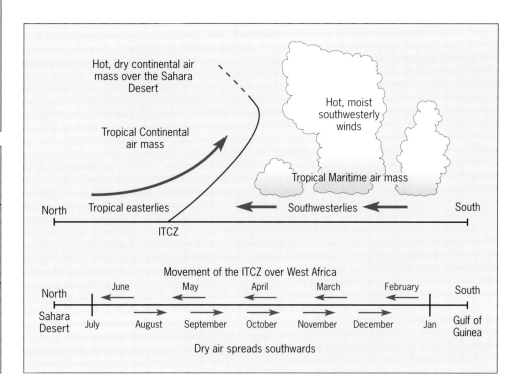

**Table 6.5 Drought, aridity and desertification (*Source:* Chapman, 1994)**

| Drought<br>A temporary phenomenon | Aridity<br>A permanent condition | Desertification<br>A human-induced condition |
| --- | --- | --- |
| Can occur in any climate<br>Unpredictable occurrence<br>Uncertain frequency<br>Uncertain duration<br>Uncertain severity<br>Long period of lower-than-average precipitation<br>Diminished water resources<br>Diminished productivity of natural ecosystems<br>Diminished productivity and deterioration of farms and rangeland | Climate state associated with global circulation patterns<br>Low annual precipitation normal<br>Rainfall highly variable in both time and space<br>High evaporation normal<br>High solar energy input<br>Large annual temperature variations normal<br>Low productivity of natural ecosystems normal<br>Low productivity of farms and rangeland normal<br>Sparse human settlement normal | *Resulting from:*<br>Groundwater abstraction<br>Overgrazing and unwise cultivation<br>Attempts to extract from land more than natural productivity allows<br>Unwise irrigation practices leading to salinisation<br><br>*and producing symptoms of:*<br>Reduction of perennial vegetation cover<br>Aquifer depletion, land subsidence<br>Damaged surface soil and subsoil, loss of soil nutrients<br>Increase in soil temperature<br>Compaction and salinisation of soils<br>Oxidisation of soil organic matter<br>Reduction of water-holding capacity of soil<br>Increased propensity for flash flooding and further erosion<br>Loss of productivity of natural ecosystems and of farms and rangeland<br>Raised surface albedo (tends to diminish rainfall)<br>Invasion of former farms and rangeland by woody weeds |

**El Niño and ocean-surface temperature changes**

If ocean-surface temperatures differ from usual, temperature and wind patterns are affected. Droughts in California and Chile are associated with lower ocean-surface temperatures than usual. El Niño events are associated with these changes, and result in droughts in Australia, Indonesia, southern Africa and Brazil.

**Changing mid-latitude depression tracks**

Changes to depression tracks can occur in two situations. Firstly, the upper westerly winds extend into lower latitudes, which results in the rain-bearing depression moving further south. Secondly, changes in the meandering paths of the upper westerlies, which are the result of changes in heat transfer from low to higher latitudes. These changes are closely related to surface weather patterns (Fig. 6.30). If the upper flow breaks down into a circular pattern, intense surface-level anticyclones develop. These can last for several weeks and block the movement of rain-bearing depressions, resulting in the term 'blocking anticyclone'. Drought in the Midwest of the USA, for example during the 1930s dust bowl event, are associated with long-lasting high-pressure ridges in the upper atmosphere (Fig. 6.30). The UK droughts of recent years (1976, 1989–92 and 1995) were the result of such blocking anticyclones.

*The characteristics of drought*

The processes that produce drought are widespread and the hazard is not confined to any geographical location. However, semi-arid areas which experience unreliable rainfall such as the Sahel, Australia and the Great Plains of the USA have suffered severe droughts. The severity of droughts in many areas, especially these semi-arid zones, have been intensified by **feedback effects** in natural systems. If fragile soils are mismanaged by overcropping, land is overgrazed, and tree cover removed, then these feedback mechanisms will operate on a wider scale than under natural vegetation or well-managed conditions. The reasons behind these mismanagement practices are complex and related to economic and social changes such as the need for cash crops to repay foreign debts, profit-making and population pressure. Many LEDCs are trapped in a cycle of land degradation which can result in desertification. This is most marked in the countries of the Sahel, which are among the poorest in the world.

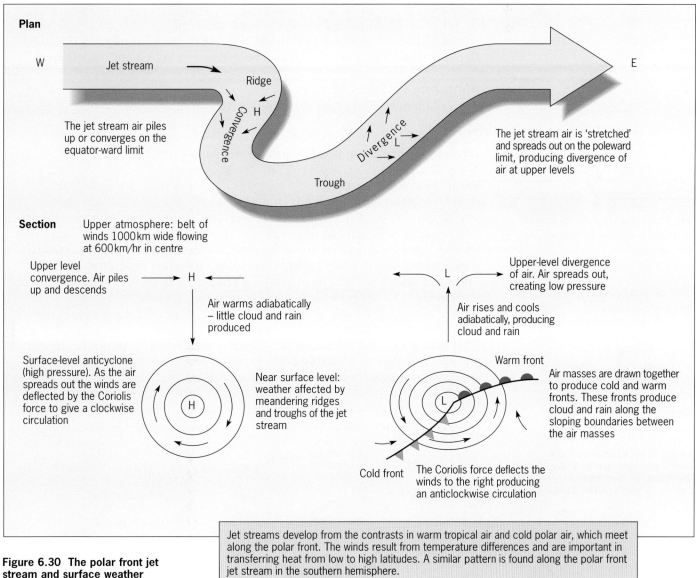

**Figure 6.30 The polar front jet stream and surface weather conditions (northern hemisphere)**

Jet streams develop from the contrasts in warm tropical air and cold polar air, which meet along the polar front. The winds result from temperature differences and are important in transferring heat from low to high latitudes. A similar pattern is found along the polar front jet stream in the southern hemisphere.

Each drought will have its own unique characteristics, and no scale of drought magnitude exists. Drought may also result in secondary natural hazards such as dust storms, disease resulting from malnutrition, pests such as locusts, and wildfires.

On its own, meteorological drought may not be a hazard to people if water-supply systems can meet the demands of agriculture, industry and the public. Drought periods may have rainfall but overall the amounts will be below average and the water stores in the environment will decline, resulting in a hydrological drought. The main impacts are on water-resource systems when rivers may be used for water supply, reservoirs emptied, water rationed and HEP production reduced. Droughts may raise issues of water-resource management, as has been the case in the UK over recent years.

Agricultural drought occurs when soil moisture is reduced and cannot maintain crop yields. This has important implications for national food production and economies exporting crops. In LEDCs drought intensifies any food-supply problems, resulting in severe hardship for individuals and increasing national debt burdens. Severe agricultural drought can result in famines, but the reasons for this are closely related to human socio-economic systems as much as to the physical drought. Many famines are closely linked with war and political upheaval. Drought and famine are difficult to separate statistically and together arguably cause the most human suffering (Fig. 1.5). Between 1968 and 1992, 59 million people were affected and 73000 died.

*Managing the drought*
Preventing or ending drought is not possible. To modify the event, though, management has concentrated on water storage. Engineering schemes involve the building of dams and storage reservoirs, often as part of multi-purpose schemes for irrigation, flood control, water supply and HEP.

**Prediction and warning**
Recent developments to modify drought and vulnerability include early warnings of drought impacts, such as crop failures. Warnings are possible because of remote sensing which detects changes such as reduced vegetation growth. Other methods of providing early warnings of drought impacts involve food and nutrition survey systems. These aim to detect food shortages before famine develops, such as by monitoring child development. Such systems were developed in Chad and Mali following the drought of the mid-1980s.

**Community preparedness**
This is an important management strategy since droughts cannot be prevented. In urban areas people may be encouraged to adopt water-conservation measures, or legislation may enforce this. It is in rural areas, especially in the LEDCs, that community preparedness is most critical. Unfortunately this is complex, since preparation for drought and avoiding famine is tied up with both environmental degradation and human socio-political systems (Fig. 6.31).

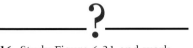

**16** Study Figure 6.31 and work through the links to answer the questions.
**a** Explain how reduced vegetation results in environmental degradation.
**b** How does environmental degradation feed back to affect national development programmes?
**c** How does debt repayment add to environmental degradation?
**d** What is the link between drought and desertification?

**Figure 6.31 Example of self-reinforcing mechanisms (positive feedback) at international, national and local levels (*After:* Scoging, 1993)**

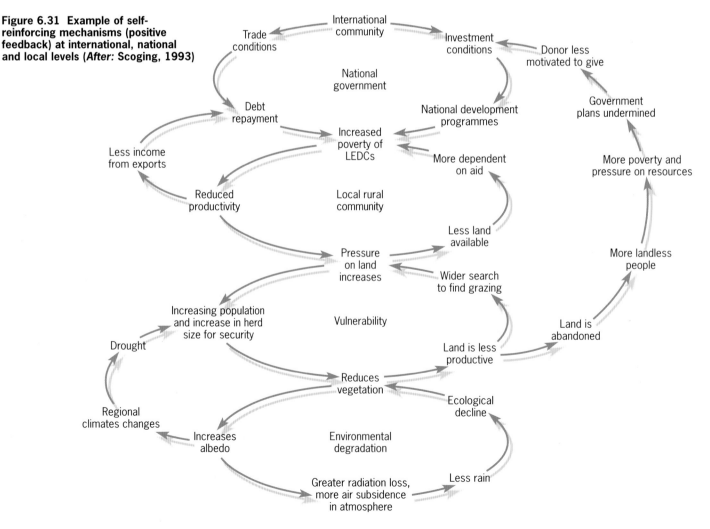

In many semi-arid areas people have developed traditional coping strategies such as herd diversification, migration and selling of surplus stock. Under severe conditions more may need to be done such as selling assets, calling in debts, or migration to urban areas. However, in reality, responses are mainly at the individual level and involve selling stock, praying, or using government aid, although many use no strategy at all. Many people would not migrate to the cities because of the fear of violence in urban areas and the lack of jobs.

**Land-use planning**

Since poor land-use practices can intensify the impacts of drought, there is a need for better land management, especially soil conservation measures. In Ethiopia, the Environmental Education Programme, started in 1985, aims to reduce environmental degradation, but unfortunately this will not tackle the wider economic and political factors involved in this degradation. In Australia farmers adopt a self-reliant approach, and land management is important in determining the farmers' ability to survive a drought. Moisture conservation and crop protection practices are used and in some cases water catchments are stripped of vegetation and compacted to increase runoff.

### ?

**17** What is meant by the term 'aid culture'?

**18** Is aid a desirable management strategy? What alternatives are there?

*Modify the loss by aid*

Acceptance of or sharing the losses are important strategies for dealing with drought. The large scale of drought usually results in aid at government or international level. In all countries, governments are involved in providing aid to drought-stricken areas. During the 1984–5 Ethiopian drought, however, the government failed to admit that there was a problem at first, mainly because the drought was in the rebellious northern provinces. This lack of action was partly responsible for the terrible famine which followed.

International aid is mainly in the form of food aid by governments, international organisations such as the United Nations Disaster Relief Organisation (UNDRO), and non-governmental organisations such as the Red Cross and Oxfam. Providing aid is not without its problems. The food aid may not reach those most in need, may create an 'aid culture' and does not address the human factors involved in the drought impacts. In the longer term, aid can be used to help farmers re-establish themselves and to improve communications and health facilities.

## The 1991–92 drought in Zambia

*Background*

Zambia in southern Africa (Fig. 6.32) has a large manufacturing and mining sector centred upon copper exports. Some 58 per cent of the population live in rural areas, though rural population growth resulted in a million more people in the 1980s. The government under Kenneth Kaunda had ruled the country as a single-party republic since independence from Britain in 1964. His government had used export earnings for industrialisation and supporting the growing of maize as a basic food and export crop. The maize subsidies resulted in large areas of monoculture, and on average the country is self-sufficient in maize production. However, food supply in Zambia is constantly threatened by droughts, as in 1982–84, 1989 and 1990. The 1991–92 drought came at a time of political and economic upheaval in the country, with a change of government in October 1991.

*The drought and its impacts*

The 1991–92 drought came at the end of a relatively dry decade. Rainfall totals were 450 mm in 1991–92 compared with 850 mm in the 1970s. The north of the country was least affected, but in total two million people were affected in rural communities. In the cities, people maintained their incomes and could buy imported food.

The rainfall totals were low, but the key problem was the lack of rainfall just after planting the maize in January and February (Fig. 6.33). The result was maize production down 40–100 per cent. Farmers tried to plant a later crop but this also failed, leaving many without their normal food supply and next year's seeds. Crops of groundnuts, beans and cowpeas were also lost. Livestock numbers were reduced by the drought and disease, but overgrazing was not a major problem because stock numbers had already been reduced by East Coast fever.

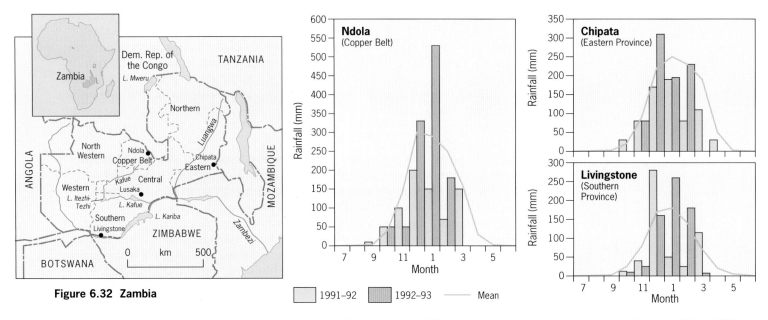

**Figure 6.32  Zambia**

**Figure 6.33  Rainfall for 1991–2, 1992–3, and the 30-year mean (*Source:* Tiffen, 1995)**

The reservoirs were already low from the dry years. Flow on the River Kafue were the lowest since 1905, with the March 1992 peak flow reduced from an average of 820 to 100 m³/s. Power generation was reduced to 30 per cent of capacity at both Victoria Falls (River Zambezi) and Kafue Gorge (River Kafue). This resulted in power rationing in urban areas and for industry. In rural areas, small streams and wetland quickly dried up, reducing water availability. This was made worse by 4000 boreholes already being out of action due to a lack of spare parts. People increasingly used wood fuel and charcoal to replace maize-stalk fuel, but there was little evidence of long-term damage to the environment. The 1992–93 rains brought a quick recovery in the natural vegetation and wildlife, but the effects on people were longer term.

## Drought response and management

The drought stripped many rural families of their assets of livestock and seed stock, with losses of between 30 and 100 per cent of income. People sold what they had in order to buy food before the relief maize arrived. There was also an increase in gathering of fruits, vegetables and insects for food.

The government responded by informing aid donors of the situation before it developed into a crisis. In March 1992, food-aid pledges were received from governments and international organisations. By August, enough food was arriving in the country to prevent famine, although there were some transport difficulties. Non-government organisations, including the Churches, distributed maize to two million people. The maize distribution was by the Food for Work Programme (FFW). This gave free maize to those without food or cash resources. In return they were required to work on self-help projects such as repairing roads, school buildings and wells. Women were mainly involved in the FFW while men engaged in income-earning activities. The government provided some credit to aid the farmers' recovery, but those who already owed money were not eligible. Their recovery was much slower and inequalities increased within villages.

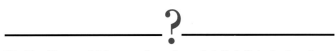

**?**

**19**  Use Figure 6.33 to analyse the rainfall deficit during the drought.

**20**  Write a government report to show why rural areas are so vulnerable to drought.

**21**  How did the rural population respond to the drought?

**22**  Assess the government's management of the drought.

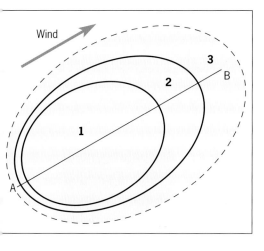

Cross-section

Flame height

A  1–2    3    2    1  B

**Stage 1: preheating**
Water is expelled from plants by nearby flames, drought or a hot dry day. Gases are released as the temperature rises and the wood breaks down by the process of pyrolysis.

**Stage 2: flaming combustion**
The wood burns fast and hot as the gases burn. Cracks develop in the wood and release more gases and flames, oils and resins. Energy is released by convection and radiation. Since wood is a poor heat conductor, the inside of the log may not burn unless the process of pyrolysis continues.

**Stage 3: glowing combustion**
Wood burns more slowly and at a lower temperature as the fire consumes the wood itself instead of the gases released by pyrolysis.

**Figure 6.34  The stages of wildfire**

# 6.7 Wildfire

Fire and human activity have been closely linked from early times when fire was first used for warmth, cooking, driving out game and clearing land for agriculture. Controlled fire is of benefit to people, but when uncontrolled, fire becomes a major hazard and is called wildfire or bushfire.

## The nature of wildfire

Fire is the rapid combination of oxygen with carbon, hydrogen and other organic material in a reaction producing flame, heat and light. The solar energy stored by plants during photosynthesis is returned to the atmosphere during fire. The fire consists of three main stages (Fig. 6.33). Wildfires may move slowly over the ground mainly as glowing combustion, advance as a wall of fire along a flaming combustion front, or move through the treetops as a crown fire. The nature of the fire itself will depend upon the types of plants, strength of the winds, topography and the fire behaviour itself (Fig. 6.35). The climate and nature of the fuel (the plants) are the two key factors.

Once the general climatic conditions have allowed the vegetation to dry out and become susceptible to burning, the nature of the fire event will depend upon wind speed and direction. The largest fires occur in dry, windy weather with low humidity. This is likely to affect a large region, resulting in a high fire frequency in one area. Major fires are of great significance, with 95 per cent of

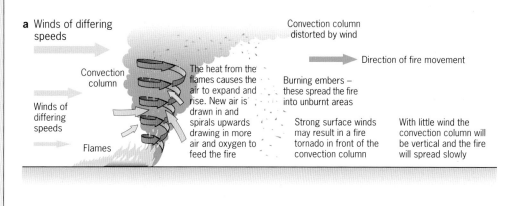

**Figure 6.35  Some fire types**

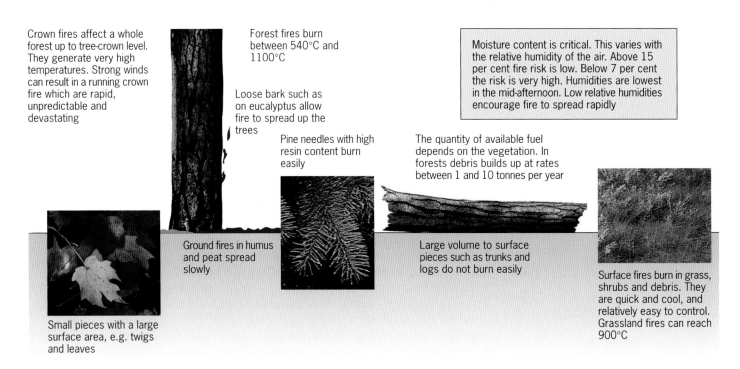

Crown fires affect a whole forest up to tree-crown level. They generate very high temperatures. Strong winds can result in a running crown fire which are rapid, unpredictable and devastating

Forest fires burn between 540°C and 1100°C

Loose bark such as on eucalyptus allow fire to spread up the trees

Pine needles with high resin content burn easily

The quantity of available fuel depends on the vegetation. In forests debris builds up at rates between 1 and 10 tonnes per year

Moisture content is critical. This varies with the relative humidity of the air. Above 15 per cent fire risk is low. Below 7 per cent the risk is very high. Humidities are lowest in the mid-afternoon. Low relative humidities encourage fire to spread rapidly

Ground fires in humus and peat spread slowly

Large volume to surface pieces such as trunks and logs do not burn easily

Surface fires burn in grass, shrubs and debris. They are quick and cool, and relatively easy to control. Grassland fires can reach 900°C

Small pieces with a large surface area, e.g. twigs and leaves

**Figure 6.36  Key characteristics of plants as fuel for wildfires**

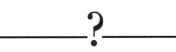

**23** Use Figure 6.36 to explain how plant fuel characteristics affect wildfire development.

Fire causes:
• worst drought for 50 years in Indonesia.
• plantation companies burning dry forest

Forest fires:
• covered 300 000 ha
• spread to 1 million ha of deep peat.
• caused smog affecting 70 million people

Air pollution:
• lasted several weeks.
• reached index of 839 (100–200 = hazardous)
• 35 000 Indonesians and 15 000 Malaysians treated for breathing problems
• haze caused two major accidents

burned land being caused by only 3 per cent of fires. Wind has the effect of driving flames forward, encouraging the pre-heating stage (Fig. 6.34). Burning embers which ignite more vegetation are more easily spread in windy conditions. The flaming edge of the fire (fire front) moves at a rate which increases with increasing wind velocity. A study of extreme fires in the eastern USA and south-east Australia found that most fire outbreaks occur near surface weather fronts, especially in warm, dry air ahead of a cold front with unstable air and strong winds at the surface. Fires are also aided by **Föhn** winds which bring hot, dry air over lowland areas, for example the Santa Ana in southern California and the Sirocco in southern Europe.

The plant fuel can vary considerably in size, arrangement, quantity and moisture content (Fig. 6.36).

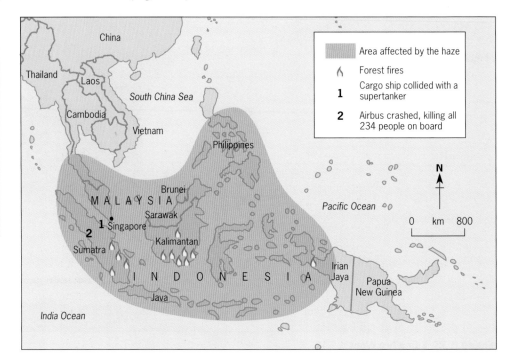

**Figure 6.37  The Indonesian forest fires of September 1997**

## Distribution and geographical location

Wildfire is mainly a rural hazard, with small communities being most at risk. However, in some areas of the world, the risk is increasing as low-density suburban development expands into vegetated areas, especially in MEDCs. These have vulnerable populations at low density in extensive suburban developments, as in California, southern Europe and Australia.

Natural fires occur in any environment where there is vegetation. Lightning strikes the earth somewhere on average 100 000 times a day, and can ignite any dry vegetation. It is the nature of that vegetation that is the key to whether fire takes hold following a lightning strike. Thus, areas of the world with a dry season, or semi-arid conditions, are most commonly affected.

The most fire-susceptible vegetation types are in the Mediterranean climatic regions. These include the Mediterranean Sea, California, parts of Australia; temperate and tropical grasslands; and forests which experience seasonal rainfall. In these areas, fire and natural ecosystem development are closely linked. Some vegetation types are very susceptible to burning. For example, eucalyptus trees have a high oil content which burns easily. These originated in Australia but have been exported to other semi-arid areas, including southern California, northern Africa, the Middle East and India. Thus, human activity has helped to spread this fire-prone vegetation. Cropland is also susceptible to burning, especially grain crops when ripening just before harvesting.

Fire is rarely a hazard in tropical rainforest environments due to high humidity and rainfall. However, a combination of forest clearance, human mismanagement and drought resulting from the El Niño event of 1997–98 produced fires burning out of control in South East Asia during September 1997 (Fig. 6.37). Temperate deciduous forests are also low risk since they lose their leaves in winter and are too humid to burn in summer, although susceptibility is higher in autumn. Tundra areas are low risk.

## Causes of wildfires

Natural fires are a frequent and regular event in grassland, bush and forest. Research in the USA shows that before human settlement, forest fires occurred with a return period of 70–80 years. Many ecosystems have been the result of, or extended by, human use of fire for clearing vegetation. This is the case with some savanna areas, temperate grasslands and maquis (chapparal) in Mediterranean regions. However, many fires are not due to lightning: between 80 and 90 per cent of fires that threaten residential areas are probably the result of human activity such as agricultural fires, children playing with matches, camp fires out of control, and carelessly discarded cigarettes. These causes have increased as leisure time and tourist activity have increased. Many fires also result from unknown causes, or arson. This may account for 32 per cent of fires in the USA.

## Impacts of wildfires

Wildfires result in loss of life, property, crops, timber and livestock. People can be easily trapped by fast-moving fire. In 1991 fires in Oakland and Berkeley Hills, California, trapped and killed 25 people and destroyed 2500 homes. In 1987, 870 000 ha of timber production forest were destroyed in the Da Xing An Ling area of north-east China. The fire killed 193 people and left 56 000 homeless.

Wildfires have environmental impacts. Intense forest fires can destroy nutrients and soil structure, and release a large amount of particulate material and toxic gases into the atmosphere (Fig. 6.38). The loss of vegetation increases soil erosion and flood risk. However, in some ecosystems fire is beneficial and vegetation is adapted to withstand fires. For example, in grassland, fire is the main agent of decomposition and nutrient recycling. In some forest ecosystems, for example Douglas fir, sequoia, and Ponderosa pine, fire is

**?**

**24** To what extent could wildfire be described as a quasi-natural hazard rather than a natural hazard?

**Figure 6.38 The Kuala Lumpur (Malaysia) skyline engulfed in haze from the Indonesian forest fires of September 1997**

**Figure 6.39 The two cycles of a pine forest with and without the benefits of frequent natural or prescribed fire**

beneficial and aids seed germination, stimulates some shrubs and herbs to regenerate and reduces insect and parasite populations. Ecosystems with natural fires have a patchwork of vegetation in different stages of maturity and a greater diversity of fauna.

## Managing wildfires

### Modify the event

In many countries the approach to fire management has been to suppress all fires, especially those near to populated areas and timber resources. Firefighting methods are dangerous and expensive, however. They include water or chemical spraying from the ground or the air to reduce heat, beating flames to smother oxygen or cutting gaps in the vegetation (firebreaks) to reduce fuel supply. Extinguishing all fires results in a build-up of vegetation and litter which will burn more intensely and destructively should a fire take hold.

In many forest areas and national parks controlled or prescribed burning is used as a management method (Fig. 6.39). This takes place under suitable weather conditions and removes the litter and lower vegetation but does not damage the trees, so the fuel availability for uncontrolled fires is reduced. A 50 per cent reduction in fuel availability results in a 50 per cent reduction in the spread of a fire, and a 75 per cent reduction in its intensity. Animal populations benefit from a more diverse ecosystem in different stages of **succession**. Controlled burning is increasingly used in the USA (Fig. 6.40) and Australia but there is some controversy over its use, especially in national park areas.

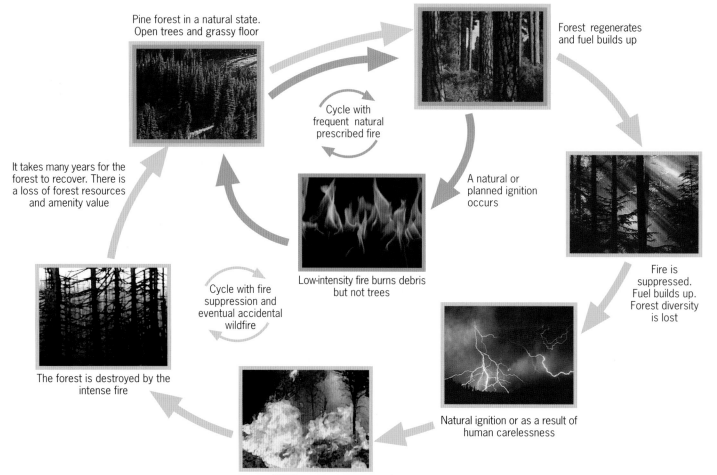

Pine forest in a natural state. Open trees and grassy floor

Forest regenerates and fuel builds up

Cycle with frequent natural prescribed fire

A natural or planned ignition occurs

Fire is suppressed. Fuel builds up. Forest diversity is lost

It takes many years for the forest to recover. There is a loss of forest resources and amenity value

Low-intensity fire burns debris but not trees

Cycle with fire suppression and eventual accidental wildfire

Natural ignition or as a result of human carelessness

The forest is destroyed by the intense fire

Wildfire occurs

Hazard-resistant design can be used in buildings to reduce the likelihood of destruction. Many homes in fire-prone areas are made of wood with vegetation close by. Fire resistance can be increased by taking preventative measures, such as making sure that there are no trees or other flammable materials near the house or that chimneys have spark arresters fitted, or using clay, concrete and firebreaks when designing houses.

### Modifying vulnerability

The weather and biomass conditions which result in fires are well understood and prediction and warning systems can convey this to the public. Notice boards in national park areas can warn tourists of the fire hazard. Lookout points and surveillance aircraft can also be used.

Since most wildfires have human causes, community preparedness is a key management approach. In many countries there are established rural firefighting groups and management systems for large fires, for example, for evacuation and co-ordination. Public education concerning home safety and the causes of wildfire by human carelessness, and the benefits of prescribed burning, are also used.

Land-use planning involves the use of firebreaks as part of rural land-use planning and mapping of fire hazards.

### Modifying the loss

Insurance is a common approach in MEDCs, run by the private sector, but this has limitations (see section 2.4). Aid has a role following fire disasters, though this is usually at the national or regional level.

**Figure 6.40 Ponderosa Pine forest, Kaibab National Forest, Arizona, USA. The forest floor has been cleared by a controlled fire to reduce the spread of fire in the litter layer. There is some scorching of lower branches, but the trees remain unburnt.**

**25** Suggest why the policy of controlled burning might be opposed and by whom.

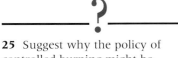

# The western USA fires, summer 2000

The worst fires in the USA for 50 years burned over parts of 11 states from late march until early autumn (Fig. 6.41). The region had been affected by widespread drought and summer dry lightning (without rain) ignited thedry vegetation. The result over the summer was 65 316 fires damaging 4.5 million acres, with 66 large fires across 11 states. The worst affected states were Montana and Idaho (Fig. 6.42). In Montana, 375 000 acres wer burnt, destroying 169 buildings including 50 homes. In California, 90 000 acres were burnt, including 72 000 in the Sequoia National Forest Park. The fires resulted in eleven deaths, including eight firefighters.

**Figure 6.41 Extent of the summer 2000 fires**

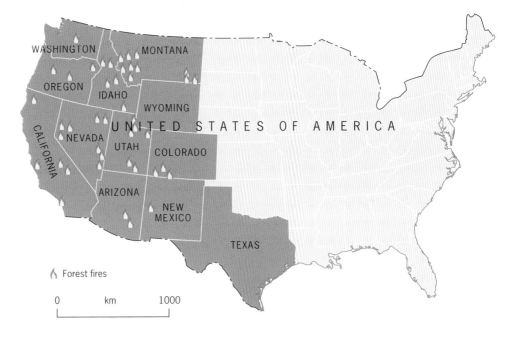

The management strategies focused on using fire fighters to stop the fires and evacuation of areas at risk. Air tankers were used to drop fire retardant or water, with up to 150 aircraft involved. The USA fire fighters consist of 13 000 fire fighters in 64 crews of 'Hot Shot'. They were supplemented at the worst times in July and August with up to 1500 US troops. At the worst of the fires, international help consisted of 79 fire fighters from Australia and New Zealand helping in the state of Montana. The costs of fire fighting were put at $15 million per day. the teams were mainly in areas where water supplies were not available due to remoteness. Thus the strategy was to clear vegetation ahead of the fires to form fire breaks. Evacuation of residents from areas at risk wa used in populated areas. For example, in Bitterroot Valley near to Hamilton, Montana, 1400 residents were evacuated as 120 000 acres burned.

**Figure 6.42 Flames leap skyward as wild fires in the American West burn uncontrolled, with the state of Montana suffering the worst effects of the inferno**

## Summary

- Atmospheric hazards are widespread in occurrence, scale and duration. They can result in a range of secondary hazards, including wildfire, landsliding and flooding.

- El Niño–Southern Oscillation events result in an increase in atmospheric and related secondary hazards in large areas of the Earth. Monitoring of El Niño events is increasingly important in hazard prediction.

- Tropical cyclones (hurricanes and typhoons) are the most significant natural hazards in terms of loss of life and damage to property. The conditions for their formation are well documented.

- Tropical cyclones are classified by their intensity and result in wind, flood and storm-surge hazards.

- Tropical cyclones are managed by prediction and warning systems, evacuation, land-use planning and hazard-resistant design.

- Tornadoes are the most violent storms but are relatively small in size and short-lived events.

- Tornado development is related to cumulonimbus cloud and thunderstorm activity. Unlike tropical cyclones, tornadoes are most common in mid-latitudes, especially the Great Plains of the USA.

- Tornadoes are managed by prediction and warning systems, and community preparedness.

- Drought is a shortfall of water (rainfall) below 'normal' conditions which results in hydrological, agricultural and ecological impacts. They are related to persistent anticyclonic conditions and El Niño events.

- The impacts of drought are long term and vary with social, economic and political factors. In extreme cases, drought can result in much human suffering and famine.

- Drought is managed by a range of methods, but aid is relatively important in its management.

- Wildfire is associated with seasonally dry climates or drought conditions. Many fires are the result of human activity (quasi-natural).

- Wildfires result in loss of life, property, crops, timber and livestock. There may be environmental impacts, although in many ecosystems fire is linked with vegetation succession.

- Management of wildfires centres upon controlling the event and public education programmes.

# 7 Geomorphological hazards

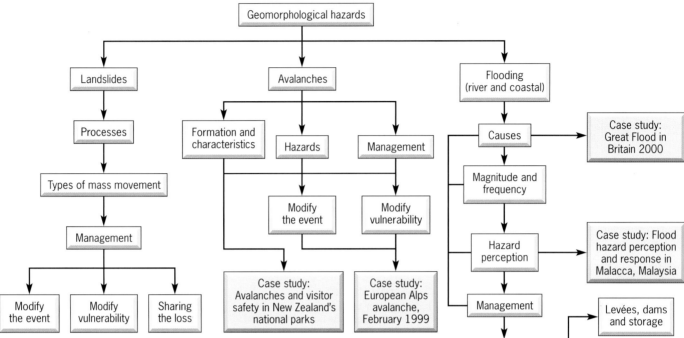

Hazards in the lithosphere are the result of the interaction of hydrological, geological and atmospheric factors. The hazards produced can also occur or be intensified as a result of human activity. People are more able to modify hydrological and geomorphological processes than other geophysical systems. Geomorphological hazards are often closely linked with atmospheric processes, and some events may be produced as secondary hazards of tectonic processes.

## 7.1 Landslides

Landslides are movements of rock, sediment or soil by falling, toppling, sliding and flowing. These mass-movement processes are part of slope evolution and mass wasting as the land surface is lowered (Fig. 7.1).

*Processes resulting in landsliding*
Most landslides involve the movement of rock or debris along a slip surface. Most of the time there is a balance between the stresses acting on material resting on or forming a hillslope. For a landslide to occur, the balance between the strength of the materials and the stresses acting on them is changed (Table 7.1).

All slopes are affected by mass movements but some have underlying geological characteristics which encourage large-scale movement. Clay absorbs water in its structure and water clings to its surface, making **internal cohesion** weak. Pre-existing slide surfaces are areas of weakness and can be reactivated. Other geological weaknesses are rock layers dipping down the hillslope, weak cement, soft layers mixed with harder layers, or heavy jointing. When a landslide occurs the failure of the materials is usually for a number of reasons (Table 7.1). Common landslide triggers are earthquakes, heavy rain, the thawing of frozen ground, and human building projects or road construction. Volcanic activity can produce lahars which are potentially lethal.

## Type of movement

**Falls**

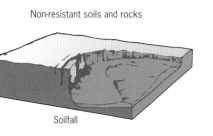

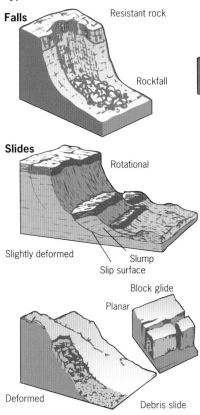

**Slides**

**Flows**

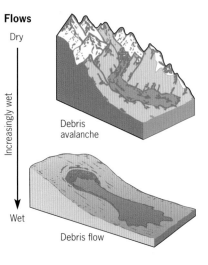

**Figure 7.1  The main mass-movement types of landslides (left and above). Mass movements are variable in size and speed, ranging from very small-volume movements of 1m³ to movements of over 1 million m³. Distances can vary from a few centimetres to tens of kilometres, and speeds from very slow (0.6 m/year) to 3 m/sec. Landslides or mass movements are classified by the type of movement, but there may be combinations of these in any one event. (*Source:* Selby, 1993)**

### Table 7.1  Forces acting on material on a slope

**Upsetting the balance – how to cause a landslide**

**Decrease the shear strength**

- Increasing the water content of the slope materials. This reduces **internal cohesion** and **internal friction**. This is the most common cause of mass movements. The role of pore-water pressure is very important. Water trapped in rock and sediment pores is under pressure from the material above it. The more the material is compressed and the higher the water content, the higher the pore-water pressure. This can be enough to lift up sediment and start movement.

- As overlying material is removed by mass movements, the material beneath has less weight on it. Expansion occurs in a 'stress-relaxation' process. This opens up cracks and gaps which increases the **porosity** and allows more water to enter.

- Weathering processes break down rock minerals into new clay and other minerals which expand when water is present. As rock weathering continues, the proportion of these clay minerals will increase in some rock types.

- Burrowing animals or the development of soil pipes by **throughflow** of water will weaken the slope materials.

- Removal of vegetation (for example, as a result of wildfires) or through human activity such as overgrazing, building and deforestation. Surface materials are looser with the loss of roots.

**Increase the shear strength**

- An increase in slope angle, especially at the base of the slope. This can result from natural processes such as river and marine erosion, but also occurs because of human activity, for example, building a road at the base of the slope.

- An additional weight on the slope due to increased water content. Sedimentary rocks have a porosity of 10–30 per cent, and when these spaces are filled with water the weight can increase greatly. Other causes are mass movement of material from upslope or human activity building on the slope.

- Shocks and vibrations from an earthquake or heavy machinery.

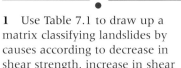

**1** Use Table 7.1 to draw up a matrix classifying landslides by causes according to decrease in shear strength, increase in shear stress, human processes and natural processes.

## Landslides as a hazard

Recent hazard assessments rank landslides as thirteenth among natural hazards in terms of human impacts. Between 1945 and 1990 there were 33 events with death tolls of 50 or more. These killer events are the result of rapid, high-energy landslides which move large amounts of material downslope and bury people and buildings. However, these events are high-magnitude, low-frequency events. They are mainly associated with geologically active fold mountain belts where uplift and erosion produce unstable steep slopes, for example, the Himalayas, Andes, Apennines and Alps.

There are also huge numbers of small and medium-sized events which may not result in loss of life, though together these result in large financial losses in damage to buildings and roads. These impacts have been used to classify landslides as a landslide damage intensity scale (Table 7.2). In hazard

**Table 7.2  Landslide damage intensity scale**

| Grade | Description of damage | Grade | Description of damage |
|---|---|---|---|
| 0 | *None:* Building is intact | | and window frames too distorted to use; occupants must be evacuated and major repairs carried out. |
| 1 | *Negligible:* Hairline cracks in walls or structural members: no distortion of structure or detachment of external architectural details. | 5 | *Very serious:* Walls out of plumb by 5–6 degrees; structure grossly distorted and differential settlement will have seriously cracked floors and walls or caused major rotation or slewing of the building (wooden buildings may have detached completely from their foundations). Partition walls and brick infill will have at least partly collapsed; roof may have partially collapsed; outhouses, porches and patios may have been damaged more seriously than the principal structure itself. Occupants will need to be rehoused on a long-term basis, and rehabilitation of the building will probably not be feasible. |
| 2 | *Light:* Building continues to be habitable: repair not urgent. Settlement of foundations, distortion of structure and inclination of walls are not sufficient to compromise overall stability. | | |
| 3 | *Moderate:* Walls out of perpendicular by 1–2 degrees, or substantial cracking has occurred to structural members, or foundations have settled during differential subsidence of at least 15 cm; building requires evacuation and rapid attention to ensure its continued life. | | |
| 4 | *Serious:* Walls out of perpendicular by several degrees; open cracks in walls; fracture of structural members; fragmentation of masonry; differential settlement of at least 25 cm compromises foundations; floors may be inclined by 1–2 degrees, or ruined by soil heave; internal partition walls will need to be replaced; door | 6 | *Partial collapse:* Requires immediate evacuation of the occupants and cordoning off the site to prevent accidents from falling masonry. |
| | | 7 | *Total collapse:* Requires clearance of the site. |

assessments, landsliding impacts may also be costed as a part of the heavy rainfall and flooding, earthquake or volcanic eruption which was the final trigger for their occurrence. This makes evaluating the significance of landsliding more difficult.

Worldwide, the average death toll from landsliding is thought to be about 600 per year. Areas in the tropics susceptible to hurricanes, earthquakes and active mountain belts are especially vulnerable. In Japan, the hazard is high because of snow melt, typhoons, susceptible geological structures and volcanic eruptions.

Human activity has been important in increasing landslide activity, some of which has been catastrophic. Urban areas are vulnerable, particularly shanty towns developed on deforested unstable slopes. The result has been landslide disasters in Caracas (Venezuela), Cuzco (Peru) and Rio de Janeiro (Brazil). In Hong Kong blocks of flats have collapsed, killing 64 people in 1966 and 138 in

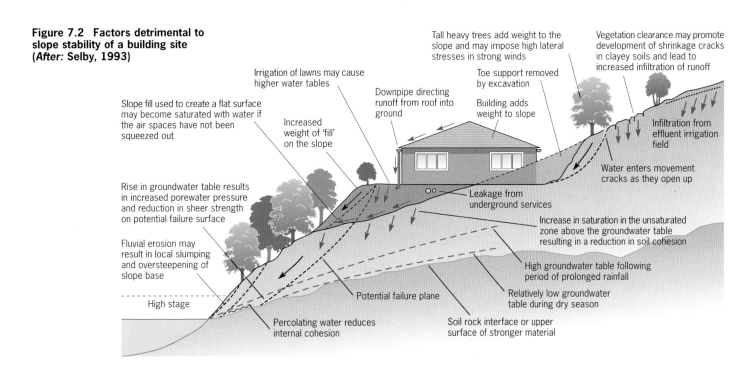

**Figure 7.2  Factors detrimental to slope stability of a building site (*After:* Selby, 1993)**

Tall heavy trees add weight to the slope and may impose high lateral stresses in strong winds

Vegetation clearance may promote development of shrinkage cracks in clayey soils and lead to increased infiltration of runoff

Irrigation of lawns may cause higher water tables

Toe support removed by excavation

Downpipe directing runoff from roof into ground

Building adds weight to slope

Slope fill used to create a flat surface may become saturated with water if the air spaces have not been squeezed out

Increased weight of 'fill' on the slope

Infiltration from effluent irrigation field

Water enters movement cracks as they open up

Rise in groundwater table results in increased porewater pressure and reduction in sheer strength on potential failure surface

Leakage from underground services

Increase in saturation in the unsaturated zone above the groundwater table resulting in a reduction in soil cohesion

Fluvial erosion may result in local slumping and oversteepening of slope base

High groundwater table following period of prolonged rainfall

Potential failure plane

Relatively low groundwater table during dry season

High stage

Percolating water reduces internal cohesion

Soil rock interface or upper surface of stronger material

**?**

**2** Why is it difficult to assess the significance of landsliding as a hazard?

**3** Use Figure 7.2 to explain how building increases the risk of slope failure. Structure your answer in terms of increasing shear stress and decreasing shear strength.

1972. Building and road developments cut sections out of slopes and fill in other areas. These may increase instability. Buildings add weight and have other impacts (Fig. 7.2). In the Mediterranean, deforestation of geologically active slopes with clay and sand deposits have resulted in catastrophic landsliding, especially in Italy. A survey in Los Angeles County, USA, shows how human activity can increase slope movement: of the landslides over 30 m in size, about 15 per cent were developed by grading activities (i.e. cutting and filling new slopes) and 25–30 per cent by building activity.

The significance of the landsliding hazard varies spatially and in time as response to both physical and human factors. Human vulnerability to landsliding is increasing as urbanisation continues and more roads are cut through mountainous regions.

## Types of mass movement

### Rockfall
The simplest mass movements are rockfalls. These occur on steep slopes, and blocks of rock are broken away along weaknesses such as joints and bedding planes. Under normal conditions only a small number of blocks fall at any one time, but large falls may be triggered by an earthquake.

### Slides
Slides occur along one or more failure surface (Fig. 7.1). A rotational slide moves downwards and outwards along a curved slip surface. The horizontal distance moved is relatively short because of this curved movement, so damage may be severe but is not widespread. Translational slides, however, can cover

**Figure 7.3 Cross-section of the 1970 Nevados Huascarán debris avalanche. Key elements were the initial vertical fall, air-launching over glacial-debris hills, splitting of the avalanche into two lobes, and flow as wet debris. (Source: Abbott, 1996)**

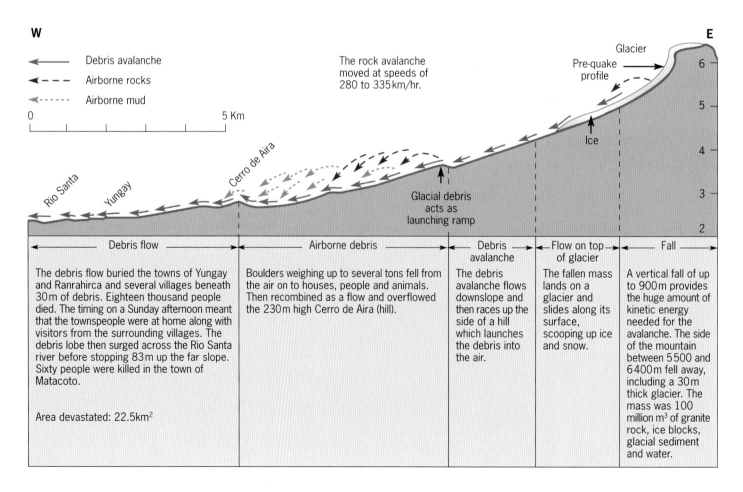

larger areas as the rock mass moves down and out and continues as far as the driving force and sloping surface allow. If the material becomes deformed the result is a debris slide.

### Flows

In a flow the moving material behaves like a fluid. The material can range in size from huge boulders (debris flow) to clay grains (mudflow). Loose, unconsolidated sediment is particularly susceptible after heavy rain or earthquake-shaking. Lahars are mudflows associated with volcanic activity which cause widespread destruction, as with the Nevado del Ruiz eruption (see page 69). Many mass movements involve complex combinations of falls, slides and flows: for example, the earthquake-triggered Nevados Huascarán rock avalanche (Fig. 7.3).

**Figure 7.4  A mudslide killed 13 people in 10 seconds in a Swiss village during October 2000. Days of heavy rain had increased the shear strength on the slope, triggering the mass movement.**

# 100 feared dead as mudslides hit south Italy

Up to 100 Italians were feared dead in a series of mudslides set off by freak heavy rains in the southern region of Campania yesterday. As hundreds of troops joined in the rescue effort, regional authorities and the Italian government were accused of failing to take steps to prevent the disaster.

At least 25 people were confirmed dead while 70 others were listed as missing and feared dead and about 800 were made homeless. Houses, apartment blocks, cars and fire engines were swept away in rivers of mud that streaked through the towns of Sarno, Siano and Bracigliano in the province of Salerno and the town of Quindici in the province of Avellino. About 2000 people had to be evacuated in Sarno, the worst-hit town, after landslides on two mountains, Mount Saro and Mount Le Porche, turned to mud.

'The mountain opened up in five places and a sea of mud poured down like lava,' explained one of the rescue workers.

The region had been doused with heavy rainfall over the previous six days.

Rescue workers used 18 helicopters to scour the stricken area for survivors. Among the dead and missing were patients and doctors at the Sarno hospital, which was engulfed by a wave of mud.

The rising death toll prompted authorities to point the finger at past corruption in local government which allowed property development in areas of high risk. Campania is prone to landslides, which have killed 372 people over the past 50 years.

Fausto Bertinotti, the leader of the left-wing Rifondazione Comunista party, said the government of Romano Prodi, the Prime Minister, and the regional administration were to blame for the mudslides as they had not carried out preventative work after five landslides last year killed 20 people in Campania.

Ecological groups, including the World Wide Fund for Nature

and Italy's Legambiente, said that the disaster 'was not a natural calamity but a disaster caused by decades of ransacking the land and sprawling construction.'

Among those criticised was Franco Barberi, the Under-secretary for Civil Defence, who replied that there had been delays in making available 53 billion lire (£17 million) earmarked by authorities in Rome for work in Campania.

Seven people died in Sarno and there were reports of 50 people missing.

Four people died when they were carried away by a mudslide at Siano.

The bodies of a 34-year-old woman and her three children aged between four and 12 were washed out into a street in Bracigliano early yesterday after a mudslide hit the village the previous night, the authorities said. Another two people were reported to have died in the village.

Landslides and flooding left five dead and several missing in Quindici while at San Felice a Cancello, near Caserte, a 73-year-old woman was crushed to death in her home by a flood of mud and stones.

About 65 per cent of Italy is classed as being at risk from landslides. The worst disaster of this kind on record happened in Campania in 1954, when heavy rains brought mass landslides which killed 205 people and made another 5466 homeless.

Luigi Manfredi, a senator for the opposition Forza Italia party, called for a parliamentary commission of inquiry to be opened into the state of civil protection in Italy.

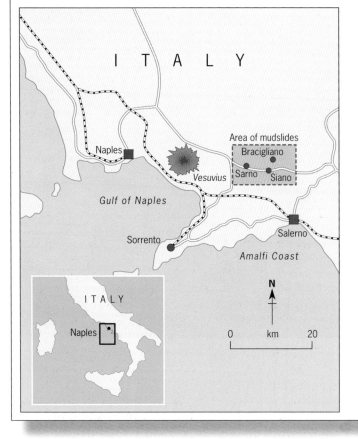

**Figure 7.5  Newspaper article: 100 feared dead as mudslides hit south Italy (*Source: The Times*, 7 May 1998)**

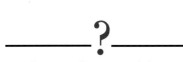

**4** What was the cause of the landslide in Southern Italy? Use a diagram to explain your answer.

**5** Why is there concern that property development had been allowed in areas of high risk? Explain how buildings would affect the stability of the slopes.

**6** Ecological groups consider the mudslides to be a quasi-natural hazard (see page 80). Explain fully their viewpoint in the case of these events.

**7** List the factors you would consider when assessing an area as a landslide risk.

**8** Suggest why hazard mapping as a technique for landslide hazard management is not widely used in LEDCs.

**9a** Is legal liability a useful hazard management strategy?
**b** Who should bear the responsibility by paying the costs – the buyer, the developer, or the local government giving the permission? Explain your answer.

# 7.2 Managing the landslide hazard

*Modifying the event*

Slope stability can be increased by a variety of engineering techniques which, although expensive, enable control of landsliding to be largely successful (Fig. 7.6). There are two key issues with this approach to landslide hazard management: cost and responsibility. Government funding may be available for emergency stabilisation techniques but only rarely for permanent slope stabilisation. However, building codes can enforce some use of these techniques by private developers.

*Modify vulnerability*

Most mass movements are not very rapid and thus forecasting, warning and evacuation are possible techniques. Community preparedness can be used if people are aware of the early signs of movement such as bulging walls, tension cracks, tilted poles and fences, and new areas of waterlogged ground.

Hazard mapping is increasingly being used, especially in MEDCs, as the factors which favour landsliding can be assessed to produce a hazard map. For vulnerability to be assessed, land uses need to be part of the mapping process. Landslide hazard assessment maps are ways of predicting the landslide threat using the factors which influence slope stability. However, forecasting the magnitude and frequency of events is not possible. Forecasts are based on work after initial signs of slope movement have been detected. Work to produce landslide susceptibility maps provides an excellent framework for land-use planning, development control, building regulations, and setting insurance premiums. For this method to be effective, however, the hazard must be perceived as being predictable and laws must be enforced. There may be problems in using this approach in already developed areas, where a high hazard rating may reduce land values.

**Sharing the loss**

Private insurance for landslide hazards is not easily available due to the high risks involved for the insurance companies. In the USA only mudslides resulting from flooding can be covered. Legal liability is becoming an increasingly common loss-sharing adjustment. Since the landslide-producing processes are well understood the 'Acts of God' argument when landslides occur is losing credibility, especially if slopes have been regraded for building in a way which has destabilised the slope. Costs in the USA have been shared by developers and in some cases local governments who have given permission for the development. Only in New Zealand is complete landslide insurance protection available.

# 7.3 Snow avalanches

*Avalanche formation and characteristics*

An avalanche is a rapid movement of snow down a slope as a result of structural weakness in the snow cover on the slope. The forces acting on a snow mass are similar to those involved in mass movements (Table 7.1).

There are three main forms of snow avalanche with different characteristics of slope failure, flow and occurrence – loose snow, slab and slush. Slab avalanches are potentially the most dangerous since large masses of snow are involved. Snow builds up in layers following each snowfall event. Initially the density is low, but as snow continues to be added the density in the lower layers increases as air is squeezed out to form **firn**. However, in some snow packs the snow becomes less dense in places as ice and snow crystals grow and the voids between them are enlarged. This forms a weak layer in the snow called a depth hoar. Thawing and refreezing between different snowfalls produces boundaries which act as weaknesses within the snow pack.

For an avalanche to occur the slope must be steep enough to allow the snow to slide. Avalanches therefore occur mainly on 25°–40° slopes. On lower slope angles the shear stresses are insufficient to encourage the snow to fail and on steeper slopes, especially above 60°, it is rare for enough snow to collect to result in an avalanche. Large avalanches are most numerous above the tree line in regions of heavy snowfall, rapid temperature changes which cause the snow to melt, or where rain falls on to the snow. Spring is the most likely season since the snow pack is large after the winter falls, and temperature changes are likely to be more frequent. In the French Alps, 77 per cent of avalanches occur between January and March.

Avalanches tend to recur at the same sites and can be detected by breaks of slope, eroded sections, damaged vegetation of different ages, and debris mounds in the runout zone. Where an avalanche has been very large or plunged over steep slopes there may be depressions formed by the impact of snow and debris. Slush avalanches form depositional features such as fans and boulder tongues.

### Avalanches as hazards

Most avalanches are too small or remote to be a problem. However, in areas of human activity they represent a major hazard. As settlement expands into

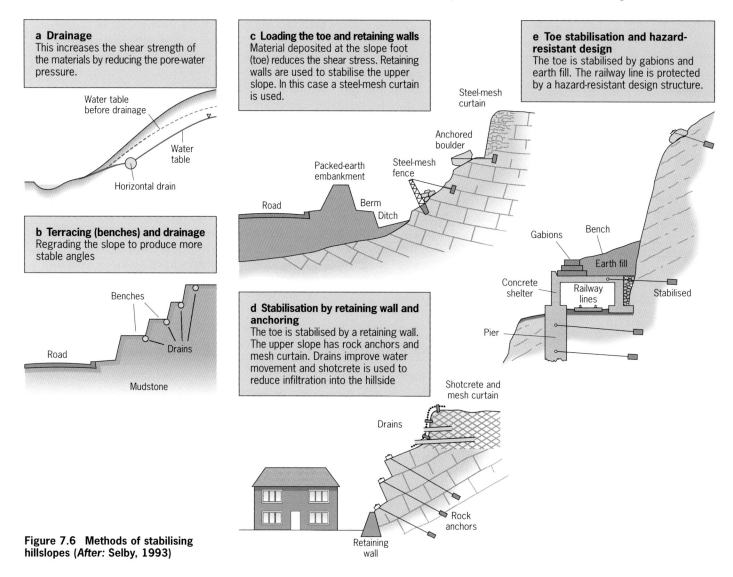

**a Drainage**
This increases the shear strength of the materials by reducing the pore-water pressure.

Water table before drainage
Water table
Horizontal drain

**b Terracing (benches) and drainage**
Regrading the slope to produce more stable angles

Benches
Drains
Road
Mudstone

**c Loading the toe and retaining walls**
Material deposited at the slope foot (toe) reduces the shear stress. Retaining walls are used to stabilise the upper slope. In this case a steel-mesh curtain is used.

Packed-earth embankment
Road
Berm
Ditch
Steel-mesh fence
Anchored boulder
Steel-mesh curtain

**d Stabilisation by retaining wall and anchoring**
The toe is stabilised by a retaining wall. The upper slope has rock anchors and mesh curtain. Drains improve water movement and shotcrete is used to reduce infiltration into the hillside

Shotcrete and mesh curtain
Drains
Rock anchors
Retaining wall

**e Toe stabilisation and hazard-resistant design**
The toe is stabilised by gabions and earth fill. The railway line is protected by a hazard-resistant design structure.

Gabions
Bench
Earth fill
Concrete shelter
Railway lines
Stabilised
Pier

**Figure 7.6 Methods of stabilising hillslopes** (*After:* Selby, 1993)

**Figure 7.7** Avalanches are a cloud of snow particles but when they hit something solid they pack together and become like concrete. A force of 100 tonnes per square metre can be exerted.

mountainous regions and tourist development increases, people are becoming increasingly vulnerable. Infrastructures such as communications, and power-line and transport routes are also at risk.

Death and injury from avalanches are the result of impacts which fracture limbs, suffocation as a result of pressure of snow, inhaling powdery snow, hypothermia, exhaustion, frostbite and shock. Buildings and structures are at risk from impact pressures of up to 100 tonnes/m² which can move reinforced concrete structures.

Avalanches are confined to mountainous regions of the world, especially in arctic and temperate regions. Their frequency is highly variable, according to local climatic and topographic conditions. The areas of highest hazard exist where there is human settlement and tourist development such as the Alps, Scandinavian countries, and the US and Canadian Rockies. Since trees make the snow cover more patchy and prevent large snow masses accumulating, deforestation for settlements, tourist development and infrastructure has added to the hazard. In the USA there are up to 10 000 potentially dangerous avalanches per year, but only about 1 per cent harm people or property. In the Andes, avalanche deaths are associated with mining developments. The higher population density of the European Alps results in a relatively high death toll which in Switzerland averages 20–30 per year. Until the mid-1980s, avalanche deaths showed an upward trend with the greatest risk in tourist towns and along transport corridors. Recent figures suggest that this trend has been halted by management methods. About 70 per cent of fatalities in MEDCs are now associated with voluntary risk, such as skiers and mountain-climbers. However, disasters still occur in all areas and mountain communities are always directly at risk or suffer being cut off as roads and infrastructure are damaged.

*Managing the snow avalanche hazard*

**Modifying the event**
In some areas of the world, avalanches are managed by environmental control through artificial avalanche creation. By creating a series of smaller avalanches at safe times, the hazard can be controlled as the snow pack is removed. This approach is expensive and uses explosives and military weapons.

Most management techniques aim to retain the snow on the mountainside or to deflect the avalanche should one occur (Fig. 7.8). The techniques are expensive and can be unsightly.

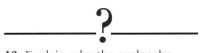

**10** Explain why the avalanche hazard has increased in recent years.

**11** Why are remote mountain regions and tourist developments particularly vulnerable?

**12** For each structure shown in Figure 7.8, explain its purpose in avalanche modification.

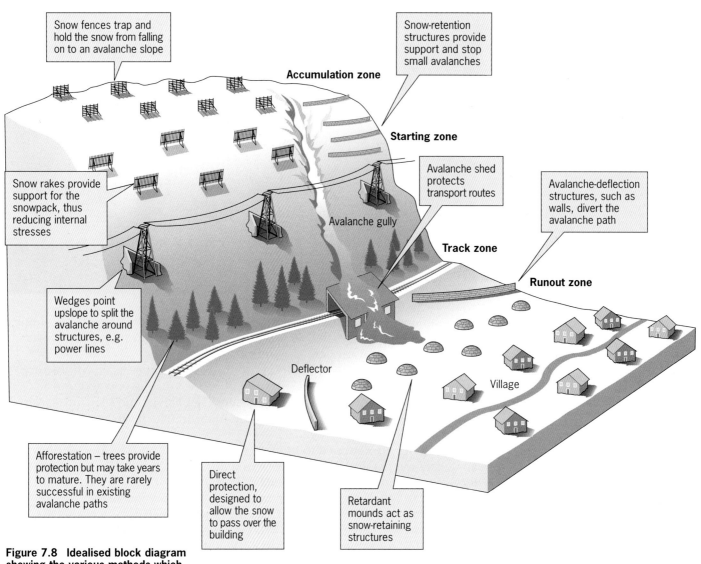

Snow fences trap and hold the snow from falling on to an avalanche slope

Snow-retention structures provide support and stop small avalanches

**Accumulation zone**

**Starting zone**

Snow rakes provide support for the snowpack, thus reducing internal stresses

Avalanche shed protects transport routes

Avalanche-deflection structures, such as walls, divert the avalanche path

Avalanche gully

**Track zone**

**Runout zone**

Wedges point upslope to split the avalanche around structures, e.g. power lines

Deflector

Village

Afforestation – trees provide protection but may take years to mature. They are rarely successful in existing avalanche paths

Direct protection, designed to allow the snow to pass over the building

Retardant mounds act as snow-retaining structures

**Figure 7.8 Idealised block diagram showing the various methods which are available for the physical modification of avalanches. Only one or two devices are likely to be in place in any one avalanche-prone vicinity. (After: Smith, 1996)**

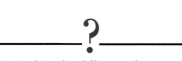

**13** Explain the difference between forecasting and prediction as applied to avalanche management.

**14** How is new technology helping in the management of avalanches?

## Modifying vulnerability

Warning systems are common for avalanche hazards, and nearly 30 countries have systems in operation which use both forecasts and prediction. Forecasts are used for day-to-day management of winter sports area, whereas predictions are used for hazard land zoning. Forecasting is not precise but involves regular snow stability tests and meteorological data. Major ski resorts may repeat these daily and offer forecasts on the Internet. Avalanches triggered by storms are the easiest to forecast but snowpack changes are more difficult.

Since avalanche tracks are often used repeatedly, land-use planning is a useful method of hazard mitigation. In Switzerland avalanche hazard maps have existed since 1878. Today, three zones are used: high potential hazard, moderate and no hazard. These are based on topographic maps, field observation, long-term records, and run-out distance. However, this approach requires much financial and time investment, which is not always possible in more remote regions such as the Himalayas. Work is under way in Switzerland to develop avalanche hazard maps using satellite imagery based upon forest cover. It is hoped that this work will enable safer route planning and tourist developments in areas lacking detailed mapping.

# The European Alps avalanches, February 1999

The Alps of Europe had one of the heaviest snowfalls of the twentieth century over the winter of 1998–99.

By the end of February 1999, 150 000 people were trapped in their villages due to impassable roads. During January and February, 70 people were killed in avalanches in the Alps (Fig. 7.9). This was more than double the usual death toll for the region which, over the last few years, has seen deaths reduced due to successful avalanche hazard management. However, global warming effects are likely to mean that snow falls in larger amounts and later in the season. This will mean that the nature and location of the avalanche hazard may need to be reconsidered. The winter of 1998–99 may be the first signs of these changes in the nature of alpine avalanches.

**Figure 7.9 Avalanches were widespread in the Alps. Here the Swiss Army join rescue workers at Evolene, Switzerland where eight people were missing**

**Figure 7.10 Progression of the avalanche**

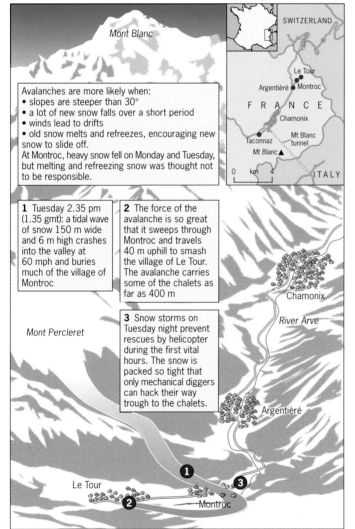

Mont Blanc

Avalanches are more likely when:
• slopes are steeper than 30°
• a lot of new snow falls over a short period
• winds lead to drifts
• old snow melts and refreezes, encouraging new snow to slide off.
At Montroc, heavy snow fell on Monday and Tuesday, but melting and refreezing snow was thought not to be responsible.

**1** Tuesday 2.35 pm (1.35 gmt): a tidal wave of snow 150 m wide and 6 m high crashes into the valley at 60 mph and buries much of the village of Montroc

**2** The force of the avalanche is so great that it sweeps through Montroc and travels 40 m uphill to smash the village of Le Tour. The avalanche carries some of the chalets as far as 400 m

**3** Snow storms on Tuesday night prevent rescues by helicopter during the first vital hours. The snow is packed so tight that only mechanical diggers can hack their way trough to the chalets.

Mont Percleret

SWITZERLAND

Le Tour
Argentière ● Montroc
F R A N C E
Chamonix
Taconnaz
Mt Blanc tunnel
Mt Blanc ▲
0   km   4
ITALY

Chamonix
River Arve
Argentière
Le Tour
Montroc

Two main events (slab avalanches) accounted for nearly half of the 1999 deaths: the village of Le Tour in the French Alps and the Austrian ski resort of Galtur.

## Le Tour, 9 February 1999

The villages of Montroc and Le Tour are close to the town of Chamonix in the French Alps. They are both in an area familiar either with the avalanche hazard but the location of the villages at the bottom of Alpine valleys were not considered at risk from avalanches. There had been no significant avalanches near to the villages for 91 years and they had been designated as 'white zone', i.e. not at risk from avalanches. The event itself (Fig. 7.10) was unusual for three reasons:

• the avalanche travelled at 97 kph
• it was at a very low altitude (low risk area)
• it was very large and powerful
• it travelled uphill.

The event destroyed 18 Alpine chalets, killing 12 people and burying another 20 people who were later rescued. The rescuers had to use heavy digging equipment as the low temperatures meant that the snow packed too hard for hands and shovels to be effective.

**Figure 7.11 Rescue workers in action carefully probe the snow for survivors**

## Galtur, Austria, 23 February 1999

The worst Austrian avalanche disaster since 1954 struck the Tyrolean village of Galtur at 4.00 p.m. The event was preceded by huge amounts of snow during February with 3.7 metres falling in the Galtur area. This was over four times the monthly average. As well as the huge amount of fresh snow, the pattern of the snowfall increased the avalanche risk. Temperatures had fluctuated so that heavy wet snow fell on top of dry snow, forming unstable boundaries in the snow pack. In addition, high winds of over 150 kph stripped snow off exposed peaks and resulted in huge accumulation elsewhere. The avalanche lasted for 16 seconds as an 800-m wide section of snow broke off the upper valley slopes and travelled at 200 kph downhill to Galtur in the valley bottom.

If people have not been crushed to death, they can survive for about 15 minutes buried in the snow before suffocating. Local people rescued 40 people but 30 died in the event. About 40 000 were stranded in the ski resorts of the area due to road closure. A 4-year-old boy was rescued after being buried for 100 minutes. This relatively long survival time is unusual and more common in the very young since their bodies can slow down more rapidly due to a relatively small surface area. The body's metabolism slows down so much that the brain and other organs require very little oxygen. The heart will beat very slowly, e.g. 2 times a minute.

This avalanche caused some concern in terms of management approaches. 300 rescuers and sniffer dogs were brought into the area although there was much concern that they took 15 hours to arrive. There was anger amongst tourists that some tour operators continued to send people to the area when they knew it was high risk. Poor visibility due to the heavy snowfall in early February meant that teams from Galtur did not remove snow from high-risk avalanche areas. Normally, they would use explosives to cause controlled avalanches. On 20 February meteorologists issued a clear avalanche warning for the area. Some tour operators had airlifted tourists out of the area but there was no overall evacuation of the area. Indeed some of the more wealthy tourists arranged private flights to escape the area.

**15** Suggest the criteria that would be used in constructing an avalanche hazard map.

**16** Could the Le Tour event have been avoided? Explain your answer.

**17** What physical events gave the ideal conditions for avalanches as in the Galtur event.

**18** What human errors added to the scale of the Galtur disaster?

**19** What lessons can be learned from the winter of 1989–99 for future avalanche hazard management?

# Avalanches and visitor safety in New Zealand's national parks

New Zealand's national parks are largely in mountainous areas with spectacular scenery. Risk from avalanches is potentially high when people congregate on ski-fields and glaciers. Visitors to the national parks have increased by 10 per cent per year as a result of a dramatic increase in outdoor recreation activities. There are now 23 ski-fields in New Zealand, the most popular being Whakapapa ski-field in Tongariro National Park which receives more than two million visits each winter season and up to 8 000 skiers at one time (Fig. 7.12).

Visitors are varied in their risk awareness. Some are motivated by the risk-taking but others are unaware of the avalanche hazard. Park managers accept a moral responsibility for visitor safety although there is no clear legal requirement. Park management assumes responsibility when accidents occur.

Avalanches are a widespread hazard since conditions are favourable for avalanche development. There is heavy precipitation, the southern hemisphere south-westerlies bring frontal rain and strong winds which can melt the snow and cause drifting. Cirque hollows and other glacial erosion sites are ideal for snow accumulation and steep slopes speed avalanche descent. The avalanche season is from May to November with peaks in August and September. The largest avalanche recorded was 200 000 tonnes with speeds of 200 km/hr.

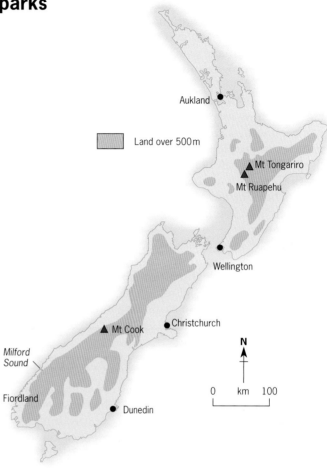

**Figure 7.12  New Zealand**

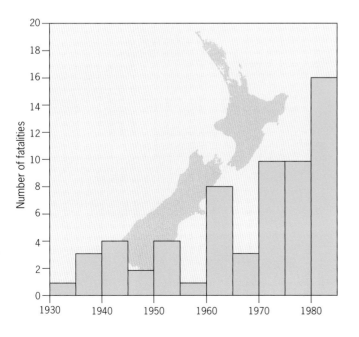

Many areas are very remote and avalanches present little danger. Areas of high hazard exist in the popular ski-fields, for example on Mount Ruapehu and Mount Cook. Between 1879 and 1986, there were 70 deaths in avalanches, but since 1930 fatalities have increased (Fig. 7.13). Most victims were climbing (50 per cent), and 25 per cent were involved in alpine training and rescue.

Buildings have also been damaged. In 1983 a tourist lodge on Milford Track in Fiordland National Park was ruined and an HEP plant damaged. Roads and bridges have also been damaged. In 1986 the property losses were about $1 million. Road closures also have a financial impact as tourist traffic and commercial fishermen are disrupted.

**Figure 7.13  Avalanche fatalities in New Zealand (five-yearly intervals, 1930–84). The deaths of 16 people between 1980 and 1984 (in a total of 458 avalanche events) puts New Zealand third in the world for avalanche deaths after Austria and Switzerland. (*Source:* Breese et al., 1986)**

## Avalanche management

This has involved studying local conditions to increase understanding of avalanche origins, and monitoring avalanche occurrences. Evaluation and forecasting schemes have been implemented at Tongariro, Mount Cook, and Fiordland National Parks based upon daily observation, snow pits and weather readings. The information is made available to park managers and users. These programmes are expensive but are proving to be successful.

The avalanche paths in most hazardous parts of the parks are now mapped. An assessment of relative risk has been undertaken based upon the probability of vehicles or people being hit by an avalanche, and is used in public safety programmes and in siting facilities. Work is under way to estimate return periods of large avalanches. Hazard zoning is not used because of the relatively low population densities but may be required in the future.

Avalanche hazards are reduced by three control methods: relocation, traffic control and direct control. Relocation is the ideal solution but can be expensive. Ski-field facilities can be relocated, but moving roads is more difficult. On some roads an emergency route to bypass areas at risk is used when the avalanche hazard is high. At times of extreme risk, tracks, roads and ski areas may be closed. There is some direct avalanche control. On ski-fields in Tongariro National Park, avalanche guns are used to release slides. In some areas, bombs are thrown from helicopters after storms to stabilise the snowpack. Engineering structures such as dams and snowsheds (Fig. 7.8) are not used because of their visual impact.

Education and safety services have been developed with training for staff, including rescue techniques, public awareness courses, publicity material and warning signs.

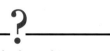

**20** Explain why the avalanche hazard is increasing in New Zealand and why public awareness of the hazard may be low.

**21** Should maintaining scenic beauty be a consideration in the management strategies used in New Zealand's national parks? Explain your answer.

# 7.4 Flooding

Flooding of river valleys and coastal areas is the most frequent of natural hazards and is one of the most significant for human activity in terms of deaths, injuries, and long-term social and economic impacts. The numbers affected can be huge and the geographical area relatively large. Flooding regularly claims over 20 000 lives a year and affects 75 million people globally. This is because the attractiveness of river valley and coastal locations for human activity and settlement places large numbers at risk. Impacts can be severe at all levels of economic development. However, flood impacts follow the pattern of other hazards, with LEDCs suffering the most deaths and MEDCs the highest total economic losses.

**Figure 7.14 The effects of the Mississippi floods in St Louis, Missouri**

## *Causes of flooding*

### River flooding

River flooding results from a number of causes. By far the most common is excessive rainfall related to atmospheric processes, which include monsoon rains with intense mid-latitude depressions, or a series of depressions bringing prolonged high rainfall amounts, and tropical cyclones which bring high rainfall totals to the areas within their tracks (see page 99). Floods are increasingly being linked with atmospheric–oceanic processes at a large scale – the 1993 Mississippi flooding in the USA has been linked with an El Niño Southern Oscillation event, and the flooding in the Sudan and Bangladesh in 1988 with a La Niña event.

The rainfall events producing flooding result in two main types of flood. Regional flooding affects large-scale river systems and may be at a national or even international scale due to high rainfall totals producing a high-magnitude, low-frequency event, as with the Mississippi flooding of 1993, the Rhine in 1995, and the Oder in 1997. Regional-scale flooding has been responsible for some of the largest death tolls in history resulting from natural hazards, especially in China and Bangladesh.

Flash floods are a consequence of intense periods of rainfall in a short time. The floods which result are high-energy and high-magnitude events but cover a relatively small area. Thus, although potentially very destructive, their effects are more localised. Flash flooding is associated with high humidity and very unstable atmospheric conditions. These are found in areas with thunderstorms, near warm oceans, and steep, high mountains in the path of moist winds. Thunderstorm events last a few hours but can result in huge amounts of rainfall.

Rainfall inputs alone to a drainage basin will not necessarily result in a flood. The capacity of the water stores and the hydrological processes operating in the **drainage basin** will also be important (Fig. 7.15). Most floods are the

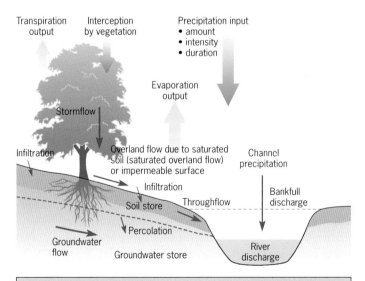

The likelihood of flooding will depend upon the nature of the precipitation input and the relative importance of the stores and flows in the drainage basin. The more overland flow and quick throughflow, generally the more the likelihood of flooding. The water stores (vegetation, soil and groundwater) are important: if these are full, the flows will transfer water rapidly to the channel. The relative importance of these flows and stores will vary in both time and space.

**Figure 7.15  Water stores and flows in a drainage basin**

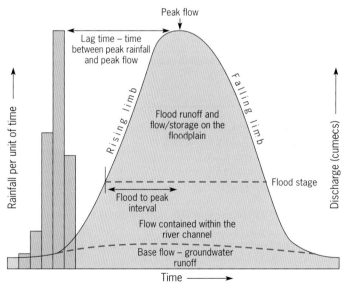

The lag time and steepness of the rising limb are related to the importance of the quickflow processes of overland flow and quick throughflow. Slow throughflow and groundwater flow transfer water to the channel more slowly and contribute less to the peak flow. Where these processes dominate, the hydrograph will have a lower peak and a longer lag time.

**Figure 7.16  The flood hydrograph**

result of quickflow processes of overland flow and rapid throughflow. These produce a rise in discharge which can be plotted as a flood hydrograph (Fig. 7.16). With flash floods the soil may be relatively dry, but the rainfall more intense than the soil's **infiltration capacity**, producing rapid overland flow.

The relative importance of quickflow and slowflow processes are variable in both time and space. Rock and soil type will affect the ability of the drainage basin to absorb rainfall. Even in areas with permeable rocks dominated by slowflow processes, rainfall over long periods will saturate the ground and result in flooding, as was the case with the Chichester flood of 1994 in an area of predominantly porous chalk bedrock. Other drainage basin characteristics are important (Fig. 7.17); these will influence flood characteristics between drainage basins but also at different points in the same drainage basin, especially large ones.

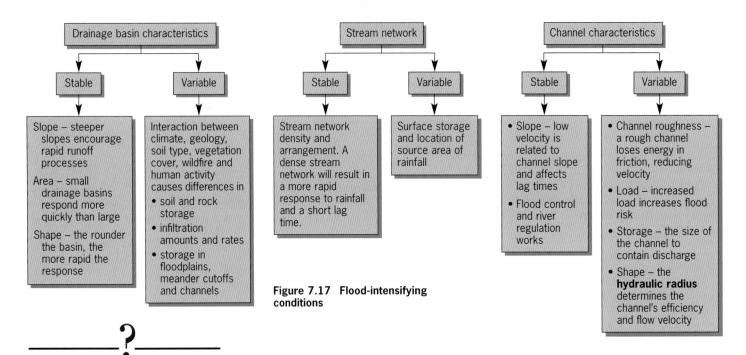

Figure 7.17 Flood-intensifying conditions

**?**

**22** Explain how the following will affect water stores and flows in a drainage basin (Fig. 7.15):
**a** prolonged rainfall in winter with low temperatures and deciduous vegetation
**b** a dry spell in summer in Britain followed by light drizzle
**c** frozen ground in high-latitude mountainous areas.

**23** Use Figure 7.16 to define the following terms: lag time, flood-to-peak interval, base flow, rising limb, falling limb.

**24** Suggest how human activity can affect the variable flood-intensifying conditions shown in Figure 7.17.

Land use can be crucial in determining the nature and intensity of flooding. Urbanisation replaces vegetation and soil cover with a larger area of impermeable surfaces on streets and roofs. Water is transferred rapidly into drains. The result is a higher peak discharge, steeper rising limb, and shorter lag time in the flood hydrograph compared with rural areas. Increases in flood peaks and reduced lag times can also be associated with deforestation, vegetation clearance, soil compaction and trampling, wildfires and land drainage. Vegetation removal and poor agricultural practices increase soil erosion and thus the sediment load of rivers. This increased sediment load increases the flood risk since deposition within the river channel reduces its capacity to hold higher discharges.

### Other causes of floods

Rapid snowmelt or snowmelt combined with rainfall can cause widespread flooding, especially in the interiors of North America and the Commonwealth of Independent States. These usually occur in late spring or early summer. In glaciated areas the flood hazard results from melting ice or the collapse of a dammed glacial meltwater lake. These glacial outbursts occurred in the Alps before management was undertaken to reduce them, and are a hazard today in the Andes. Meltwater pockets may collect over time within a glacier mass. When these burst they add rapidly to the discharge of glacial streams, forming a sudden flood wave. Outbursts can also occur as a result of volcanic activity causing ice melt. In Iceland these are called *jökulhlaup*. Although rare, the effects can be spectacular, with roads and bridges being swept away and considerable turbulence in the sea if the flood waters spill over the coast and hit the seabed. Flooding can also result from landslides and dam failures.

## Coastal flooding

Coastal floods can be caused by tropical cyclones (see Chapter 6) and tsunami (see Chapter 5). Storms in mid-latitudes can also result in serious coastal flooding. The degree of flooding will depend upon the severity of the storm and the storm surge effect (see Fig. 6.13), plus the level of the tide at the time of the event. The risk of coastal flooding is increasing in many locations as a result of long-term regional-scale sinking of the land mass and global (eustatic) sea-level rise. The latter will be an increasingly important factor if the predicted sea-level rises resulting from global warming do occur. This effect can be seen in the UK. Southern Britain is subsiding at 1–3 mm per year, and sea level is rising. Coastal lowlands consisting of post-glacial deposits are most at risk from this increasing high-water level on to which the storm surge effect (2 m or more in Britain) needs to be added. The surge effect is increased in shallow coastal water such as the southern North Sea. The combined effects of an intense depression with strong winds producing high waves occurring at the time of the highest tide of the year produced a flood event with a return period of over 1:500 years at Towyn in North Wales. Other locations were also flooded (see Dinas Dinlle case study). River estuaries can be the locations for severe **estuarine flooding** with the combined effects of a storm surge and river flooding caused by rainstorms inland. Coastal flooding is probably the most severe natural hazard threat to the UK.

**Figure 7.18 Stranded people await rescue by helicopter on a bridge over the Limpopo River near Xai-Xai, Mozambique, March 2000. The regional-scale flooding was due to exceptionally heavy rains during the rainy season followed by Cyclone Eline hitting the area.**

## Flood magnitude and frequency

Flooding is a worldwide hazard and can occur in all environments, including flash flooding in desert and semi-arid areas. Floods show the magnitude and frequency relationship in Figure 1.9 and magnitude and return period relationships in Figure 1.10. The actual figures vary for each river system and coastal location, and are important information for planners and inhabitants at risk, as well as engineers planning flood alleviation schemes. Recurrence intervals of specific events are calculated using the formula

$$\text{Recurrence interval} \atop \text{(return period)} = \frac{(n+1)}{r}$$

where $n$ is the number of discharge/storm surge levels in the record and $r$ is the rank of that discharge/surge level. The data record shows that the flood hazard has increased over the last few decades. Using return period information, the statistical probability that a magnitude will be equalled or exceeded can be calculated.

## The flood hazard

Flooding is a regular occurrence in many river systems. Although the magnitude of the flood may vary, floods probably offer more opportunities for people than any other hazard. Flooding maintains soil fertility by depositing fresh layers of alluvium and flushing salt out of soils. The Euphrates, Ganges, Nile, Tigris and Yangtze have all supported important civilisations as a result of their fertile floodplains. Even today many agricultural systems on floodplains are in harmony with low-magnitude, high-frequency floods.

**Figure 7.19 The floodplain of a river and flood risk**

Most of the time the river's discharge is contained within the channel. A flood occurs when the discharge exceeds the maximum the channel can hold (the bankfull discharge). During a flood the floodplain becomes part of the river's channel. Floodplains evolve by shifting channel positions and sediments deposited as the flood waters recede.

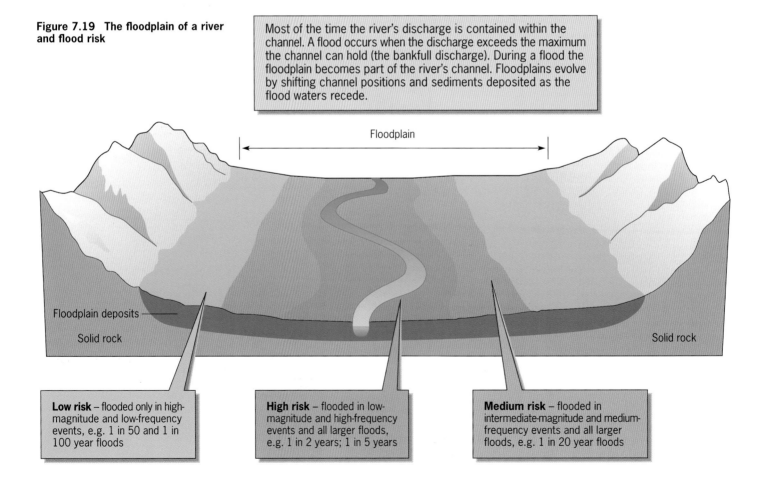

Floodplain

Floodplain deposits

Solid rock

Solid rock

**Low risk** – flooded only in high-magnitude and low-frequency events, e.g. 1 in 50 and 1 in 100 year floods

**High risk** – flooded in low-magnitude and high-frequency events and all larger floods, e.g. 1 in 2 years; 1 in 5 years

**Medium risk** – flooded in intermediate-magnitude and medium-frequency events and all larger floods, e.g. 1 in 20 year floods

The floodplain has locational advantages alongside water sources, river transport and for waste disposal. Flat floodplain areas are often used for buildings and routeways due to the relative ease of construction.

Human habitation of floodplain locations, including higher risk areas (Fig. 7.19), has increased in the twentieth century. This is due to urban development, population pressure, and more road and rail routeways. Thus people have increasingly become exposed to the flood risk and the hazard has increased in relative importance without an actual increase in flood events. In England and Wales less than 2 per cent of the population live on the 1:100 year floodplain. In the USA it is 10 per cent and involves 26.8 million. In MEDCs the flood hazard is highest in urban areas. Urban development increases the severity of flooding because of hydrological changes and also the use of storm drains for clearing water. These can quickly become blocked by debris or unable to cope with the volumes of water. In LEDCs floodplains in cities are often the sites of shanty town development. In rural areas agricultural practices are increasingly not suited to flood cycles due to increasing population pressures and the need for cash and food crops.

The impacts of a flood are wide-ranging. During the event deaths and injury may result from people being swept away by the force of water. The damage increases with the velocity of the water and the depth of the flood surge. The force of the water can damage buildings, with foundations being damaged by speeds above 3 m/s and by debris being swept along. The largest death tolls are recorded in the LEDCs, where high populations may live on floodplains or deltas with limited flood warning systems. China has the greatest number of people affected by floods, and between 1860 and 1960 five million Chinese were killed by flooding. In MEDCs loss of life is reduced but economic losses can be huge.

Economic losses do not just involve property damage. The impacts can affect national economies in the longer term. Following the July 1997 floods in eastern Europe, the Polish economy suffered the loss of fertile farmland and damage of several billion dollars which resulted in emergency loans from the

**Figure 7.20 The 'intangible' effects of flooding: rating scale results from three case studies**

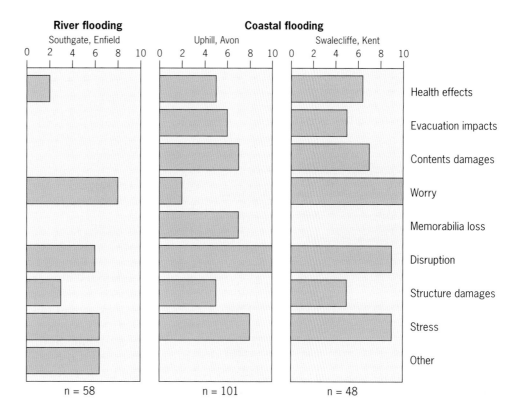

?

**25** How do the more intangible impacts of flooding compare with the more tangible impacts of contents damage and structure damage for the flood events (Fig. 7.12)?

World Bank to aid recovery. In the Czech Republic, 30 per cent of the country was affected and the costs were estimated at up to US$3 billion. Although LEDCs may sustain fewer total economic losses, relatively these may be severe as the economies are less able to contain the losses and recovery is slower.

Regional flooding may be followed by increased disease risk from cholera and dysentery as sewage contaminates drinking water and dead animals contaminate the supply. Following the Mozambique floods of February/March (Fig. 7.18) 2000, nearly 2000 cases of cholera were confirmed and hundreds of cases of malaria. In tropical regions increasing insect numbers may spread diseases such as malaria and yellow fever. Longer-term illnesses, especially respiratory diseases, increase, particularly among the old and young. Impacts on livelihoods can be severe. Labourers are not needed on flooded fields, and it may take years to recover from the loss of possessions and work animals. Vulnerability is highest among the poorer members of all societies due to lower levels of preparedness, economic resilience and health.

The intangible effects of flooding on people's lives can be dramatic and long term. These impacts often feature more highly than economic losses (Fig. 7.20).

# The Great Flood of 2000 in the British Isles

## Causes

The autumn of 2000 (September, October, November) was the wettest in England and Wales since records began in 1766. This was due to a series of unusually intense and slow-moving depression crossing the country, especially between mid-October and mid-November. During September rainfall was high for the whole country with some regional variations (Fig. 7.21). For example, rainfall was 41 per cent above average in south-east England. This high rainfall quickly replenished the soil moisture stores from the drier conditions and high evaporation rates of the summer. Thus when heavy rainfall arrived in October, there were high antecedent soil moisture conditions, allowing runoff to add quickly to river discharge.

The high mid-October rainfall was due to very slow moving depression called an 'anchored low'. Due to a

wave in the usually straight upper jet stream (Figure 6.30), it took nearly a week to cross the British Isles. The frontal and cyclonic rainfall caused widespread flooding with the worst effects in the South-East, which had the worst floods for 40 years. East Sussex had 255 mm of rainfall in the first twelve days of October. This was 25 per cent more rainfall than the average for the whole month.

In early November, the flood misery continued with a mid-latitude depression crossing the British Isles from 4 November. This developed 3000 miles from the country in the area known for the 'perfect storm' (Fig. 7.22). The depression was at its occluded stage for most of its long time over the British Isles (Fig. 7.23) and thus huge amounts of rainfall fell onto the country which already had high water levels in rivers and saturated soils. For example, the Met. Office recorded 50 mm of rain in 24 hours in Anglesey, a figure just below the whole monthly average. To complete the rainfall impacts even more, there was a family of depressions for the weekend of 11 November.

## Impacts

There were 12 deaths from floods and a total of £2 billion of damage. 5500 homes had been flooded and the flooded area reached an estimated 700 000 acres. Transport routes were disrupted with roads impassable (Fig. 7.24) and railways paralysed by flooding in hundreds of places. More than 1000 trees had fallen onto the line in the Southern Region alone, and a landslide south of Lancaster shut the North Western Rail Line. Figure 7.25 summarises some of the main flood warnings and impacts across the country.

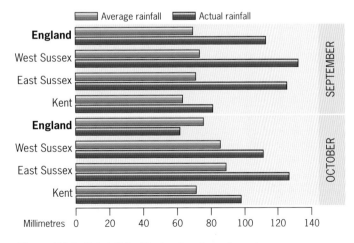

**Figure 7.21 Rainfall for England and south-east England, September and October 2000**

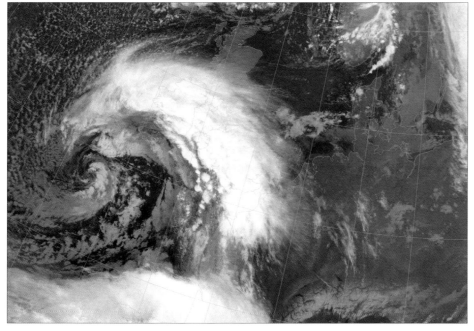

**Figure 7.22 The approach of 'the perfect storm'. The north of Scotland can just be seen at the top of the picture.**

**Figure 7.23 The arrival of the storm**

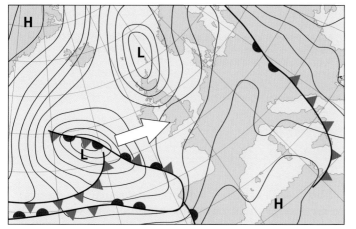

**1** Midnight Saturday 4 November: storm moves in from mid-Atlantic. Depression 975 mb, moving east at 30 mph.

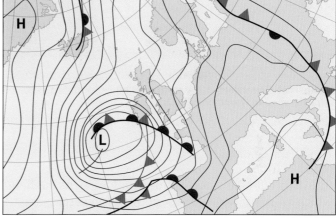

**2** Midday Sunday 5 November: rain begins to affect West Country. Winds begin to increase in west.

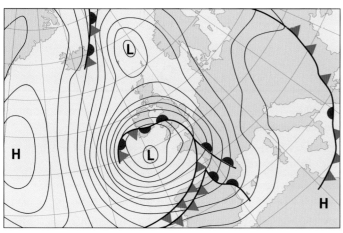

**3** Midnight Sunday 5 November: downpours widespread throughout the country. Storm stays almost stationary.

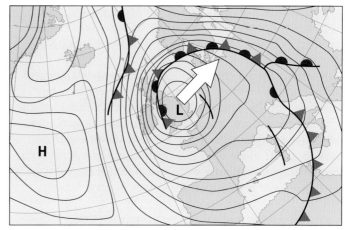

**4** Midday Monday 6 November: rain still affecting many areas as storm moves away. Storm will not move away until Wednesday.

Warm front    Cold front    Occluded front    Isobar     **H** High pressure    **L** Low pressure    Movement of storm

**Figure 7.24 The effect of the storm that hit Leicestershire in November 2000**

**SCOTLAND AND NORTH WEST**
**RAIL**
**Huyton to Liverpool**
Olive Mount cutting collapsed
**ROAD**
**B977** Kintore to Fintray road flooded at Kintore Golf Club

**MIDLANDS**
**SEVERE FLOOD WARNINGS**
**River Teme** Bransford Bridge to Powick
**River Severn** Bevere to Powick and Worcester to Gloucester
**RAIL**
**Lichfield to Rugely** Flooding at Armitage blocking down line
**Rugby to Hanslope** Flooding at Weedon
**Derby to Stoke** Flooding at Uttoxeter Flooding at Clay Mills
**ROADS**
**A57** Dunham flooded at Dunham Bridge
**A5132** Between Eggington and Hilton closed both ways at Stutterford Bridge – bridge unsafe
**A52** Between Eastgate: Derby (A601) and the Pentagon: Derby (A61) closed due to flooding
**A1133** Bestorpe closed by flooding
**A6097** Between Gunthorpe and New Road East, Nottingham flooded both ways

**A617** Between Kelham and Newark Bypass (A46/A616) flooded

**SOUTH WEST AND WALES**
**SEVERE FLOOD WARNINGS**
**River Dee** Llangollen to Chester, Bangor on Dee, Wrexham
**RAIL**
**Tiverton to Exeter** St David's Track bed washed away
**Barnstaple branch line** Damaged bridge
**Swindon to Gloucester** Sapperton tunnel floor collapsed
**ROADS**
**A4104** Upton on Severn flooded along **B4211** Hanley Road, and most routes in and out of Upton
**A417** Maisemore flooded
**A470** Llanrwst (B5427) flooded – passable with care
**A542** Horeshoe Pass flooded
**A541** Tremeirchion turning: Bodfari (B5429) flooded
**A525** Bangor on Dee Bypass (B5069) flooded along with B5426 from Bangor to the A528. Diversion via B5130 and the A528
**A525** Flooded between Rhewl and Llyfasi College of Agriculture (B5429)
**A5** Capel Curig (A4086) flooded – passable with care
**A5** Corwen village, flooded road passable with care

## Management

In Britain, flood is managed using a variety of methods which were used for this event, with forecasting and warning, and insurance being of key importance. In many cases the hard engineering flood defences were unable to withstand the high water volumes. Flood warnings are a crucial part of the strategy. By 30 October there were 25 severe flood warnings in the country. This had risen to 41 severe warnings by 6 November. There were 200 general warnings in operation. Media coverage is also extremely high and effective in providing the public with weather and flood warnings. The flood warnings enable residents to clear ground floor and basements of at-risk properties; they use sand bags to try to prevent water entering buildings. In more extreme cases, areas are evacuated. For example, residents were evacuated from parts of York and 300 residents from Lewes in East Sussex during the October floods.

Insurance is another important part of flood management in Britain. The average claim was thought to be about £12 000; 25 per cent of claims were from businesses. However, it is estimated that 30 per cent of people in the worst-hit areas did not have flood insurance.

This flood event has led some insurance companies to reconsider their premiums and the excesses for residents. In some areas insurance is not given at all or there are new clauses about the higher standards of rebuilding and repair if properties are to be insured again.

**?**

**26** Compare the rainfall for September and October 2000 for England and the South-East (Figure 7.21).

**27** Describe the passage of the depression over the British Isles from Saturday 4 November (Figure 7.23).

**28** Library research/revision: Explain why fronts and occluded fronts produce high amounts of rainfall.

**29** Use the information in Figure 7.25 to annotate an outline map of the British Isles with the impacts of the floods.

**30** Should flood insurance premiums be increased and clauses be included for floodplain residents? Explain you viewpoint.

**A548** Flooded north of Llanfair Tlhaiarn (A544)
**A541** The Rhosemor turning (B5123) flood at Hendre

**SOUTH EAST AND EAST ANGLIA**
**SEVERE FLOOD WARNINGS**
**River Lavant** East Dean to Chichester city centre
**River Ems** Westbourne Estate and Lumley Mill
**RAIL**
**Manningtree to Wrabness** Single line operating
**Hayward's Heath to Preston Park** Flooding at Hassock and Patcham Tunnel
**ROADS**
**A27** Old Shoreham Road, Lancing, flooded east bound form Manor roundabout and Old Sussex Pad public house
**A1067** Between Norwich and Attlebridge, crossings over River Wensum flooded. Costessey Mill, Mill Pit Lane and Helsdon Road bridge
**A23** Patcham interchange (A27) flooded both ways at junction with Varndean Road
**A1123** Earith bridge closed due to flooding
**B1134** Diss flooded at Pulham Market
**B1066** Whepstead flooded both ways.

Woodhurst Road, Maidenhead, flooded both ways
**A4094** Ray Mead Road, Maidenhead, flooded between Maidenhead bridge and Boulters Lock. Diversions in place
**B4009** Lower Icknield Way, Chinnor, flooded

**NORTH EAST**
**SEVERE FLOOD WARNINGS**
**River Derwent** Elvington to Barmby. River levels at Malton and Norton, Howden and environs
**River Ouse** Naburn, Acaster Malbis, Barlby and Selby
**River Aire** Gowdall and Kellington
**River Rother** Rotherham
**River Don** Kellington
**RAIL**
**York to Scarborough** Flooding at Malton
**York to Church Fenton** Flooding at Ulleskelf
**York to Knaresborough** Flooding Doncaster to York
Flooding at Marshgate and embankment slip at Heck
**Doncaster to Stainforth** Flooding at Marshgate
**Sheffield to Chesterfield** Flooding at Renishaw Park
**Selby** Embankment slip at Barlby
**Goole to Knottingley** Embankment slip

Hartlepool to Sunderland Flooding single line in operation
**Durham/Croxdale** All lines blocked by flooded River Wear
**Berwick to Alnmouth** Embankment slip-down line blocked
**Wakefield to Pontefract** Flooding at Featherstone
**Connisbrough to Swinton** Flooding at Mexborough
**ROADS**
**A656** Lock Lane, Castleford, flodded
**A63** Between Thorpe Willoughby and Selby 9A19/A1041) flooding between Thorpe Willoughby and Gowthorpe
**A169** Howe bridge, Goathland, area flooded
**A19** Selby (A63) flooded at the toll bridge. Also closed between Eggborough power station and Chapel Haddlesey
**A614** M62 interchange: Golle (M62) flooded approaching motorway. Opposite carriageway still open
**A1406** Port Clarence Road, Billingham, flooded both ways from B1275 Hope Street to A178 Seaton Carew Road
**A163** Bubwith near Barlby
**A166** Stamford Bridge
**A645** Little Heck railway bridge between Low Eggborough and West Cowick (off A19)

**Figure 7.25 Region by region guide to flooding chaos (*Source: The Times*, 11 November 2000)**

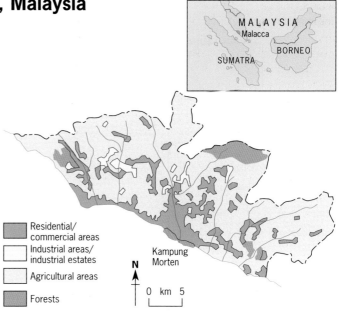

# Flood hazard perception and response in Malacca, Malaysia

The village of Kampung Morten is a traditional Malay settlement within the built-up area of Malacca (Fig. 7.26). The village is situated on the lower reaches of the Malacca River and is frequently flooded, especially during the north-east monsoon season (December–January). The houses show the traditional flooding adjustment of being raised 1.5–2 m above the ground on stilts, and villagers also use tyres, sandbags and wooden barricades to reduce flood impacts. Only during larger events are the houses flooded, since water levels must be high enough to rise above the stilts. This occurs relatively frequently – 1939, 1952, 1954, 1961, 1971, 1975 and 1985. Heavy rainfall in the upper Malacca catchment area produces most of the flooding and there is a lag time of about 18 hours, so there is time for evacuation if warnings are given and residents are responsive to them.

Residential/commercial areas
Industrial areas/industrial estates
Agricultural areas
Forests

N

Kampung Morten

0 km 5

**Figure 7.26 The location of Kampung Morten and the general land-use patterns of Central District, Malacca**

**Table 7.3  The perceived gravity of the flood hazard during the 1971 floods (*Source:* Khairulmaini, 1994)**

| Food risk | Frequency | Percentage |
|---|---|---|
| Potential death | 3 | 8.6 |
| Health hazard | 3 | 8.6 |
| Loss of property | 17 | 48.6 |
| Loss of working hours | 10 | 28.6 |
| Communication problems | 1 | 2.9 |
| Do not know | 1 | 2.9 |
| Total | 35 | 100.0 |

**Table 7.4  Residents' perception to a hypothetical warning of an impending flood (*Source:* Khairulmaini, 1994)**

| Perceived response | Frequency | Percentage |
|---|---|---|
| Do nothing | 7 | 20.0 |
| Keep watch | 15 | 42.9 |
| Consult others | 4 | 11.4 |
| Temporary flood-proofing measures | 2 | 5.7 |
| Move valuables/properties | 1 | 2.9 |
| Evacuate premises | 6 | 17.1 |
| Total | 35 | 100.0 |

The residents were surveyed to understand their perception and response to the flood hazard (Tables 7.3 and 7.4). Only 10 per cent of residents linked flooding to natural processes. Some 70 per cent thought that the rapid development of the state had increased the flood hazard, and 5 per cent thought that floods were 'Acts of God'. Their perception of the flood hazard and the degree of anxiety was shown to be important in how they responded to the flood hazard (Fig. 7.27). About 80 per cent of residents wanted a flood warning system, and 54 per cent would relocate if they were given enough compensation. This latter figure is relatively low. Nearly half the residents seem prepared to accept the flood hazard.

**?**

**31** How do Kampung Morten residents perceive the flood hazard as threatening their lives (Table 7.3)?

**32** Suggest why the residents accept the flood hazard and continue to live in this location.

**33a** Use Figure 7.27 to suggest how the physical factors, dwelling characteristics and personal factors will affect flood hazard perception.
**b** Why is the degree of concern important in how residents respond?
**c** What actions can residents take if they have a high degree of concern?

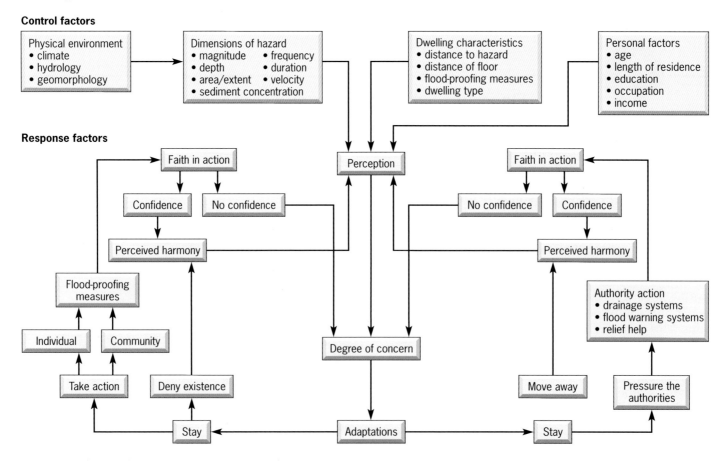

**Figure 7.27  Model of flood hazard perception and adaptation of an individual dweller in Kampung Morten (*Source:* Khairulmaini, 1994)**

## Managing the flood hazard

### Modify the event

Flood abatement measures focus upon the water stores and processes operating in the drainage basin by aiming to increase the size of the stores and the importance of slowflow processes. Local measures involve reafforestation and revegetation to increase evapotranspiration losses, and land management to reduce soil erosion.

Flood diversion measures aim to control and divert flood waters by hard-engineering schemes. A number of techniques are used.

LEVÉES OR DYKES These are a common form of flood control (Fig. 7.28). Levées are relatively cheap if they are built of earth or clay. They are a major part of flood defences on the Mississippi (USA), Rhine (W. Europe) and Chinese rivers such as the Yellow River. Well-maintained levées are an effective management approach within the flood size that they are designed to contain.

However, if levées fail the results can be disastrous and the flood event worse. Under natural conditions, water floods out of the channel and is stored on the floodplain, and the discharge is reduced downstream. Flood waters contained within the levées, however, continue to flow rapidly downstream. If the levées fail the area inundated will be more severely affected as water pours through the breach.

Coastal flooding is managed by hard-engineering schemes, most commonly embankments (dykes) and barriers made of earth, clay or shingle. The largest such scheme is the Dutch Delta Plan protecting the deltas of the Rhine–Meuse–Scheldt which was started in 1958 following the death of 1835 people in the 1953 North Sea floods. The scheme has cost £2.3 billion, protects against the 1:500 year event, and was completed in 1986. Britain has 800 km of sea defences, many built after 1953 floods which killed over 300 people on the East Coast. The Thames Barrier scheme involves a barrage to prevent a storm surge moving upstream to central London and embankments along
the estuary coastline.

DAMS AND FLOOD WATER STORAGE Reservoirs behind dams built for river flood control or as part of multipurpose schemes are used for flood control throughout the world. These schemes are expensive but can provide multipurpose benefits of irrigation, water supply, improved navigation
and hydro-electric power (Fig. 7.29).

Flood water storage can also occur in flood relief channels and storage basins located on floodplains, for example the Washlands scheme, Northampton. These schemes are often used in or near urban areas.

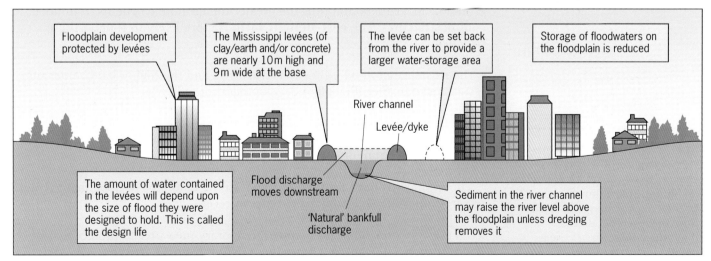

**Figure 7.28  Levées (dykes) as a flood-diversion measure**

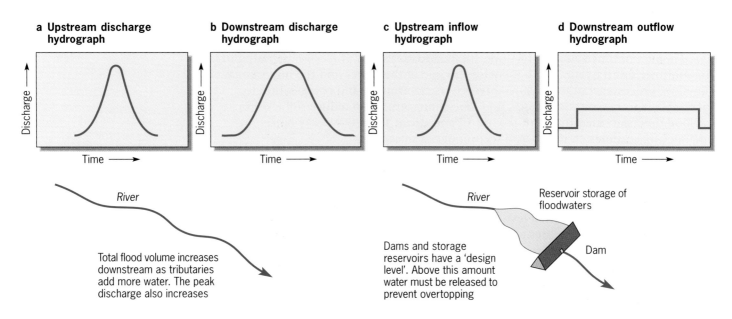

**Figure 7.29 Hypothetical hydrographs of (a) an uncontrolled river and (b) reservoir-regulated outflow. All or part of the flood discharge is stored in the reservoir for release later at a reduced rate. Dam releases of water can take into account the impacts from uncontrolled tributaries downstream to reduce or prevent flooding.**

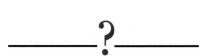

**34a** Annotate a copy of Figure 7.29 to explain how discharge changes downstream for controlled and uncontrolled flows.
**b** How might emergency releases from the reservoir affect downstream discharge? Use a graph to illustrate your answer.

CHANNEL MANAGEMENT Channel management aims to reduce flooding by increasing either the capacity of the channel or its efficiency as a conveyor of water. Channel capacity is increased by dredging to enlarge the cross-sectional area. Channel efficiency is increased by changing the channel shape to increase the **hydraulic radius**. If there is less energy loss through friction of water with the bed and banks, velocity will increase and more water will move more quickly through the channel. The likelihood of flooding will therefore be reduced. These changes are called **channelisation**. Meanders may be removed by being cut off so that water flows along a more direct course downstream. In its extreme form, channelisation results in a straight, concrete-lined channel which may reduce flooding but lacks ecological diversity and amenity value. This approach is most commonly used in urban areas where levées or other measures are not possible because of building right up to the river's edge.

There is increasing concern about the continued use of these structural measures. Where they exist, development of floodplains is likely to continue with demands for more and higher-level protection works. This link between flood control works and floodplain development is called the **levée effect**. It results from three factors (Smith, 1996).

• The greater the amount of floodplain development, the greater the existing economic investment and thus the greater the economic benefits from flood control structures. The **cost–benefit ratio** is more likely to support these schemes.

• The existence of flood protection structures, and the higher land values that result, make further floodplain development more likely.

• The floodplain dwellers and users have not borne the costs of these protection works directly. Flood control schemes are usually financed by local or national government.

These concerns have resulted in a shift in the emphasis of flood management towards other management approaches in recent years.

HAZARD-RESISTANT DESIGN This involves temporary measures to protect against floods such as sandbags, but permanent design features are more effective. Houses can be raised on stilts, and basements and low floors waterproofed.

*Modifying vulnerability*

## Forecasting and warning

This is one of the most important ways of managing flood hazards, especially regional-scale and coastal flooding. Flash flooding is more difficult to forecast because of the speed and often localised nature of the event. Increasing technology has allowed meteorological, discharge and tidal data to be collected more efficiently. Computer modelling enables scientists to predict how individual river systems will react to precipitation inputs, or tide levels relate to forecasted storms.

Improved communication technology has also enabled more efficient dissemination of warnings to the public. However, as with all such systems, the public must understand and respond to the warnings if they are to be effective. For example, in September 1996 the Environment Agency linked homes and businesses in the Soar Valley, Leicestershire, to a new computer-controlled telephone system. This automatically sends recorded flood warnings to people in high-risk locations. Before this new system, local police officers had to knock on doors to give out warnings.

In more remote regions, especially in LEDCs, lack of communication technology makes this process difficult. Warnings, if they are available, will need to be disseminated by local officials. It is estimated that there are 15 flood-prone countries with no warning system at all, and at least 40 more with inadequate systems.

## Community preparedness

Community preparedness is closely linked with the use of flood warning systems. Public response to these warnings by evacuation, and the removal of valuables to higher levels in buildings, can save lives and property loss.

## Land-use planning

Land-use planning aims to use floodplains in a way which restricts development in high-risk areas of the floodplain (Fig. 7.19) to only those land uses which will not be damaged by flooding such as pasture, leisure uses and wildlife areas. This approach is most effective for the future use of undeveloped areas of the floodplain. However, even in areas which have been developed there are attempts to relocate land uses away from high-risk areas.

**a  Site prior to implementation of managed retreat scheme**

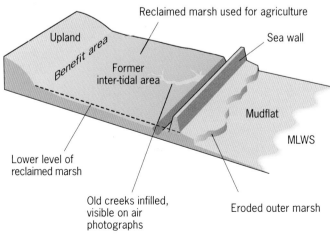

**b  Implementation of managed retreat**

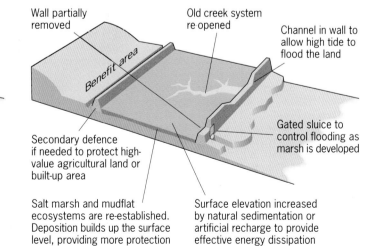

**Figure 7.30  Managed retreat for flood defence (*Source:* MAFF, 1993)**

This approach is closely linked with detailed flood hazard mapping which aims to aid the decision-making process. However, there can be conflict as floodplain residents fear a reduction in their property values once the high-risk areas have been identified in print or on the internet (Fig. 7.31). The Environment Agency estimate that two million houses valued at £35 billion have been built on floodplains and are therefore at risk from flooding. The hope is that future developments estimated at between 3 to 4.4 million new houses by 2016 will be away from floodplain areas.

Land-use planning is becoming increasingly important in managing coastal flooding. With rising sea levels the cost of building and maintaining sea defences will increase. A report in 1996 concluded that the current sea defences in the UK may be up to 2 m too low to contain the 1:100 event predictions over the next century. As a result, in some locations a soft-engineering approach called **managed retreat** is being adopted (Fig. 7.30). This is mainly for inter-tidal locations which would once have been flooded by high tides. These areas of former salt-marsh and mud-flats have often been drained and used for agriculture. By allowing this land to revert to natural flooding the shoreline will build up by deposition to provide a wider foreshore to reduce the impacts of storms. Any secondary defence needed would be lower in height and therefore cheaper. The wider foreshore allows salt-marsh and mud-flat ecosystems to develop again.

**35** How will house prices be affected by publishing this information on flooding?

**36** The map does not indicate the level of risk. Why may this anger residents in flood-prone areas?

**37** What other agencies may find this information useful?

**38** Write a brief flood risk report for the region where you live.

# Internet map pinpoints flooding perils

HOUSE PURCHASERS can now check on the Internet if a potential home is prone to flooding. The Environment Agency introduces a free service today on which the public can check the risk against a property's postcode.

When users key in a postcode or the name of a town or city, the flood plains emerge as blue tubes snaking across the countryside and though urban areas. People can then focus on a site of interest such as Uckfield, East Sussex, where homes and buildings have been under several feet of water recently. The system based on Ordnance Survey maps, can zoom down to individual streets and fields.

York, another city to suffer floods regularly, is seen as having several big flood plains, including that of the Ouse, weaving through its suburbs and centre. Someone buying a house in the Huntington area of York would see that it is flanked on two sides by flood-prone land, with only a band of streets and a school in the centre safe from the threat of flood.

A spokesperson for the agency said that the fact that a property was on a flood plain did not mean it would definitely experience flooding.

London is in the tidal flood plain of the Thames but is unlikely to suffer because of protection from the Thames Barrier at Woolwich. London is most at risk from storm surges coming form the sea up the Thames estuary which the barrier, when raised, holds back.

The maps do not indicate the level of risk. People who need more information are urged to contact their local Environment Agency office.

The announcement came as the agency published findings showing that more than half the people living in a flood plain are still not aware that their property may be vulnerable to flood damage.

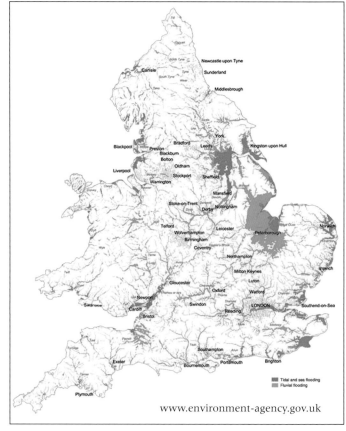

www.environment-agency.gov.uk

**Figure 7.31  Internet information affects property values (*Source: The Times 7 December 2000*)**

# Coastal flooding defence scheme at Dinas Dinlle, Gwynedd, Wales

## Background

The village of Dinas Dinlle in North Wales (Fig. 7.32) is situated on low-lying land in Caernarfon Bay. The area consists of recent alluvium, coastal and blown sand deposits, with boulder clay cliffs to the south of 'The Mound' archaeological site (436564).

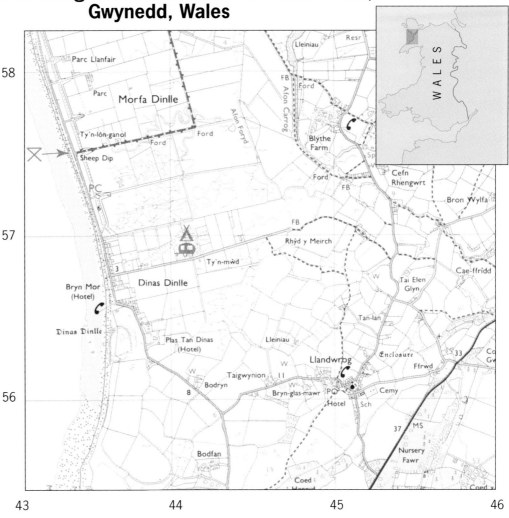

**Figure 7.32  Dinas Dinlle
(© Crown copyright)**

The area has suffered from flooding since the nineteenth century but the frequency of events has increased in recent years. In 1976–7 a gabion wall was built to defend the area and was fronted by a narrow shingle beach and a flat sandy foreshore (Fig. 7.33). The south to north longshore drift of material across the village has reduced in recent years, and as a result the beach has been eroded and the wall undermined.

By the early 1990s the area was suffering from increased wave overtopping of the sea wall and flooding of the coastal road and low-lying land. In February 1990 a severe storm resulted in overtopping the sea wall near the hotel (435566), and to the north of the village the sea wall was breached (Fig. 7.35). The hotel and properties with basements were flooded, along with the coastal road which resulted in the village being cut off for several days. The pasture-land to the north of the village was flooded to a depth of 0.3 m. Although there were no casualties, there was much distress and economic hardship as a result of the

event. The return period of this storm was estimated to be between 5 and 10 years, so without further defence works flooding would have been frequent.

**Figure 7.33  Dinas Dinlle before the defence scheme**

**Figure 7.34  Dinas Dinlle after the defence scheme**

## The scheme

The scheme that was implemented was designed to protect the village from flooding and maintain the area's attractiveness for tourists (Fig. 7.36). The engineering structures protect the village area and work with coastal processes to build up a protective beach which dissipates wave energy. North of the village the scheme involves managed retreat (Fig. 7.30). The coastal road will be relocated inland over time as the shingle ridge moves inland to a naturally stable position. The works involved four main components (Fig. 7.36).

## The cost–benefit analysis

The scheme has a design life of 50 years. During this time there are likely to be a number of small flooding events, and a calculated probability of 99.5 per cent for a 1:10 year event and a 63.60 per cent probability of a 1:50 event. Without a new scheme (i.e. the 'do nothing' approach), all these events would result in economic losses including property flooding, business disruption, road access problems, and intangible losses such as impacts on tourism and personal distress. Where possible, economic values are given to these losses. These are totalled for the losses expected over the 50-year design life and become the benefits of the scheme. This is because these losses will not occur if the scheme goes ahead. The costs of the scheme are the engineering works, beach nourishment, road embankment, drainage, compensation and fees. The resulting cost–benefit ratio of the implemented scheme was 1:2.24. However, the scheme needs full justification before grant aid is received. This includes a consideration of the alternatives available, and an environmental impact assessment. The most favourable cost–benefit ratio (1:2.84) was for the 'do minimum' approach. This would maintain the existing level of defence. However, the MAFF guidelines state that areas such as Dinas Dinlle should be protected up to at least

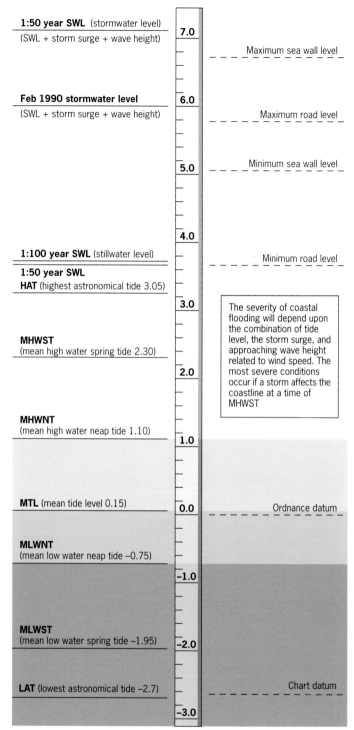

**Figure 7.35  Dinas Dinlle tide and topographic data (*Source:* Welsh Environment Agency)**

the 1:50 year event level. The 'do minimum' approach would not provide this level of protection. Other schemes were considered, including a sea wall, but these had less beneficial cost–benefit ratios, and so were not justified economically as a suitable alternative existed.

**?**

**39** Use the OS extract (Fig. 7.32) to describe the relief and landforms of the Dinas Dinlle area.

**40** What are the land uses of the area?

**41** Use Figure 7.35 to comment upon the old defence levels and road heights compared with observed and predicted storm levels.

**42** What are the key features of the scheme (Figs 7.34 and 7.36)?

**43** Explain why the managed retreat approach will enhance the ecological diversity of the area (refer to Fig. 7.30).

**44** Why was managed retreat not acceptable for the whole area?

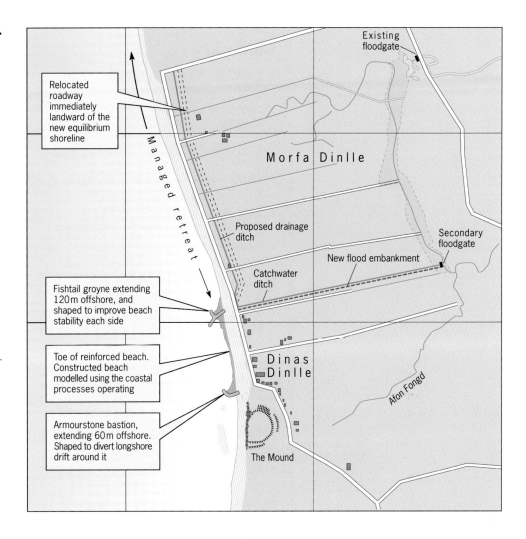

**Figure 7.36    Details of the scheme for Dinas Dinlle**

## Modifying the loss

Aid is a common response to flood losses and may involve governments or international organisations such as the European Union. In MEDCs there is some reluctance on the part of governments to provide disaster aid to flood-hit communities which should have been insured, so aid may then be limited to uninsurable losses. The effectiveness of insurance as a management approach depends upon the uptake by households and the provision of cover by insurance companies. In parts of the Netherlands, for example, flood insurance is not available, but in the USA, the National Flood Insurance Program (NFIP) was introduced in 1968 to help manage river flooding based on land-use zoning.

## Summary

- Landslides result from a range of slope processes and can be increased by human activity.

- Landslides occur when the balance between shear stress and shear strength is changed.

- Landslides are particularly associated with geologically active fold mountains and areas with high rainfall.

- Landslides can be managed by a range of engineering techniques, but these are expensive.

- Vulnerability to landsliding can be reduced by hazard mapping, land use, building regulations and community preparedness.

- An avalanche is a mass movement of snow and debris in mountainous regions, especially in active and temperate regions.

- Increasing population, road and tourist development is increasing human vulnerability to the avalanche hazard.

- Avalanches can be managed by artificial avalanche creation, or a range of engineering techniques. Forecasting and warning systems are increasingly used, especially in tourist areas.

- Flooding is the most frequently occurring natural hazard and has significant human impacts.

- Flooding results from a range of causes, including high rainfall amounts, intense downpours, snowmelt, glacial outbursts, *jökulhlaup*, landsliding and dam failure.

- Coastal flooding is a serious hazard in low-lying areas due to storm surge from tropical cyclones and mid-latitude depressions or tsunamis.

- As with all hazards, flood perception is important as regards the human response and management approaches used.

- Flooding of all types can be managed by hand-engineering structures, channel-scale control, forecasting and warning, community preparedness and land-use planning.

# References

Abbott, P L (1996), *Natural Disasters*, Wm C Brown.

Alexander, D (1993), *Natural Disasters*, UCL Press.

Asian Development Bank (1991), 'Disaster mitigation in Asia and the Pacific'.

Atsuyaki, S (1995), 'Fault lines in our emergency management system', *Japan Echo*, vol.22, no.2.

Barry, R G and Chorly, R J (1992), *Atmosphere, Weather and Climate* (6th edn), Routledge.

Blaikie, P, Cannon, T, Davis, I and Wisner, B (1994), *At Risk: Natural Hazards, People's Vulnerability and Disasters*, Routledge.

Bryant, E A (1991), *Natural Hazards*, Cambridge University Press.

Buckle, C (1996), *Climate and Weather in Africa*, Longman.

Cannon, T (1994), 'Vulnerability analysis and "natural" disasters', in Varley (1994).

Chapman, D (1994), *Natural Hazards*, Oxford University Press.

Chester, D (1993), *Volcanoes and Society*, Edward Arnold.

Cooke, R U and Doornkamp, J C (1990), *Geomorphology in Environmental Management*, Clarendon Press.

Delos Reyes, Perla J (1992), 'Volunteer observers' program: a tool for monitoring volcanic and seismic events in the Philippines', in *Geohazards: Natural and Man-made* (eds G J H McCall, D J C Laming and S C Scott), Chapman and Hall.

Dingwall, P R, Fitzharris, B B and Owens, I F (1989), 'Natural hazards in New Zealand's national parks', *New Zealand Geographer*, vol.45, no.2.

Dregg, M (1992), 'Natural disasters: recent trends and future prospects', *Geography*, vol.77, no.336, July.

Dregg, M (1993), 'Earthquake hazard, vulnerability and response', *Geography*, April.

Freeth, S (1992), 'The deadly cloud hanging over Cameroon', *New Scientist*, 15 August.

*Geographical Magazine* (1993), October.

Goudie, A S and Brunsden, D (1994), *The Environment of the British Isles: An Atlas*, Clarendon Press.

Gruber, U and Haefner, H (1995), 'Avalanche hazard mapping with satellite data and a digital elevation model', *Applied Geography*, vol.15, no.2.

Hicks, N (1993), 'Into the lava lab', *Geographical Magazine*, October.

Jones, D (1993), 'Landsliding as a hazard', *Geography*, vol.78, no.339, April.

Jones, D K C (1992), 'Landslide hazard assessment in the context of development', in *Geohazards: Natural and Man-made* (ed. G J H McCall et al.), Chapman and Hall.

Keller, E A and Pinter, N (1996), *Active Tectonics: Earthquakes, Uplift and Landscape*, Prentice-Hall.

Khairulmaini bin Osman Sallah (1994), 'Perception and adaptation to flood hazard: a preliminary study', *Malaysian Journal of Tropical Geography*, vol.25, no.2.

Lacayo, R (1989), 'Is California worth the risk?', *Time*, 6 November.

Lavell, A (1994), 'Prevention and mitigation of disasters in Central America: vulnerability at the local level', in Varley (1994).

Leigh, C H and Sim, L K (1983), 'Attitudes and adjustments to the flood hazard in a mixed community in Malacca Town, Peninsula Malaysia', *Singapore Journal of Tropical Geography*, vol.4, no.1.

MAFF (1993), *Coastal Defence and the Environment: A Guide to Good Practice*, Stationery Office.

May, P J *et al.* (1996), *Environmental Management and Governance: Intergovernmental Approaches to Hazards and Sustainability*, Routledge.

Moody, J A (1994), 'Propagation and composition of the flood wave on the upper Mississippi River, 1993', US Geological Survey, Circular 1120-F.

Musk, L F (1988), *Weather Systems*, Cambridge University Press.

Nash, J M (1996), 'Unravelling the mysteries of twisters', *Time International*, 20 May.

Oliver-Smith, A (1994), 'Peru's five-hundred-year earthquake: vulnerability in historical context', in Varley (1994).

Oppenheimer, C (1996), 'Volcanism', *Geography*, vol.81, no.350, January.

Palm, R and Hodgson, M E (1992), 'After a Californian earthquake', University of Chicago Geography Research Paper 233.

Park, C C (1992), *Environmental Hazards*, 2nd edn, Nelson.

Penning-Roswell, E C and Hanmer, J W (1988), 'Flood hazard management in Britain: a changing scene', *Geographical Journal*, vol.154, no.2, July.

Perry, A and Reynolds, D (1993), 'Tornadoes: the most violent of all atmospheric phenomena', *Geography*, vol.78, no.338, April.

Perry, C A (1994) 'Effects of reservoirs on flood discharges in the Kansas and Missouri River basins, 1993', US Geological Survey, Circular 1120-E.

Rantucci, G (1994), *Geological Disasters in the Philippines*, IDNDR and Cooperazione Italiana.

Scoging, H (1993), 'The assessment of desertification', *Geography*, vol.78, no.339, April.

Selby, M J (1993), *Hillslope Materials and Processes*, Oxford University Press.

Shennan, I (1993), 'Sea-level changes and the threat of coastal inundation', *Geographical Journal*, vol.159, no.2, July.

Smith, K (1996), *Environmental Hazards: Assessing Risk and Reducing Disaster*, Routledge.

Soloviev, V (1978), 'Tsunamis', in *The Assessment and Mitigation of Earthquake Risk*, UNESCO Press.

Summerfield, M A (1991), *Global Morphology*, Longman.

Swiss Reinsurance Co. (1996), 'Natural catastrophes and major losses in 1989', Sigma Economic Studies 2/90.

Tiffen, M (1995), 'The impact of the 1991–2 drought on environment and people in Zambia', in *People and Environment in Africa* (ed. T Binns), Wiley.

Tomblin, J (1987), 'Management of volcanic emergencies', *UNDRO News*, 17, July–August.

US Geological Survey (1985), 'Evaluating earthquake hazards in the Los Angeles region: an earth science perspective,' Professional Paper 1360.

US Geological Survey (1989a), 'Seismographs – keeping track of earthquakes', in *Earthquakes and Volcanoes*, vol.21, no.1.

US Geological Survey (1989b) *Earthquakes and Volcanoes*, vol.21, no.5.

US Geological Survey (1989c), 'Citizen participation in emergency response', in 'The Loma Prieta earthquake of 17 October 1989 – the public response', Professional Paper 1553b.

US Geological Survey (1990), 'The San Andreas fault system, California', Professional Paper 1515.

US Geological Survey (1992), 'Human behavior during and immediately after the earthquake', Professional Paper 1553.

US Geological Survey (1992a), *Earthquakes and Volcanoes*, vol.23, no.1.

US Geological Survey (1992b), 'Living with volcanoes', Circular 1073.

US Geological Survey (1994), *Earthquakes and Volcanoes*, vol.25.

US Geological Survey (1995), 'Look before you build', Circular 1130.

Varley, A (1994), *Disasters, Development and Environment*, Wiley.

Wolfe, E W (1992), 'The 1991 eruptions of Mount Pinatubo, Philippines', *Earthquakes and Volcanoes*, USGS, vol.23, no.1.

# Glossary

**Adiabatic**  Change of temperature without external exchange of heat. An air parcel which expands due to decreasing pressure will cool on rising. The opposite effect is an air parcel warming as it sinks and pressure increases.

**Aftershock**  Small earthquake following a major earthquake near the original earth movement. Can occur in large numbers following a major earthquake.

**Asthenosphere**  The upper mantle between 50 and 300 km deep to about 700 km which deforms relatively easily. Represents the base of lithospheric plate movement.

**Benioff zone**  Sloping zone of earthquake foci as plates are subducted.

**Channelisation**  Modifying of river channels by straightening, deepening or reshaping for flood control, drainage and navigation.

**Cold front**  Boundary between two air masses with relatively cold air behind the boundary in the direction of movement.

**Condensation nuclei**  Dust and pollen particles which encourage condensation of water from the atmosphere.

**Convection**  Transfer of heat energy by motion of air, with warm air rising and cold air sinking.

**Coriolis force**  Force resulting from the Earth's rotation which diverts air movements (winds) to the right in the Northern Hemisphere and to the left in the Southern Hemisphere.

**Cost-benefit ratio**  Ratio between costs and benefits of a proposed scheme. The benefits must be greater than the costs for the scheme to be viable. To some impacts, e.g. environmental, it may be difficult to assign a monetary value.

**Cumulonimbus**  Cloud type ('cumulo' meaning heap or pile, and 'nimbus' meaning rain). Large vertical development often several kilometres high. Associated with thunderstorms.

**Debris avalanche**  Mass movement type where a large mass of relatively dry material flows downslope.

**Drawdown**  Retreat of sea level as a tsunami wave trough approaches land.

**Epicentre**  Point on the Earth's surface directly above the site of movement (focus).

**Estuarine flooding**  Flooding of a low-lying river estuary resulting from a combination of river flooding and high tides.

**Fault**  Crack in rocks resulting from stresses in the Earth's crust. Faults can vary in scale from small cracks to major fractures.

**Fault zone**  Group of faults occurring in the same region. They are usually parallel/sub-parallel to each other, and result from tectonic plate movement.

**Feedback effects**  Effects which cause change in environmental systems. Positive effects result in system change. Negative feedback causes the system to revert to its original state.

**Fissure eruption**  Volcanic activity through a crack or fissure rather than through a central volcanic core – usually basaltic magma.

**Focus**  Site of movement inside the Earth's crust, resulting in an earthquake.

**Föhn**  Wind on the lee side of a mountain range. Usually warm and dry as a result of adiabatic warming.

**Geophysical processes**  Physical processes operating in the environment including geological, biological, geomorphological and atmospheric processes.

**Geostationary satellite**  Satellite which maintains the same position above the Earth's surface. Rotates at the same speed as the Earth.

**Ground deformation**  Movement of the surface materials of the earth as a result of earthquake waves, including uplift and subsidence.

**Hazard salience**  The relative importance of hazards compared with other human concerns, e.g. unemployment, poverty, crime.

**Hydraulic radius**  A measure of the efficiency of a river channel as a conveyor of water. Calculated by dividing the cross-sectional area by the wetted perimeter. The higher the figure, the more efficient the channel.

**Hypocentre**  The focus of an earthquake (*see* **Focus**).

**Infiltration capacity**  The rate at which water can enter or infiltrate into the soil (usually measured in mm per hour).

**Internal cohesion**  The internal strength of materials such as clays where particles are held together by chemical or electrostatic forces.

**Internal friction**  The force between grains of sediment such as sand particles which hold the mass together. For movement to occur, the forces applied must be greater than the internal friction between the particles.

**Intertropical Convergence Zone**  The zone where the trade winds meet at the thermal equator. Its position moves with the overhead sun.

**Island arc**  A chain of volcanic islands resulting from subducting lithospheric plates.

**Isostatic recoil**  The recovery of the earth's crust following compression by the weight of large ice sheets. This process is occurring today in temperate latitudes which were glaciated during the Pleistocene.

**Jet stream**  Upper-level (9000–15 000 m) winds which blow with great speeds of over 100 km/hr. Most developed in temperate latitudes and sub-tropics.

**Lava**  Molten rock or magma when it reaches the earth's surface.

**Levée effect**  The impact of river flood protection measures on human activity, e.g. rising land values due to the reassurance provided by the defences built.

**Lithospheric plates**  The divisions of the crust and upper mantle which form distinctive plates and which move relative to each other.

**Magma**  Molten rock.

**Managed retreat**  Policy to move back (inland) coastal flood defences to allow natural processes to build up a protective foreshore.

**Mantle**  The layer of the earth about 2800 km thick between the thin outer crust and the central core. Consists of dense rock rich in iron and magnesium minerals.

**Mercalli scale**  A 12-point scale measuring the intensity of ground movement resulting from an earthquake based upon the visual impacts on buildings.

**Moment magnitude**  A measure of earthquake size related to the rigidity of the rock times the area of faulting times the amount of slip on the fault plane.

**Monsoon season**  A distinct annual wet season related to seasonal changes in wind direction.

**Plate tectonics**  A geological model that advances the idea that the earth's crust and upper mantle are divided into rigid sections or plates.

**Pore-water pressure**  The pressure exerted on rocks and soil particles by the water in the pores between them.

**Porosity**   The percentage of pores (air spaces) in a rock or soil.

**Pyroclastic flow**   Flow of a mixture of hot gases, lava particles and rock fragments (tephra), produced by explosive volcanic eruptions. Movement is at a high velocity close to the ground surface due to the dense nature of the mixture.

**Richter scale**   Logarithmic scale measuring the magnitude of an earthquake related to earthquake wave amplitude.

**Run-up stage**   The stage where a tsumani makes landfall. Wave height increases.

**Sea-floor spreading**   The creation on new oceanic crust along a constructive plate margin. The new crust is added along the mid-ocean ridges as the plates move apart, causing the sea floor to widen or spread.

**Stratosphere**   The layer of the atmosphere above the troposphere characterised by no variation of temperature with height.

**Subduction zone**   The zone where an oceanic plate descends back into the mantle.

**Sublimation**   A direct change of state of water from a solid to a gas, omitting the liquid stage.

**Succession**   The change in plant communities over time from early colonisation to the most developed community for the environmental conditions of the area.

**Supercell thunderstorm**   Thunderstorm associated with one giant updraught of air and localised strong downdraughts.

**Symbolisation**   The concept that disasters create an image that is simple and shared by those who experience the event due to the following factors:  the event is 'outside' the community; an agreement on a hierarchy of values quickly emerges; problems need immediate action; previous conflicts are minimised; status differences are reduced; and the community identity is strengthened.

**Tephra**   All the rock fragments that are ejected through the volcanic vent – ash, cinders and volcanic bombs. When consolidated, they form pyroclastic rocks.

**Throughflow**   The downslope movment of water through the soil.

**Thrust fault**   A low-angled reverse fault in which the upper rocks move up and over the lower rocks so that older rock layers are placed on top of younger rocks.

**Tropopause**   The top of the troposphere. Varies from 8 to 16 km in height above the earth's surface.

**Troposphere**   The lower layer of the atmosphere characterised by a decrease of temperature with height.

**Unstable**   A state of the atmosphere where an air parcel which is forced to rise (e.g. at a front or over a mountain range) becomes warmer than the surrounding air and therefore continues to rise.

**Wave refraction**   The change in the approach angle of a wave as it moves towards the shore.

**Wind shear**   The gradient of wind velocity with height related to the temperature structure of the air.

# Index